DEATH UNDERGROUND

DEATH UNDERGROUND

The Centralia and West Frankfort Mine Disasters

Robert E. Hartley and David Kenney

Southern Illinois University Press / Carbondale

Copyright © 2006 by Robert E. Hartley and David Kenney
All rights reserved
Printed in the United States of America
09 08 07   4

Library of Congress Cataloging-in-Publication Data
Hartley, Robert E.
Death underground : the Centralia and West Frankfort
mine disasters / Robert E. Hartley and David Kenney.
    p. cm.
Includes bibliographical references and index.
1. Coal mine accidents—Illinois—Centralia. 2. Mine
explosions—Illinois—Centralia. 3. Coal mine accidents—
Illinois—West Frankfort. 4. Mine explosions—Illinois—
West Frankfort. I. Kenney, David, 1922– II. Title.
TN805.I3H37 2006
363.11'962233409773875—dc22
  ISBN-13: 978-0-8093-2705-8 (cloth : alk. paper)
  ISBN-10: 0-8093-2705-8 (cloth : alk. paper)
  ISBN-13: 978-0-8093-2706-5 (pbk. : alk. paper)
  ISBN-10: 0-8093-2706-6 (pbk. : alk. paper)   2006001169

Printed on recycled paper. ♻

The paper used in this publication meets the minimum
requirements of American National Standard for Information Sciences—Permanence of Paper for Printed Library
Materials, ANSI Z39.48-1992. ∞

To all coal miners and their families everywhere
And for Grace Ann

Contents

List of Illustrations   IX
Preface   XI
Map of Illinois   XV

Introduction: Prelude to the Disasters   1

PART ONE. THE 1947 CENTRALIA MINE DISASTER

1. More Than a Coal Town   23
2. "Please Save Our Lives"   30
3. Day of Reckoning   58
4. Years of Strife   73
5. A Pox on All Houses   82
6. Miners' Lives   105
7. The Reality of Coal Politics   121

PART TWO. THE 1951 WEST FRANKFORT MINE DISASTER

8. "It's All Blown to Hell"   137
9. Burying the Dead   148
10. Seeking the Cause and Greater Safety   156
11. Affected Lives   175

Conclusion: After the Disasters   181

Appendix 1. Miners Killed in the Centralia Mine Disaster   193
Appendix 2. Miners Killed in the West Frankfort Mine Disaster   197
Notes   201
Glossary of Coal Mining Terms   219
Bibliography   221
Index   227

Illustrations

Map of Illinois   xv

Following page   104

The List by Georges Schreiber, depicting widows of the Centralia mine disaster

Bodies of men killed in the Centralia mine are placed in a hearse

Copy of the mine inspection report made a week before the Centralia explosion

Illinois state legislators prepare to conduct investigation underground

Throngs of citizens gather at Centralia First Methodist Church

Mourners gather outside St. Mary's Catholic Church in Centralia

Governor Dwight Green meets with reporters in Centralia

U.S. Senate subcommittee holds hearings in Centralia

Senator Henry Dworshak scans copy of *Centralia Sentinel* extra edition

William P. Young and Driscoll Scanlan at Senate hearing

John Lorenzini and William P. Young at Senate hearing

Harry Niermann speaks with Senators O'Mahoney of Wyoming and Cordon of Oregon

Robert Medill, former Department of Mines and Minerals director, testifies before Senate subcommittee

Joe Vancil, last survivor of the Centralia disaster

Fred Bright at 1982 reunion of Centralia mine survivors

Fred Hellmeyer at 1982 reunion of Centralia mine survivors

Earl Wilkinson at 1982 reunion of Centralia mine survivors

L. G. Sprehe at 1982 reunion of Centralia mine survivors

Lynn Sharp at 1982 reunion of Centralia mine survivors

Elvera Kirkland looks at photograph of her father, Gus Hohman, who was killed in the mine explosion

Photograph of Jack Pick Jr., Centralia No. 5 survivor, with medals and memorabilia of his air force career during World War II

John L. Lewis, who built and ran the United Mine Workers of America

Rescue workers prepare to enter New Orient No. 2 mine at West Frankfort

A rescue squad, burdened with oxygen tanks and tools, waits to enter the mine

Fearing the worst, miners' wives wait for word of their loved ones

Faces tell the story as another body is brought out of New Orient No. 2

A victim is carried from the mine before a cluster of rescue workers and officials

Relatives and friends wait for bodies to be delivered to the temporary morgue at West Frankfort Junior High School

Omar Lingo, a weary mine inspector, who declared that rock dusting was not adequate in the mine

Preface

TWO CALAMITOUS COAL MINE DISASTERS OCCURRED IN
the southern portion of Illinois in the middle of the twentieth century that
were linked by history, culture, politics, and danger. The first, at Centralia
No. 5 mine in 1947, killed 111 men. The second, at New Orient No. 2 mine
in West Frankfort in 1951, killed 119. The stories of the two events as told
in this book provide sufficient information for readers to understand what
happened and why, with many details previously unreported.

We spare little in telling how 230 men lost their lives, leaving hundreds,
probably thousands, of widows, children, other relatives, and dear friends
in deep mourning, for this is the core of knowledge of the disasters. Their
stories deserve full treatment because the tragedies stand among the worst
in U.S. coal mining history. In fact, they are first and second in the number
of lives lost since 1928.

Having accomplished that account, it is the authors' goal to go well beyond the basic disasters. The passage of time—in each case, more than fifty
years—allows us to explore local events on a larger stage and draw a more
complete picture than was possible at the time or even a few years later. We
put the two locations in a geographic context with the development of coal
mining in the United States, Illinois, and more particularly, southern Illinois,
and we address the often-asked question "Why would anyone want to work
in a coal mine?" We explain how generations of men in a single family worked
below ground, in many instances beginning in their teenage years.

The tradition of mining coal is a fixture in Illinois history, although not
well known to today's residents and less so to those outside the state. With the
fading of coal mining as a high-profile business and employer, many people
have little appreciation of coal's importance to the state's economy, now and
in the past. There are good stories to be told that embellish that tradition.

But this history has its dark side, too. While no group or individual violence was involved in either of the two disasters, that is not the case during earlier generations in the coal mines. The brutal business of mining coal, the union wars with management, and the effects of economic depression and world war must be understood to appreciate the conditions at Centralia No. 5 in 1947 and at New Orient No. 2 in 1951.

Early in our research, we recognized that above all this was a drama about miners' lives and their families. All parties to the drama are important—unions, coal mine operators, state officials—but we want to present a distinctly human side to what happened. Consequently, we trace the lives of several men from their first work in the mines to the day of their death or survival. This journey led us to some heartrending accounts but also to uplifting stories of kindness, courage, and determination.

Among our discoveries is one of the featured individuals in the book. Of all the persons and organizations that fill out the accounts of Centralia and West Frankfort, his name stands forth: Driscoll O. Scanlan. Surrounded by the tales of sorrow, shame, and blame, Scanlan, a state mine inspector whose responsibilities included Centralia No. 5, reaches near-hero status. For years, Scanlan repeatedly told state officials and mine owners of the dangers to safety in the mine and pleaded for corrective action. Unfortunately, his efforts were ignored. Scanlan's experience reminds us of the futility of being a single warning voice in a highly politicized system. He faced a moral dilemma that haunted him for the rest of his life.

We also provide the results of our search for individuals and organizations that must shoulder responsibility for the two disasters. No one was arrested, charged, or brought before a jury. The only persons officially to lose a job were Robert Medill, director of the Illinois Department of Mines and Minerals, after Centralia, and James Wilson, state inspector, after West Frankfort. There were investigations of each explosion, with plenty of fingerpointing, bluster, and political posturing, but little accountability. However, the record is clearer than people were willing to acknowledge in the immediate aftermath, and it takes shape as the narrative unfolds with revelations in sworn testimony.

The politics of coal at the national level and across the state is one of the more intriguing aspects of mining history and relates directly to the two tragedies. One example is the impact of partisanship in the appointment of mine inspectors who were officials of the Illinois Department of Mines and Minerals. The politics of coal after Centralia played a significant role in the 1948 gubernatorial election contest between Governor Dwight Green and challenger Adlai E. Stevenson II.

When all is said, these pages are a memorial to the millions of miners who went underground, and still do, at great personal risk to bring coal to the surface so the rest of us can enjoy warm homes in the winter, cool buildings in the hot summers, and the multitude of convenience goods produced by coal energy.

This book, our second collaboration, has been another comfortably shared journey. Each of us discovered much about the history and traditions of coal mining, which we hope is apparent in the narrative. Our enduring friendship, mutual interest in Illinois history, and ease in blending research and writing habits make these projects a pleasure.

We are indebted to the many people who contributed experience, knowledge, time, and energy to our exploration of coal mining and the two disasters. From the beginning, the idea sparked interest among those who believe the written history of coal mining in Illinois has been inadequate. Thankfully, writing this book brought us in touch with old friends and helpmates and introduced us to new acquaintances whose interest in the project and in the accurate telling of history kept us motivated.

Our friends at the Illinois State Library, headed by Cheryl Schnirring, are always at the top of the thank-you list. They patiently answer questions and lead us to important documents and materials. Once again, researcher Claire Fuller Martin of Springfield added value to our project. Art Rice at the Benton office of the Illinois Department of Mines and Minerals made a major contribution to our work. He provided state files on both disasters and assisted in reading portions of the manuscript. Without his care and interest, the state's records might have been destroyed years ago. The Centralia story was enriched by Gerald Scanlan, nephew of Driscoll O. Scanlan, the state mining inspector so closely associated with events at the No. 5 mine. Files carefully maintained by the two Scanlans provided details unavailable from any other source.

Tammy Wendling at the Centralia Public Library responded to every request with pertinent information and guidance. Linda Krutsinger, editor of the *West Frankfort Daily American*, was generously helpful. Charles Brown at the St. Louis Mercantile Library and Jean E. Meeh Gosebrink at the St. Louis Public Library willingly discovered materials from the archives of the *St. Louis Globe-Democrat*, *St. Louis Post-Dispatch*, and *St. Louis Star-Times*.

The outpouring of assistance from people amazed us. Marietta Broughton and Mike Jones of the *Centralia Sentinel* made newspaper files and photographs available for the asking. Their deep roots in the community and commitment to accuracy led us to important sources of information. Both of them had relatives in the No. 5 mine on March 25, 1947. Mike read portions of the manuscript, as did Art Rice, D. G. Schumacher, Fletcher Farrar Jr., and Mary Hartley.

Bob Rogers of West Frankfort, himself a miner for twenty-four years, led one of us around the coal miners' room in the museum of the Frankfort Area Historical Society, displaying artifacts and answering a host of questions. Jak Tichenor, of Southern Illinois University Broadcasting Service, contributed his deep understanding of coal culture and shared images of coal mine life.

For the use of material from interviews and correspondence, we are grateful to Georgia Colp, Karen S. Crouse, Saundra Ebbs, Wilma Gutzler, Elvera I. Kirkland, William P. Knight, Charles McDaniel, Bill Niepoetter, Betty Pick, Sharon Raymond, Ralph Spinner, Ella Sweet, Joe T. Vancil, Jack Westray, and Sam Wilkinson.

We are appreciative, too, of our continuing relationship with Southern Illinois University Press and its commitment to publish Illinois history. Our special thanks go to editors Karl Kageff, Carol Burns, and John Wilson for their devotion to this project. We reserve highest praise for those closest to us and for their understanding of our labors.

Chicago

Springfield

St. Louis

Centralia

West
Frankfort

N

0   50 Miles

DEATH UNDERGROUND

Introduction: Prelude to the Disasters

THE MAGIC OF "ROCKS THAT WILL BURN" HAS intrigued the human consciousness for centuries. The power that nature stored deep in the earth for millions of years has been employed to heat homes, drive steamships and locomotives, aid in the making of steel, and generate electricity for all its many uses.[1] It is estimated that currently 500 billion tons of coal are in reserve and accessible to mining in the United States. At the rate of usage today, that is a three-hundred-year supply. That amount of coal contains as much energy as 2 trillion barrels of crude oil, which is more than three times the world's known oil reserves.[2]

Significant use of coal in England began in the thirteenth century. Gradually, British miners found solutions to the problems of drainage, ventilation, hoisting the coal, preventing explosions of gas and coal dust, and providing safer individual lighting devices.[3] Still, mining coal in Great Britain was a dangerous trade. An explosion in 1812 took 92 lives. One of the greatest of British disasters occurred in 1862 in the Hartley mine, killing 204 men and boys. Disasters in Great Britain, tragic as they were, pale before comparisons with other countries. At Courrières, France, in 1906, 1,100 men and 98 horses died in an explosion. The all-time record was set in 1942, in China, when 1,549 died in an explosion in the Honkeiko mine.[4]

The earliest-known written record of coal observed in what became the United States was in a map drawn by the seventeenth-century explorer Louis Joliet showing *charbon de terra* along the Illinois River. The first great commercialization of coal in the United States took place in the anthracite fields of Pennsylvania about the time of the American Revolution. Coal oil and gas were used to light the cities of the East as early as the first quarter of the nineteenth century. Eventually, steamboats and railroad locomotives turned from burning wood to coal. Railroads also provided the essential means of moving coal from mine to market.

When an expanding U.S. coal industry needed experienced miners, many emigrated from Great Britain, an influence that did much to shape the mining of coal in the United States. The "Great Hunger" in Ireland during the 1840s caused many thousands to immigrate to the United States and seek employment. By 1870, one-half of the coal miners in the United States were immigrants.

During the nineteenth century, coal mining in the anthracite fields of Pennsylvania utilized techniques that had been employed in Great Britain for centuries. Each miner was a craftsman who worked largely without supervision, accompanied by another miner referred to as his *buddy*, in a room eighteen to thirty feet wide, cut into the coal seam off one of the passageways, or entries. The miner often hired the buddy to do the heavy work of shoveling coal. Frequently, fathers, sons, and brothers worked together. Methods employed in the anthracite fields were carried into bituminous mining in other states.

Typically, each entry, or passageway, was intersected at right angles by other entries. These would then spawn cross entries of their own, with the whole layout appearing somewhat like the array of streets in a town or village. The rooms in which the miners worked opened off the entries. As the rooms moved farther into the seam, they were crosscut every sixty to seventy feet for the sake of ventilation. The remaining coal between rooms and crosscuts formed the pillars that supported the roof of the mine. This method was called *room-and-pillar*. It left a great deal of coal in the pillars.[5]

The labor of getting out the coal was arduous in the extreme. Miners used picks, shovels, sledges, steel wedges, and drilling tools. The process began with an undermining, or *undercutting*, in the bottom of the face of the coal seam. This was also called *holing* and usually was done with a pick. The miner often had to work sitting down or lying on his side, and usually it took two men half a day to do a proper undercutting.

When all or a portion of the face of the room was undercut to a distance of four to six feet, one or more holes were drilled in the face near the top of the room and above the undercut. A charge of black powder was tamped into the holes, and a fuse was attached. The miner lighted the fuse and ran for cover. The explosion of the charge brought the coal above the undercut to the floor of the room, where it could be shoveled into a wooden cart. In some cases, the undercut was not employed; instead, a heavy charge of powder was used to blast the coal forward onto the floor of the room. This was called *shot out of the solid*. The choice of method reflected the nature of the coal, the industry of the miner, and the thickness of the seam.

In 1869, a fire in the Avondale mine on the Susquehanna River near Plymouth, Pennsylvania, killed 108 men and boys. A contemporary account of the Avondale tragedy in the words of Andrew Roy, an experienced miner from Great Britain who was chief mine inspector for Ohio at the time, provides details of the inferno. The Avondale mine had only one shaft. To provide a complete circuit for the ventilating system, the single shaft was divided in two by a wooden partition. The ventilating furnace at the bottom of the shaft that created a draft of air set fire to the woodwork within the shaft. Only minutes later, a burst of flame emerged on top from the output half of the shaft. It became a virtual chimney for the conflagration, the fire spreading quickly to the engine room and the coal-breaker structure. No one could escape.[6]

The Avondale tragedy brought a new awareness of the need for the regulation of coal mine operations, resulting in the first state statutes. Never again in the anthracite fields did a single disaster claim as many lives. From 15 fatalities for each million tons of anthracite coal mined in 1870, the figure dropped to 6.5 in 1931 and to 1.86 in 1950.

The work of mining coal in the nineteenth century was hard and dangerous, in view of the meager wage. A miner could not be certain of week-long, much less year-round, employment, which depended on the demand for coal and the diligence of management. During the latter half of the century, it was not unusual for a miner and his family to subsist on a few hundred dollars a year. An anthracite miner literate enough to write about the conditions of his work in the 1890s reported that for eleven months in 1890–91, his wages amounted to $368.72, an average of $33.52 a month. The rent for a company house was $10 a month. His bill at the company store was never less than $20 a month. He was a *contract miner*, meaning that he was the lead worker in a team of two. The laborer who assisted him was paid a little more than two-thirds of the contract miner's wage.[7]

Sometimes the miner's pay was in scrip that could be spent only at the company store. Often the rent of a house and the bill at the store amounted in a month to more than the miner had earned. The song "Sixteen Tons," popular in the United States during the 1950s, lamented the fact that with each passing day the miner grew older and further in debt. "Tennessee Ernie" Ford, who sang and promoted the tune, was from Bristol, Tennessee, in coal country. Merle Travis, who wrote the words and music, had a father and two older brothers who were coal miners. One of his albums from the 1940s included "Sixteen Tons" and other songs titled "John Henry," "Nine Pound Hammer," and "Dark as a Dungeon," all with coal mine themes.

By 1900, coal was mined in at least twenty-five states. Production approximately doubled each decade from 1840 to 1910. As competition grew in proportion to production, profits declined, affecting the entire structure of the industry. Skimping on safety helped balance the books.

After 1880, a steady stream of immigrants entered the coal mine labor force. Their willingness to work for the meager pay coal companies were offering kept wages low. Ethnic divisions and differences of language and religion hindered the development of a class consciousness among miners. Mine operators encouraged those differences as a means of discouraging worker solidarity. By 1900, nearly half of the immigrant miners were from southern and eastern Europe; by 1910, the figure was 71 percent. Usually the immigrant miners had little education, and many could not speak or read English, limiting their ability to understand mining safety directions, whether oral or written. Payment of wages based on the individual's production often put pressure on the miner to enlarge his output at the expense of safety.[8]

The first decade of the twentieth century recorded an unprecedented number of disasters in the nation's coal mines. Two hundred and one men died in a mine disaster at Schofield, Utah, in 1900. Seventeen major disasters killed 235 in 1906, eighteen took 918 lives in 1907, eleven killed 348 in 1908, nineteen took the lives of 498 persons in 1909, and there were 485 fatalities in nineteen disasters in 1910. It was "an epidemic of crisis proportions."[9]

The greatest loss of life in coal mine history in the United States occurred in 1907, caused by explosions at the No. 6 and No. 8 mines of the Fairmont Coal Company at Monongah, West Virginia, a coal camp village near the city of Fairmont. Before the carnage at Monongah ended, at least 362 men died. The dead left at least 250 widows and more than 1,000 children. The impact on the community and survivors was incalculable.[10]

At the time of the Monongah disaster, "American society was at the apex of its brutality," according to one report. The nation's values lay in production and distribution rather than in human life. To the operators of coal mines, greater safety was valued for efficiency in production rather than human welfare. Monongah triggered a greater public attention to the coal mine safety problem. Coupled with the Cherry, Illinois, coal mine holocaust two years later, Monongah turned the mind and heart of the nation to the improvement of safety.[11]

Coal Mining Comes to Illinois

The first commercial coal mine in the state of Illinois was located on the banks of the Big Muddy River near the present city of Murphysboro, in Jackson County. In today's terms, the site was about one hundred yards downstream from the old Illinois Route 13 bridge, where an outcropping of coal could be dug out from the face of the hillside bluff, loaded on flatboats, and floated down the river. That stream emptied into the Mississippi a few miles below the village of Grand Tower, in Jackson County, where at one time an attempt was made to process iron ore.[12]

Illinois coal mines first reached an annual production of 1 million bituminous tons in 1864. The yield increased to 5 million tons in 1879, 15 million in 1890, 20 million by 1897, and a record high of 89 million tons in 1918, more than a fourfold increase in twenty years. Fatalities underground reached an all-time high during those last two decades. In the latter part of the nineteenth century, Illinois miners often put in workdays of ten to twelve hours. Each miner and his helper together were paid a total of a dollar a ton for coal delivered to the bottom of the shaft. Five or six tons were a good day's work.[13]

The "coal camps," villages that grew up around the pit heads, often were solely owned by the coal companies. Owners built and rented marginal housing to the miners and operated the company store where miners were compelled by circumstance to do most of their buying, usually at inflated prices. This pattern predominated in the anthracite fields of other states and in the bituminous mines of Illinois. In the camps, coal miners' wives worked as hard as their spouses. They cleaned the homes, cooked the big meals that the labor of their husbands made necessary, and did the never-ending laundering of grimy clothing, bearing and caring for the children, planting and tending a garden, and other household tasks.

Year after year, the list of major Illinois coal mine disasters grew: the Diamond mine at Braidwood in 1883, with 61 dead; Zeigler in 1905, with 51 killed; 259 dead in 1909 at Cherry; Zeigler again in 1909, with 26 fatalities; and 52 dead at the North mine at Royalton in 1914. The toll averaged one death every six days from 1882 to 1913.[14]

The worst mine calamity in Illinois history, the disaster at Cherry in 1909, ranks third in terms of lives lost in the history of coal mining in the United States. The village of Cherry, in Bureau County, grew up near a site chosen by the St. Paul Coal Company in 1905. Proclaimed as the very model of a company town, Cherry had company-built houses and the usual company stores, bank, hotel, park, and school. For the most part, the houses were "differentially constructed," with variations in design. Miners cut and shoveled coal by hand in the Cherry mine, and each worker was paid by the amount he loaded. In 1909, each team of two—father-son and brother-brother teams were common—was paid an average of $1.08 a ton, with five tons considered a good day's work. That meant less than $6 a day, divided between the two.

Mules pulled the loaded three-by-six-foot wooden carts along tracks to the shaft where coal was hoisted to the surface. Two young miners made their way on November 13 along a passageway of the mine, with bales of hay for the mules. Inadvertently, they left the hay cart standing under one of the kerosene torches that temporarily lighted the mine, due to an electrical system failure a short time before. Kerosene dripped onto the bales of hay, and soon they began to burn, igniting the timbers shoring up the roof of the passageway. In the depths of the mine, men and boys struggled through thick smoke and flames for a way to safety by means of one of the two shafts where cages and a stairway connected with the top. Two hundred fifty-nine of them died, leaving 200 widows and almost 1,000 children, in a community of 2,500 persons.

Soon after the Cherry disaster, Illinois governor Charles S. Deneen convened a special session of the legislature in an effort to strengthen mining safety laws. Lawmakers provided for mine rescue stations and certification standards for certain key positions. The first state mine investigation commission in the nation was established. In 1910, under the impact of Cherry, the Illinois legislature approved an employer liability law that eventually became the state's Workmen's Compensation Act.

Following the Monongah and Cherry disasters, Congress created the U.S. Bureau of Mines in 1910 but did not give it power to enforce regulations. Mine operators were a powerful force in determining the bureau's scope of work. The bureau, basically a research and education agency, stressed rescue, an activity none could oppose. Work by the bureau, along with state regulation, made coal mining a safer industry. Fatalities for each million tons produced fell by about two-thirds from 1907 to 1919, due in part to limiting the number of gas and dust explosions. Mandated state inspection helped, and the United Mine Workers of America (UMWA) assisted in some safety matters. However, the regulators gave little attention to preventing roof falls, haulage road accidents, and death and injury resulting from the use of high-voltage electricity.[15]

In spite of regulatory progress, continued growth of the industry and mechanization of the mines worked against improved safety. Mines became deeper, increasing the presence of methane gas, a volatile explosive. Digging and loading coal by machine increased the amount of dust in mines, and the greater use of explosive powder to bring down the coal, in place of the traditional undercutting, posed a threat.[16]

Coal Mining in Southern Illinois

It has been said that southern Illinois is much more than a geographic region—it is a state of mind. As one observer noted, it seems often to be its own state, in the fashion of South Dakota. Poor farmers, mainly from the South, of Scotch, Scotch-Irish, Irish, English, and German bloodlines were among the original settlers. They were not slave owners, nor did they aspire to be. In the main, they were subsistence farmers, living in isolated farm homes, usually built of logs and having a dirt floor.[17]

Once settlers cut the forests of southern Illinois, the thin forest soil leached away rapidly, until only the bare clay remained. At best, agriculture became a poor way of making a living. Often the farmers of "Egypt," the name given to the region early in Illinois statehood, resigned themselves to a marginal existence. Ignorance and superstition in some cases resulted in regard to the healing arts, education, and religion.

Traditions of violence in the settlement of personal differences came into southern Illinois from the Appalachian highlands of the South. It was the *code duelle* in all its many forms. In the words of a one-time popular song, "The Hatfields and McCoys, they were daring mountain boys" and also confirmed feudists, according to popular folklore. Strains of violence appeared throughout nineteenth-century life in Egypt. Into that setting came coal mining on an industrial basis. Coal had been dug out of the hillsides for local uses since before statehood. In the first years of the twentieth century, however, commercial mining encountered the background of resignation, superstition, and violence that decades of marginal farming by southern highlanders had produced.

Shortly before the end of the nineteenth century, tests made by local interests between Carterville and Johnston City identified a nine-foot seam of high-quality coal at a depth of 150 feet. These people made the first investments in developing the seam, but major corporations soon entered the picture. Since railroads burned coal and hauled it for use by others, they were deeply interested in the development of new coalfields near the great industrial and rail centers in Chicago. The Missouri Pacific was the first to exploit the newly discovered seam, but the Illinois Central Railroad soon followed, taking fifteen sections of land east of Johnston City.

The railroads wanted to organize the bituminous coal industry as a subsidiary of their operations, just as the anthracite field in eastern Pennsylvania had been structured earlier. However, the congressional Hepburn Act of 1906 ruled against the railroads taking part in the coal business except to satisfy their own needs for fuel. Other major investors soon took an interest, bringing wealthy speculators and corporations into development of the Williamson-Franklin-Saline counties field.

A "wildcat" operator funded by John W. "Bet-a-Million" Gates took a large holding north of Herrin. The Illinois Steel Company, interested in the coking quality of southern Illinois coal for use in its mills, acquired 4,000 acres. A Chicago coal dealer bought two mines already in production near Marion and built a rail line deep into Saline County, acquiring coal rights along the right-of-way.[18]

There were few if any experienced miners among the early settlers and their descendants of central and southern Illinois. As commercial mining grew, immigrants with technical skills developed in coal production came from the British Isles. Longtime residents of the region resented the presence of the British newcomers who spoke differently and were culturally distinctive. Divisions persisted between them and the settlers. The workforce conditions existed in part because native farmers did not make good industrial workers. They lacked the routine discipline required by investors, coming and going from work in the mines as needed to accomplish seasonal farm tasks. Many looked with disfavor on the mechanization being introduced in mining, which exceeded that of the farm. At the same time, miners' wages represented more dollars than the land would yield to those in agriculture. Resentment of newcomers increased with the arrival of mine workers from eastern and southern Europe and of blacks from the American South. Rampant racism was directed toward the blacks.

According to Malcolm Brown and John N. Webb, alienation, lack of personal relationships, distrust, and suspicion ruled the landscape.[19] European immigrants to the mining region of central and southern Illinois came from Poland, Russia, France, Czechoslovakia, Austria, Hungary, Croatia, Montenegro, Rumania, Bulgaria, Greece, Italy, Estonia, Lithuania, Syria, and other parts of the world. Their religion differed from the native Protestantism, increasing the local resentment. Feelings were strong against intermarriage with Roman Catholics. The lasting effect of that influx of workers from other lands is indicated by the fact that in 1930 one-fifth of the persons living in the counties of Franklin, Saline, and Williamson, the core of bituminous coal mining in southern Illinois, were either foreign-born or had at least one foreign-born parent.[20]

Nowhere in the region was the interaction between coal culture and community more intense than in Williamson and Franklin counties. Settlers had come to that area as early as 1804, attracted by the forested land with great, level bottom tracts in the floodplains of the Big and Little Muddy rivers. Prairies large and small were sprinkled about. There was an abundance of wild game—deer, elk, bear, turkey, and the smaller creatures of the field and forest. Fur-bearing animals were plentiful, and the streams were full of fish. Domestic livestock often ranged at large. Early settlers fished and farmed, hunted and trapped, and altogether lived a life close to the soil.

The pace quickened with the coming of the railroads at the time of the Civil War. Much of the industrial growth that brought great changes to places like St. Louis, Memphis, and Chicago had at first little discernible effect on the southern half of Illinois. Then came the realization that great riches lay beneath the worked-out soil in the form of "the rock that burns." Mining began in earnest in many parts of Illinois in the early years of the twentieth century. Friction in southern Illinois between the farm-centered culture and coal operations spread throughout the region.[21]

Conflict was inevitable between the newly formed UMWA and mine operators in southern Illinois. The national financial panic of 1893, a major economic depression, forced wages down. In 1895, in the region including southern Illinois, the average daily earning of production miners paid by the ton was $1.58, with average annual income about $235. In the prevailing hard times, men fought for the privilege of earning those meager returns. In 1898, the Illinois UMWA district negotiated a contract with most of the state's mine operators, with two conspicuous exceptions.

The St. Louis and Big Muddy mine opened near Carterville in 1898. In Williamson County, it became the scene of repeated clashes between the UMWA and the mine's owner-operator, Samuel Brush of Carbondale. Brush, raised in the home of his uncle, Daniel Harmon Brush, the founder of Carbondale, displayed the same stiff-necked sense of high moral purpose that characterized his Uncle Daniel.

Strike after strike took place at the St. Louis and Big Muddy. When operators imported black nonunion workers from the South, armed conflict between striking union men and those at work caused injury and death. Officials sent the National Guard to restore order. It was a fearful and bloody time, with public opinion clearly on the union side. Samuel Brush continued to operate a nonunion mine, but with diminishing success. Production declined, and the costs of transporting miners and their families and maintaining a heavily guarded pit head climbed. Finally, in 1906, he sold the mine to the Madison Coal Company, which thereafter operated it as Madison No. 8, a UMWA shop. Half a century later, a friend of Samuel Brush said of him, "He was the typical early American individualist who would not count the cost. He thought he was right."[22]

The Zeigler Coal Company, owned by wealthy Joseph Leiter and his father, Levi, of Chicago, began sinking a shaft in 1903 near what became the village of Zeigler, six miles west of West Frankfort. Zeigler was the elder Leiter's middle name. Joseph Leiter bought a square block of 7,000 acres of land for a mining venture after he found a seam of good coking coal at a depth of 400 feet.

Leiter's findings touched off additional corporate interest in acquiring land and coal rights in Franklin County. The Chicago, Burlington, and Quincy Railroad bought 10,000 acres at Valier and ran a line into the field.

U.S. Steel purchased most of two townships—seventy-two sections—east of Benton. The Missouri Pacific solidified its major holdings at Bush. The Illinois Central increased its domain to 20,000 or more acres north of Carterville that contained a working mine. The Frisco Lines established ownership of a large tract between Benton and West Frankfort. And the New York Central Railroad gained title to a major holding between Eldorado and Carrier Mills. By 1907, control of most of the coal in the Franklin-Williamson-Saline triangle rested in the hands of about a dozen giant corporations in railroads, steel, and coal dealerships. Thereafter, decisions were to be made at the pleasure of absentee owners and investors in Chicago, New York, and Boston.[23]

Operations began in 1904 at Zeigler No. 1, a technically advanced mine for its time. It featured machines for undercutting and loading the coal and a room where the miners could bathe and change their clothing. Workers with their families and single men arrived to fill the company houses and apartments. Zeigler became a model company town. The Zeigler Coal Company built and owned the houses and apartments, the company store, a brick school, and an up-to-date hospital. Its owners sought complete control of the community. Employees policed the streets, and mine officials provided the services of a physician. Owning several thousand acres in the vicinity, the company attempted operations of farms and orchards to produce food for sale to the miners.

Company houses at the time usually were little more than shacks. Many had no weatherboarding on the outside nor plaster inside. They lacked running water, and a single outhouse served three or four families. Zeigler company houses were better built, with none smaller than three rooms. Rents ranged from $6 to $9 a month, and that charge included running water, a luxury for the time. For an additional $.25 per month, the company provided electricity.[24] The appearance of company houses in the region was documented in the photographs of Bill Horrell and those taken during the Great Depression of the 1930s by employees of the U.S. Farm Security Administration. They revealed the grim reality of living conditions in the coal camps, showing rows of identical small houses along poorly paved streets, lacking curbs and gutters and any attempt at landscaping.[25]

The square in Zeigler, Joseph Leiter's town, was in reality a circle, with broad main streets radiating from it after the fashion of Washington, D.C. In the nation's capital, that was said to allow cannon strategically placed to sweep the streets in case of invasion or rebellion. In Zeigler, where the mine office was within the circle, observers said the arrangement allowed the placement of a machine gun that would have each of the principal streets in its field of fire.

Miners hoisted the first coal out of Zeigler No. 1 on June 9, 1904. Immediately, the UMWA local demanded the standard rate of pay established in Illinois for each ton of coal loaded in less mechanized mines. Leiter refused to meet that scale, saying that coal could be loaded faster with available machinery. He believed the union objected to a mechanized mine because it would employ fewer miners for each ton of coal produced. Legend has it that he and the union representatives were close to agreement on a compromise when one of the negotiators for the union spoke scornfully of Leiter. Thereupon, the owner threw an ink-filled pen and the unsigned contract at his opponent and declared, "Zeigler will run scab forever!"[26]

Union miners struck on July 8, and Leiter retaliated by making the mine site a heavily guarded fortress, manned by strikebreakers. The presence of forty deputy U.S. marshals and two companies of state militia guarding the mine made Zeigler appear to be a battlefield. A giant searchlight mounted on the mine tipple swept the surrounding countryside each night. Gradually, the tension eased. Still, Leiter found it difficult to keep nonunion men at work, and his expenses mounted. Striking union men and families were evicted from their homes in Zeigler and moved to a tent encampment five miles away, near Christopher. More and more, the struggle seemed to be over the future of mine unionism.

Early in the morning on April 3, 1905, soon after the day shift had gone underground, a tremendous explosion shook the mine. Union men offered to do rescue work but were rejected. A state inspector, a mine examiner, and the assistant mine manager finally went below. They all perished from the deadly gas that filled the mine. When others inspected the mine, they found evidence of a massive explosion that killed fifty-one men and boys. Only one previous disaster in the history of coal mining in Illinois—Braidwood in 1883, where sixty-one lives were lost—had taken a greater toll. Company officers called it a powder explosion and blamed the striking miners. The secretary of the State Mining Board doubted that was the case. The official finding stated that methane gas ignited by a miner's lamp caused an explosion that set off forty-one kegs of powder. Ventilation had been inadequate to keep the mine clear of gas.

The mine was cleaned up and production restored. All went well until early in 1909, when another explosion took twenty-six lives. After a third explosion and loss of life in February, Joseph Leiter gave up operation of the mine and leased it to the Bell and Zoller Mining Company, also owner of mines in the Centralia vicinity. When it resumed operation in 1910, every miner on the payroll was a member of the UMWA.[27]

Although Joseph Leiter gave up management of the mine, he continued as proprietor of the settlement called Zeigler. In 1917, he arranged to have one hundred houses built to meet the demand generated by wartime prosperity. When asked for specifications, he replied, "Oh hell, build them as cheaply as possible, just one degree from a hog pen. That's all these devils need down here. They'll tear them down anyway." Bell and Zoller closed Zeigler No. 1 in December 1949. Forty million tons of coal had been taken from the mine, including a one-day record of 9,000 set in 1928.[28]

Collapse of the Coal-Based Economy

The strains of violence evident at the St. Louis and Big Muddy and the Zeigler mines came together near the city of Herrin, in Williamson County, in what became known as the Herrin Massacre. On June 22, 1922, nineteen men working at a nonunion mine midway between Marion and Herrin were taken from the mine, marched across country, and shot, beaten, and slashed to death. Two trials on charges of murder ended in jury verdicts of "not guilty."[29]

In 1939, *Life* magazine invited the artist Paul Cadmus to portray an incident from labor history. He chose the Herrin Massacre because, in his words, "Violence appalls me and I thought I would demonstrate my horror." He painted a picture that stirred an enormous controversy because it didn't depict a historical event so much as it spoke to the universal theme of man's inhumanity to man. Cadmus chose as the setting for his painting the rural cemetery where several of the killings took place. The painting is rich in religious symbolism, depicting the brutality of the attackers on the one hand and the suffering bodies of their victims on the other. He spoke out for tolerance and kindness by depicting their opposites.[30]

While conflict and tragedy framed an ugly picture of coal mining from the turn of the century until the mid-1920s, the coal industry enjoyed continual growth and increasing employment. In Franklin, Williamson, and Saline counties, there were more than one hundred mines. Johnston City had eight, and around Herrin, there were sixteen.[31] In the three counties, the average annual increase in employment at the mines reached 1,400, and the annual increase in production, one million tons. The population of "seven stranded coal towns"—West Frankfort, Herrin, Bush, Johnston City, Eldorado, Carrier Mills, and Zeigler—grew from a total of 4,200 in 1900 to 41,000 in 1920. By 1923, the three counties formed the leading coal producing area west of the Allegheny Mountains and one of the three major regions in the United States.[32]

Signs of the growing coal-based economy appeared throughout central and southern Illinois. When coal production expanded in 1917 with the entry of the United States into World War I, the rising population of the coal towns so increased the need for shelter that hundreds of houses were built "shotgun" style, often in twenty-four hours. They joined the ranks of the company houses of earlier construction in their lack of quality. With mine ownership in absentee hands, the basis of the local economy in the coal towns became real estate value. Rising populations made town lots and houses increasingly costly. Banks and savings and loan associations put much of their wealth into real estate and business loans. The whole structure was built on coal, and when that structure ultimately failed, economic disaster struck. Before that happened, however, as one editorial put it, people enjoyed "contentment and satisfaction."[33]

The culture of the growing southern Illinois coal towns was more akin to that of the South than of such places as St. Louis and Chicago. There was an influx of workers from the South—primarily from western Kentucky—after 1900. In speech and ways of thought, the people of southern Illinois differed from those of the central and northern portions of the state.[34] In the 1920s, many of the young boys chose to work in the mines rather than continue in school. Higher education was not an option in most families, and local school districts spent little on education. Men who worked underground enjoyed being in the open air and sunshine in their off-duty hours. That feeling led them to take up hunting, fishing, and gardening, activities that had the added value of supplementing the family's food supply. Southern Illinois's forests, rivers, and small-farm agriculture provided opportunities for those pursuits.

Children of the coal towns often played their games without adult supervision, baseball being the most popular sport. Almost every town had its team, with Sunday games common in the warmer months of the year. Dancing was a common pastime of young people in the mining communities, and like baseball, required little investment. People danced in homes and in dance halls. The White City dance hall in Herrin once refused admission to teenagers, so they danced in the parking lot to music coming from open windows.[35]

Real estate values built on the growth of coal operations provided substantial local property tax revenues in the Franklin-Williamson-Saline counties area. During the early 1920s, communities built roads, graveled streets, began to provide water and sewer services, and improved schools. Handsome new high schools appeared, in contrast to years when school districts spent almost nothing on education beyond the eighth grade. By 1923, signs of depression appeared in the southern Illinois coal industry. Increased competition came from coalfields in other locations and from alternative fuel sources such as natural gas, oil, and hydroelectric. Still, employment in the mines continued at a high level. The payroll for the three counties in 1926 reached approximately $40 million. Miners averaged $50 to $60 for each two-week pay period.

Triggered by decisions made in corporate boardrooms hundreds and thousands of miles away, the collapse of the economy came suddenly. The beginning of the Great Depression only made things worse.[36] Banks and savings and loan associations, the latter once numbering thirty-five in the region, dropped to six, including only two banks, causing major losses among stockholders and frightening customers. Thirty-four coal-town banks failed during a two-year period, with great losses of depositors' dollars. Large and small businesses went bankrupt, driving the local tax structure into shock.[37]

By 1930, hundreds of citizens defaulted on property taxes. The whole system collapsed. Delinquencies piled up faster than local officials could process them. Schools could not pay teachers. In Benton, a community of 8,000 persons, officials turned off street lights and reduced the police force to one poorly paid officer.[38] By 1931, Illinois had 700,000 unemployed workers, with the worst problems in Cook County and the "southern Illinois mining counties like Franklin and Williamson. . . . Many families in the mining communities lived in actual destitution."[39]

Overall, coal industry values plummeted from $2 billion in the early 1920s to $795 million in 1930. The number of coal miners in the United States declined from 694,000 in 1919 to 602,000 in 1929.[40] The capacity of the mines in southern Illinois to produce coal consistently ran ahead of demand, meaning fewer days of employment and fewer dollars for each miner. Gradually, those who had purchased homes fell further behind in payments, and foreclosures followed. So many houses became vacant that the savings and loans, wanting to avoid paying property taxes, had them torn down. Some communities lost one-third of their buildings.

During the Depression that began in 1929, the economic condition of all Illinois coal towns worsened. Community morale in the Franklin-Williamson-Saline counties triangle declined, and pessimism and dispiritedness increased, resulting in the stagnation of businesses.[41] Photographers of the Farm Security Administration captured images of the "faces of defeat" on unemployed miners.[42] Unemployed workers comprised about one-third of the Illinois labor force by late 1931. In January 1933, after the election of Franklin D. Roosevelt as president of the United States but before his inauguration, the total neared one-half. Local relief efforts in the coal towns soon were overwhelmed, leaving UMWA locals to provide assistance for families.

In the three-county area, the coal market declined by half, reducing jobs by three-quarters and payrolls by four-fifths. No economic alternatives could fill any of those gaps. The prevailing dominance of the powerful UMWA in coal towns convinced prospective new employers to favor places where labor was weaker. An employment census taken in 1938 and 1939 in seven coal towns of the three-county area showed 41 percent of all workers unemployed. At one time, Franklin County had the highest rate of unemployment of any county in the nation. Many of those considered employed worked only one or two days a week.[43]

Longtime unemployment was most severe among older miners with few technical skills and young men who had not found jobs of any sort. Average family income in the seven coal towns was $39 a month and $472 a year. A family spent approximately one-half of its income for food and little on clothing—an average of $3.60 a month for the family. Feed, flour, and sugar sacks were made over into articles of clothing, dish towels, and wash cloths. Some people had no shoes; others had shoes only in the winter months. Many of the long-unemployed had given up city water and electricity, with outdoor toilets used by 95 percent.[44] While all of Illinois suffered from unemployment and increased poverty, the three-county area in southern Illinois was left "economically prostrate" by the late 1930s. Operators abandoned four of the larger mines in 1940 that had employed 1,200 workers.[45]

Some better-educated, more ambitious young people left the three-county area in search of education or work elsewhere during this period. Some made their way into the armed forces and colleges and universities. For other age groups, the choices were fewer. One unemployed older miner said, "Everybody that was able to get out left a long time ago."[46] Unemployment continued to be a severe problem until wartime conditions restored a degree of prosperity in 1941 and the years that followed.

Just as the Civil War and World War I provided gargantuan appetites for the industrial power that coal represented, so did World War II. World conflict brought prosperity back to the coalfields, and workers responded with record production. By March 1945, the unemployment rate in Illinois was .7 percent.[47]

John L. Lewis, Labor Baron

In the first six decades of the twentieth century, John Llewellyn Lewis was the most powerful and charismatic labor leader in the United States. He seized power and then held onto and exercised it with a closed fist in an iron hand over the UMWA. He rose to power in the coal mining industry from a brief background as mule driver, coal digger, and local union leader.[48] He gained a toehold in mine union affairs while working in an Illinois mine in 1909 and rose rapidly in union management circles to the heights of national leadership.

John L. Lewis was the son of Tom Lewis, a coal miner who emigrated from Wales to the United States. His mother was Ann Watkins Lewis, also an immigrant from Wales, whose father founded a Church of Jesus Christ of Latter-day Saints (Mormon) congregation in Lucas, Iowa. John was born in Lucas, or some say in Cleveland, Iowa, on February 12, 1880, the oldest of seven children. In addition to sharing the birthday, there are a few other similarities between Lewis and Abraham Lincoln. Both lived for a considerable time in Springfield, Illinois, and the two are buried only a few yards apart in Springfield's Oak Ridge Cemetery.

Little is known about John as a child and youth. Biographers believe he attended school until age sixteen, completing three and a half years of high school in Des Moines. Immediately, he joined his father underground working coal. Four years later, he began a five-year stretch of travel about the West, working here and there in mining and construction and gaining a feel for the working person's point of view. Lewis returned to Lucas, presumably to stay, in 1905. He ran for mayor and lost, and he failed in the feed and grain business. In 1907, Lewis married Myrta Bell, daughter of a physician and leading citizen of the local community.[49]

One of John's brothers, George, found work in an expanding mine at Panama, Illinois, a few miles south of Hillsboro, in Montgomery County. In 1908, John and Myrta, his father, mother, sister, and several of his brothers joined George in Panama. All of the males worked at the large and somewhat mechanized Sandy Shoal mine. They had an almost immediate impact on the UMWA local with direct, powerful, and sometimes physical methods. They became a political machine, aimed at advancing John's career in union management and their own in related fields. There can be little doubt that the extended Lewis family learned of the dangers of underground mining as dramatized by the Cherry disaster in 1909. Such happenings would have influenced John's thinking about the need for greater safety in the mines and the role that unions could play in improving working conditions and wages.

Lewis became a lobbyist in Springfield for the UMWA district in 1909 and was elected president of the union local at Panama a year later. In 1911, he quit work in the mines and became an organizer for the American Federation of Labor (AFL), then the strongest labor organization in the United States. After moving his home to Springfield, his career in labor skyrocketed. The coal-rich state of Illinois formed an excellent base for the exercise of his ambition. Of the nation's 710,000 coal miners, 90,000 labored in the state.

Predecessor officials of the UMWA had seen the large miner employment in Illinois and its potential for union organizing. One of the most successful was John Mitchell, whose roots and sentiments ran deep in Illinois soil.

Born in Braidwood in 1870, Mitchell worked his way through the ranks of various union organizations. With hard work, and some luck, he became acting UMWA president in 1898, eight years after he helped create the organization, and president a year later.[50] Much of Mitchell's early work in recruiting UMWA members had occurred in southern Illinois. Scotch-Irish in heritage and married to an Irish Catholic, he was especially skillful in bridging the gap between the sons and daughters of Erin and immigrant arrivals in the coalfield. He enlisted local community leaders to integrate the coal camps and villages, and membership in the UMWA grew from 34,000 to 300,000 during his presidency.[51]

Mitchell took the view that labor and management could each maximize its advantage by harmonious cooperation rather than confrontation. In 1903, with the assistance of journalist Walter Weyl, he wrote and published a book titled *Organized Labor*, which stressed his belief in collaboration, relationships, and the importance to society of trade unionism. Some in the labor movement regarded him as too accommodating to the owners and managers of the coal industry and too willing to compromise. He resigned as president in 1908 and died of pneumonia following surgery in 1919.[52]

Lewis left his post with the AFL in 1916, worked with the president of the UMWA, and in 1917 was appointed international statistician and business manager of the union's journal. He soon became the strongest figure in UMWA management and was named acting vice president. In the view of Priscilla Long, a labor historian, Lewis was "shrewd, less ethical than [John] Mitchell," "ruthless," "intelligent, and often emotional." She wrote that Lewis benefited from patronage and practiced election fraud over and over, and that he rose in UMWA ranks by appointment rather than election.[53]

In cooperation with the federal government during World War I, Lewis helped bring management and labor closer together to meet wartime needs for coal. During that time, wages in the bituminous fields increased. He was appointed the UMWA's acting president in 1918, during the alcohol-induced illness of President Frank Hayes, who had succeeded Mitchell. Two years later, he became president by election, a position he held for forty stormy years.

Utilizing strikes as bargaining weapons, including one notable labor stoppage that lasted five months, Lewis by 1924 was the acknowledged premier labor statesman of the United States. According to Dan Reitz, once a miner and union official and now a member of the Illinois House of Representatives, "Within the union, Lewis ruled with . . . [an] iron hand. When District 2 President John Brophy ran against him for the UMWA presidency in 1926, Lewis beat him in a 'questionable' election and then expelled Brophy from the Union. As Lewis appointed his allies to coalfield positions, the right to vote for district officers was taken away from the rank-and-file miners."[54]

Lewis's iron rule had repercussions for UMWA operations in Illinois. Alleging financial irregularities, the increasingly autocratic Lewis dictated the establishment of a "provisional government" for District 12 (Illinois), creating widespread opposition within the state to the central office of the UMWA in Washington, D.C.[55]

The beginning of the Depression further harmed an already ailing coal industry. Economic conditions in the industry hit an all-time low. By 1932, UMWA membership had declined from a high of 500,000 to 75,000. It also was a low point for Lewis personally. He was grieved by the death of his favorite brother, George, who had been a lobbyist for the UMWA in Springfield and Washington.

Although Lewis came from a Republican family and had been viewed as a Republican during the 1920s, he privately supported Franklin D. Roosevelt in 1932, while publicly endorsing President Herbert Hoover. After Roosevelt won, "Lewis's speeches and public statements . . . presaged the New Deal reforms and the 1935–1936 industrial union rebellion against the AF of L."[56] With the assistance of Lewis and the UMWA, New Deal legislation and codes served to confer on workers the right to join labor unions. Lewis drew 92 percent of all coal miners into union ranks, and UMWA membership grew to 400,000 within a year. Still the coal industry remained in a depressed condition. Production during the 1930s fell well below that of the 1920s. Hourly wages improved somewhat, but limited work weeks kept the mine workers' average weekly pay in 1939 to approximately $23.[57]

In 1933 and 1934, Lewis sought to open the AFL, traditionally an alliance of craft unions, to industrial unions such as the UMWA. At the AFL convention in 1935, it became apparent to Lewis that the AFL did not intend to organize and charter industrial unions. Angry and feisty, Lewis goaded the president of the Carpenters Union, William Hutcheson, into speaking disrespectfully of Lewis's ancestry. Lewis leaped over chairs to get to Hutcheson and punched him in the face. That blow signaled to industrial workers that they had gained a champion.[58]

From his position as leader, Lewis used UMWA funds to help organize unions in the auto, rubber, communications, and steel industries. With Lewis embroiled in dozens of union activities, the Depression-era 1930s became a boiling cauldron of labor strife. "By mid-1937, Lewis had become both the nation's most admired and most feared labor leader."[59] According to one labor historian, "The birth and rise of the CIO [Congress of Industrial Organizations] represent his most outstanding and enduring contribution to American life."[60] The industrial unions came together in the CIO with Lewis as its president in 1938. During the CIO's first year, almost four million people joined labor unions, and their wages increased by more than a billion dollars.

Lewis supported Roosevelt in the 1936 presidential election but opposed FDR's seeking a third term in 1940. Differing with the president in both domestic and foreign policy, Lewis supported the Republican candidate, Wendell Willkie, and when labor generally stayed on Roosevelt's side, Lewis resigned the presidency of the CIO. In 1942, he took the UMWA out of CIO ranks. He led the UMWA aggressively during World War II, calling strikes even in wartime.

Eight months after the war ended, on April 1, 1946, Lewis called a strike. It was a time of strikes in almost every industry, as workers sought to "catch up" after wartime curtailment of wage increases. President Harry S. Truman stood firm, calling for workers who struck to be drafted into the military forces.[61] The House of Representatives concurred, amidst a storm of protest from many quarters, but the Senate did not. On May 22, the federal government "seized" the coal mines.

The miners returned to work on May 29. Lewis and the coal operators came to the White House, where Lewis signed an agreement with Secretary of the Interior Julius Krug that specified a $1.85 per day pay raise, $100 in vacation pay, the guarantee of a five-day work week—opening the door to overtime pay—and a royalty of $.05 per ton on all coal mined to fund a miners' Welfare and Retirement program. The welfare program was to provide medical care, rehabilitation treatment, and death benefits "from the cradle to the grave."[62] The agreement provided authority for the director of the U.S. Bureau of Mines to establish a Federal Mine Safety Code, which became effective on July 29, 1946. The code conferred power on the coal mines administrator, a federal official, to enforce mine safety regulations and provided the first legal authority for federal inspectors to close mines found to be dangerous.[63] These changes would have significance for both the Centralia and West Frankfort mine disasters.

Shortly after the elections in November 1946, in which the Democratic Party was soundly beaten, Lewis again threatened a strike. This time, President Truman resisted. His adviser Clark Clifford later remembered that "it looked like Lewis had violated the law. . . . Roosevelt had toadied to him time and again. But now he pushed the President [Truman] the wrong way. And he just said one day, 'Okay, we're going to go!'" That meant federal court action. The government contended that since the coal industry was still technically in a state of seizure, the Smith-Connally Act, prohibiting strikes against facilities held by the government, ruled. A federal judge handed down an injunction against the strike, but still Lewis called the miners out on November 20. On a charge of contempt, the court fined the UMWA $3 million and Lewis $10,000. On December 7, the strike ended in a victory for Truman, with strong public support, and a defeat for Lewis. The two remained at odds until Truman left office in 1953.[64]

Miners trusted Lewis's leadership and persisted in striking even when ordered back to work by the U.S. government. Those actions made him and the unions less popular with the public, resulting in the Taft-Hartley Act of 1947 that regulated certain aspects of union activity. Lewis aggressively opposed it.[65] He would become a central figure in the aftermaths of the great coal mine disasters at Centralia in 1947 and West Frankfort in 1951.

Part One

The 1947 Centralia
Mine Disaster

1

More Than a Coal Town

THE PHYSICAL SCARS OF THE PAST TELL STO-
ries of Centralia's history. Tracks of the Illinois Central Railroad carved the
city in half midway through the nineteenth century, and they remain there
today. Empty buildings are reminders that railroad shops once hummed
with activity. Over the nearby countryside, remnants of the oil-well era
are echoes of the good times, the flow of money, and how swiftly the black
gold was depleted. Above ground, there is little to recall the decades of
coal mining. Deep scars underground run for miles in darkened and silent
tunnels. At the surface, shafts are plugged with concrete, isolated and mute
evidence of the bustle that brought to Centralia a rich ethnic mix of people
looking for a better life. The psychological scars are harder to identify.
They include memories of death and suffering, highlighted by the tragedy
of Centralia No. 5 mine.

In 1850, Illinois had only ten incorporated towns—Chicago, Alton,
Springfield, Beardstown, Pekin, Quincy, Peoria, Bloomington, Galena, and
Rock Island—most developed along the rivers or waterways that provided
opportunities for commercial transportation and personal travel. Chicago
was still mostly uninviting swampland with a population of about twenty
thousand people. Dust covered everything in the city, except when it rained,
and then mud covered everything.[1]

In thinly populated central and southern Illinois, farmers subsisted off
the land, bartered with their neighbors, and prayed for good crops. The
fertile land produced fruit—strawberries and peaches dominated—and
vegetables primarily for consumption by the families of farmers. Almost
every farmer had livestock. Land could be purchased for $.665 to $1.25
an acre, with few takers. Then came the railroads, and the face of Illinois
changed forever.

Spurred by the arrival of rail lines throughout the state during the 1850s, the population of Illinois doubled.[2] The state ranked eleventh in U.S. population in 1850, and fourth in 1860. The number of people in Chicago almost quadrupled during the decade, and towns sprouted along the prairie rail lines. In 1850, Illinois stood eighteenth among states in miles of railroad tracks, with only a few hundred in operation. A decade later, the state ranked second only to Ohio, with 2,781 miles completed. Centralia came to life in the exuberant 1850s, an integral part of the birth of the Illinois Central Railroad.[3]

A central railroad for Illinois from north to south had been the dream of public officials before action by Congress and President Millard Fillmore in 1850. Leading support in Congress and in the state was Senator Stephen A. Douglas, a champion of westward expansion. Legislation authorized a grant of 2.5 million acres of federal land in the state for what became the Illinois Central (IC). The land grant consisted of track right-of-way and alternate sections of land on either side of the route. In exchange for the land, the railroad agreed to transport forever all troops and government property at one-half the standard rate, and mail was to be carried for 80 percent of the standard rate. In 1851, the railroad received its federal charter.

Sale of the lands and bonds provided financing for construction of a 700-mile rail line on two distinct routes. The first ran from Cairo to Centralia and northward to Dunleith, west of Galena and across the Mississippi River from Dubuque, Iowa. The second also started in Cairo and continued to Centralia, where it split from the first and went to Chicago. Construction of the primary lines took five years, from 1851 to 1856, and cost $26,568,017, or about $37,600 per mile. Groundbreaking for construction was held on December 23, 1851, with the last rail laid and the last spike driven on September 27, 1856. Workers built the 250-mile segment from Chicago to Centralia between the spring of 1852 and the summer of 1856, with the final piece from Mattoon to Centralia finished in the spring and summer of 1856.

In 1853, the railroad established Centralia from the public land grant, the name identifying the town's location in the rail system. Towns sprouted and grew rapidly along the route north, including Decatur, Bloomington, Dixon, Freeport, and Galena. On the route to Chicago, the communities of Effingham, Mattoon, Urbana, Champaign, and Kankakee blossomed. Many of the towns did not exist before the railroad, and those that did had few residents.[4]

Within a year, the railroad laid out a plan for Centralia, erected a combination passenger station and hotel, and began construction of its terminal.

The first unit of the rail shops opened in the center of town. Centralia had an instant connection to markets and travel destinations throughout the eastern half of the nation and celebrity, too. George B. McClellan lived for a time in Centralia as chief engineer of the IC. He later became a controversial Union army general during the Civil War.[5]

The first engines on the IC were wood-burners, but a shortage of wood soon caused officials to look for alternative fuels. This led to experiments with coal, one of the first of which occurred in Centralia. A master mechanic in the town rigged one locomotive to burn coal and one to burn coke. The test did not go well, but officials knew coal would become the alternative to wood, and experiments continued. By the beginning of the Civil War in 1861, more than half of the IC locomotives burned coal.[6]

The IC provided economic stability in Centralia. Well into the mid-1900s, the railroad employed up to a thousand people in the shops as engineers, conductors, flagmen, porters, baggage handlers, and station personnel. The importance of Centralia's location brought other rail lines to the town, one of the largest operations being the Chicago, Burlington, and Quincy route. The CB&Q employed almost as many people as the IC. Other rail lines eventually routed trains through Centralia, making it a railroad town in the truest sense of the word. By 1917, passenger and freight trains traveled through Centralia every ten minutes.[7] Today the traffic is almost as heavy, but the trains carry freight.

The town's location made it ideal for transporting goods, crops, and livestock raised in central Illinois. By 1860, half of the railroad's freight tonnage resulted from the shipment of corn, wheat, fruits, potatoes, nuts, rocks, and Illinois coal. Merchants and tradesmen in the growing towns on the lines accounted for another large chunk of freight business.

The importance of the IC to Centralia was demonstrated in an unusual way when the state fair came to town in 1858. State officials worried that the upstart community could not accommodate the fair and house all the patrons. The IC came to the rescue by offering its newly constructed shops as areas for exhibits. The railroad also placed passenger cars on sidings for visitors' sleeping quarters.[8]

The firing of a Civil War cannon on October 29, 1874, announced the next major economic development for Centralia and vicinity: coal. Ferdinand Kohl and A. M. Warner, along with a number of other investors, had formed the Central Mining Company in 1869, but it wasn't until 1874 that coal was discovered about 600 feet underground, south of town. By then, only Kohl and Warner remained involved. They called this Centralia No. 1 mine.[9]

Kohl discovered that residents of the rural Centralia area welcomed more economic diversity but had little interest in working underground. With its long history of coal mining, Europe provided a source of experienced coal mine workers not available in the region. The first immigrants came from England, Scotland, Ireland, Wales, and Germany. Others soon followed from Italy, Poland, Spain, Austria, Hungary, Bohemia, Moravia, and Lithuania. The influx produced an instant diversity of the population, not always to the liking of native residents and early settlers of the town. Unable to speak English and unfamiliar with the culture of rural Illinois, many of the workers suffered social injustices before being accepted in the community. Descendants of those first miners are residents and leaders of Centralia today.

The discovery of coal and the opportunity of shipping by rail to points throughout the nation added further incentive to the search for coal seams. In the decade from 1855 to 1865, coalfields in Alton, Rock Island, Danville, Braceville, and Braidwood opened along the lines of new railroads, and in the decades following, mines opened in southern Illinois. A separate company, the Centralia Mining and Manufacturing Company, sank the Centralia No. 2 shaft and announced it to the citizens in the acceptable manner: Owners blew a loud whistle taken from a wrecked Mississippi River steamboat. New entrepreneurs sank shafts of Centralia No. 3 and No. 4 and purchased No. 1 and No. 2 from Kohl, all before 1900. Consolidation and new ventures continued into the early twentieth century. In 1905, the Bell and Zoller Coal Company of Chicago bought out owners of the mines and organized the Centralia Coal Company. Bell and Zoller was one of the Big Six among Illinois coal operators, and the Centralia company was one of its subsidiaries.[10]

About two miles south of Centralia, the company sank the shaft of No. 5 mine and reached coal on August 6, 1907. At the same time, a group of men active in the Old National Bank organized the Marion County Coal Company and sank a shaft at Glenridge, a few miles north of Centralia. By the end of 1908, there were seven active mines in the Centralia area. That was the peak in operations. Soon thereafter, mines began closing for various reasons. Mine No. 2 closed in 1913 after being condemned by the state, and in 1921, the walls of No. 4 mine east of the CB&Q roundhouse in Centralia collapsed. By 1940, all but No. 5 and Glenridge had closed because of falling production or other problems.[11]

With many of the mines outside Centralia city boundaries, it was only natural that housing for miners and families was concentrated near the work site. In the days before every family had an automobile, proximity to work was essential. Property near the Glenridge and Centralia No. 5 mines provided the locations for neighborhood housing. This was characteristic of mine locations in southern Illinois, where towns primarily for miners sprang up quickly after the sinking of a mine shaft. Operating companies often developed the "company town," staffed the stores, and rented housing, tying the economy exclusively to mining. The Glenridge mine company store, Glenridge Mercantile Company, served the community from 1912 to 1941. All the houses were similar in design and poorly built. When mines failed, so did the communities. The mines outside Centralia had the added benefit of a town nearby that was not totally dependent on mining for work and social opportunities. Many families had members working in the mines, for the railroads, or in Centralia's retail shops. As transportation became more convenient, miners chose to live in all parts of Centralia.

Until 1915, the housing settlement and the few businesses near No. 5 mine outside Centralia had no community name. In that year, Centralia voted to ban the sale of liquor. Soon after, saloons—someone counted sixteen initially—as well as liquor wholesalers, prostitutes, and gamblers, moved south of the city near the IC roundhouse. They not only wanted to remain in business but also to escape taxes being levied for paving the main street in west Centralia. When businessmen and residents decided to establish a village, they received a charter under the name Wamac, an acronym for Washington, Marion, and Clinton, the three counties that joined nearby.

For two years, Wamac ran wide open, with a one-man police department that provided virtually no law enforcement. His efforts consisted of arresting drunks and preparing lists of the names of habitual drunks for posting on the doors of each tavern. The two-cell jail overflowed, and bootleggers thrived by supplying Centralia residents with booze. With matters clearly out of hand, Wamac "went dry" by a vote of its citizens in 1917. With 5,500 votes cast, drys won over wets by 303. While legitimate liquor outlets shut down, the activity of bootleggers increased.

Bootleggers showed uncommon creativity, given the laws in Centralia and Wamac. One entrepreneur established a still not far from Wamac in Clinton County and then secured a contract for removal of garbage in Centralia. He picked up garbage in town, ostensibly to be fed to his hogs. Instead, he used it to make booze at the still and then returned to Centralia with liquor to sell.[12]

In the first eighty-four years of Centralia's life, up to 1937, economic developments progressed slowly and changed gradually, providing a stable environment for community growth. The highs and lows of the railroad business, coal mining, and farming the rich central Illinois soil balanced out, making Centralia a fairly typical, prosperous Midwestern community, not solely dependent on one business or industry. That tranquility was lost on November 30, 1937.

Oil was struck on a farm northwest of Centralia that day, and wells soon popped up all over the region. The highest concentration occurred on the west side of town, including popular Fairview Park. In short order, there were 102 wells, producing 6,200 barrels a day. That brought unaccustomed change to Centralia, but it was a drop in the bucket compared with what happened a year later. Leaders of the big oil firms, such as the Texas Oil Company, waited patiently to see if the 1937 discovery amounted to more than a local phenomenon. There were oil fields elsewhere in Illinois, but none rivaled the productive fields of Texas and Oklahoma. The answer came with a gusher on the Ed Tate farm, about one-half mile west of the Lake Centralia spillway northeast of town in June 1938. It opened what became known as the Lake Centralia-Salem field.[13]

Centralia discovered quickly what the word *boom* means in oil language. Every large oil company—Texas and Shell among them—and many independents sent men and machinery to the region, taking all available rooms and office space for rent at inflated prices. Residents converted garages, attics, basements, spare rooms, railroad cars, and even chicken houses to living quarters on a moment's notice. A flood of oil-field workers and camp followers descended on Centralia from Texas, Kentucky, Louisiana, Oklahoma, and Kansas. Miles of pipeline were laid. By the end of 1938, the new field had close to 500 wells pumping more than 50,000 barrels a day. No one knew the limits. A year later, the number of wells had increased to 1,581.

By April 1, 1940, the Lake Centralia field ranked as the largest in the nation in daily production, outranking the giant East Texas field. The largest oil companies built their own "camps" and office buildings when Centralia ran out of space. Oil derricks blanketed the region and obscured the horizon. Black gold made untold numbers of residents rich overnight, and royalty checks to families continued long after the boom ended and the oil companies left town. The City of Centralia became one of the grandest beneficiaries of the boom, thanks to a purchase in 1910 of 437 acres for use as a reservoir. During the boom, companies drilled seventy-four wells on the property, providing a flow of cash to the city that continues to this day. The money built a city hall and a community center, maintained infrastructure, and increased city services and employment. City schools benefited, too.[14]

Hardworking oil-field people also lived hard when they weren't working, and they spent recklessly. The streets of Centralia became action centers twenty-four hours a day. Impact on the city's culture and entertainment made merchants and retailers happy and others less so. On Saturday nights, stores filled with shoppers. With oil-field operations continuing around the clock, businesses provided food and drink on the same schedule. Nightclubs with gambling operations opened just beyond the north and south city limits. When the money flowed, it brought less desirable elements to town, including con artists, gamblers, and prostitutes. At the boom's peak, the population of Centralia topped nineteen thousand. In a short time, Centralia dropped any pretense of innocence.

In the twenty-first century, Centralia is only a shadow of its economic past. Railroad passenger business has declined, the railroad shops have closed, and employment has dropped. Trains rumble through town, but the economic impact on Centralia is less than at any time since the 1950s. Since the 1940s, the coal mining has largely disappeared with the closing of most operations. Employment opportunities in the oil fields have diminished. While the community struggles to remain an attractive presence for prospective businesses and industries, it takes pride in smaller achievements such as the growth of nearby Kaskaskia Community College. Meanwhile, those steeped in Centralia's history know that a boom or an uplifting business cycle has happened before, and it can happen again.

2

"Please Save Our Lives"

FOR AS LONG AS ANYONE COULD REMEMBER, from the opening of Centralia No. 5 in 1907 to the 1940s, the mine had been dusty and dry. Coal dust accumulated everywhere, reducing visibility, complicating ventilation, and making life miserable for workers. Dust is not just an irritant underground. When the mine air is saturated with dust particles, it becomes a safety hazard. A spark or a flame can ignite the highly combustible dust and touch off an explosion that roars through the tunnels and rooms, claiming everything in its path.

Strangely, though, not many fatal accidents were recorded in the first four decades of operations at No. 5. On December 27, 1909, four men were killed, one died in 1915, and on February 23, 1921, three died. These instances involved shot firers, the men who set and discharged explosives at the faces of a mine where coal is dislodged from the vein and later loaded in pit cars and taken to the surface. Other Illinois mines had more frequent accidents and larger numbers of dead. Methane gas was the culprit at some of these mines. Centralia No. 5 had virtually no methane.[1]

The dust hazard could be minimized in several ways. One was to remove the dust by hauling it out of the mine. This required frequent interruptions in production, and that caused a loss of revenues. Another procedure was to mix the coal dust with incombustible rock, pulverized stone in most cases, which neutralized the explosive potential of the dust. This was called *rock dusting*, by far the most accepted method of reducing risk. The technique did not prevent explosions but could localize a blast and reduce casualties. For example, rock dusting near the faces of the seam of coal where blasting occurred could short-circuit a chain reaction explosion. By dusting the main roads used to haul coal, but not every workroom, the same result could be achieved. The objective was to reduce risk, not eliminate it. This tactic took the steam out of an explosion that otherwise might race through the entire mine wherever coal dust particles could be found. In a few mines, coal dust was sprinkled with water to achieve the same effect, although it had to be done frequently to be effective. But no matter what methods miners used, they faced this inevitability: Coal dust would return and thicken, and it would fill the air again.[2]

Economics influenced the decisions that were made about managing the risk. Controlling dust cost money, and coal companies watched their pennies closely. In order to keep mines safe and coal dust neutralized, operations would have to be partly curtailed while crews rock dusted or removed dust. This resulted in a loss of production and revenue. Also, many operators resisted buying equipment to wet the dust because of concerns about the cost and doubts about the effectiveness of wetting. Adding to the pressures during World War II was the high demand for coal to fuel the war effort. The government requested mines to produce at maximum potential, and operators gladly obliged. This provided operators an excuse to maintain the highest levels of production while ignoring the dangers of coal dust. They considered any interruption or delay inappropriate, unprofitable, and unpatriotic.

While miners complained about dusty conditions, they did not enjoy removing coal dust or rock dusting. They viewed the tasks as dirty, tiresome, and undesirable. Consequently, workers rarely lobbied for that work. As with workers in almost any walk of life, it was easier to complain and point the finger at management. With younger men at war and replacement workers at a minimum, the average age of men in the mines increased, and there was a shortage of workers when illness or injuries occurred. Mine operators often delayed rock dusting because of high absenteeism among workers.

Accordingly, mine operators postponed or delayed critical preventive measures. In the case of Centralia No. 5, nothing cataclysmic had occurred despite the dusty conditions for years, making living on borrowed time appear to be an acceptable risk.[3] William P. Young, executive vice president of the Centralia Coal Company (a subsidiary of Bell and Zoller), would later admit he ignored warnings about dust and rejected recommendations to rock dust. In comments at a public hearing by U.S. senators, Young explained the company's attitude toward years of warnings about dusty conditions at the mine. "I don't know of any mine in which working rooms are rock-dusted." Young's official disinterest in rock dusting explains to a certain degree why the company ignored reports of coal dust hazards from state and federal inspectors and did little to improve mine safety. Young dismissed the seriousness of the inspections. "It's my honest conviction that the recommendation of the inspectors regarding coal dust was only for the convenience of the men."[4]

Inspection of mines and remedies, if any, were exclusively the responsibilities of states until 1941, when Congress passed and President Franklin D. Roosevelt signed Public Law 49. It empowered the U.S. Bureau of Mines to make inspections and investigations of health and safety conditions in coal mines. Congress required annual reports, including observations and recommendations for additional safety measures. However, the law contained no authorization to enforce safety standards.[5]

The Bureau of Mines hired and trained 107 inspectors for the first inspections in December 1941. Reports on the conditions and hazards found in each mine, with recommendations for safeguarding against dangers, were sent to mine operators, national and local union offices, and state authorities. Young knew he had no obligation to act on the recommendations, especially if he disagreed with the findings and the remedies. He later acknowledged that he differed with many of the suggested preventive measures, including rock dusting and sprinkling. Since he did not routinely see the state reports, he was under no obligation to accept those either. As events unfolded between 1944 and 1947, Young assumed he could deal with state recommendations at a political level.

The federal inspection process lacked consistency, and actual visits by inspectors were spotty, in spite of published inspection standards. From 1942 to 1944, federal inspectors made just three visits to Centralia No. 5, although semiannual inspections were required. The first federal inspection of No. 5 was conducted September 1–3, 1942. Inspectors L. W. Kelly and T. H. O'Neal made a total of 103 recommendations, 33 listed as "major." A major recommendation identified a condition that could result in a disaster.[6]

Frank Perz, appointed a federal inspector in 1944, made five inspections and reports before March 1947, often in concert with the visit by a state inspector. State and federal inspectors saw the same conditions and often made similar recommendations. Until 1946, when the federal government seized the mines by court order, the primary difference in the responsibilities of federal inspector Perz and those of his state counterpart, Driscoll O. Scanlan, was the authority to shut down a mine if working conditions threatened the lives of miners. A state mine inspector could, by law, shut down a mine if laws were violated. Perz did not have that authority until the federal seizure.

Perz, who in 1947 worked out of the U.S. Bureau of Mines in Indiana, started life in the coal mining business in 1909, helping his father load coal cars and later working at mines in Illinois. His jobs included handling mules that pulled coal cars and loading coal in the mines. In 1924, he became a mine examiner and held that position for six years. Mine examiners inspected the mine daily before each shift to assure safe working conditions. From 1930 to 1942, Perz served in mine supervisory positions, including assistant mine foreman and mine foreman. After more than thirty years' experience at various levels of the mining business, Perz appeared to be fully qualified for the federal inspector position.[7]

On the State of Illinois side, Scanlan carried the responsibility of inspecting Centralia No. 5, in addition to other mines in central and southern Illinois. He reported to his superiors in the Department of Mines and Minerals and on the State Mining Board, who sent copies of his reports to mine operators and supervisory personnel at the site. He, too, spent years working in the mines before his appointment by the Republican state administration of Governor Dwight Green in April 1941. From 1920 to the day of his appointment, Scanlan worked at Illinois coal mine locations, first with his father and then at a series of mines where he held positions of responsibility, including mine examiner. Ambitious and energetic, he added to his knowledge of mining by attending night mining school. Although Scanlan's appointment came with recommendations from Republican politicians, his party activities included work mostly for local candidates and support of Republicans for state office. The term *political hack* was never applied to Driscoll Scanlan.[8]

Scanlan avoided even the appearance of being beholden to mine operators or other special interests. If he talked with anyone, it was the miners. He went about the business of inspections without chatting or socializing with company officials. He wrote inspection reports on a portable typewriter in his car rather than use typewriters in the company offices. Some state inspectors wrote brief reports after their inspections, making few recommendations. Scanlan's reports ran to the extreme in detail, listing every violation and making repeated recommendations. A magazine writer described Scanlan as a stubborn, righteous, and zealous man of fierce integrity.[9]

Divisions of the Illinois Department of Mines and Minerals and appointed officials administered state mining laws and regulations. Those with enforcement responsibilities were the director of the department, members of the State Mining Board, and mine inspectors representing geographic districts across the state. The State Mining Board had specific responsibilities under the law for oversight of inspectors. The legislative act approved June 6, 1911, stated the board "shall in person and through the State Mine Inspectors, see that all of the provisions of the State Mining Laws are enforced."[10] The board consisted of five members, each representing a coal mining constituency: coal mine operators, coal producers, each of the two major coal miners' unions (the Progressive Mine Workers, or PMW, and the UMWA), and the Department of Mines and Minerals (represented by its director).

State law also addressed the responsibilities of mine inspectors, an important point in the unfolding of history at No. 5. The Illinois Mining Act stated, "Any inspector who shall discover that any section of this Act, or part thereof, is being neglected or violated, shall order an immediate compliance therewith, and in case of continued failure to comply, shall have power to stop the operation of the mine, or to remove any offending person or persons from the mine until the law is complied with."[11]

The department director reported to the governor and served on the State Mining Board. Beginning in 1941, Robert M. Medill held that position and reported to Governor Green. Born in 1882, Medill had gone to work at age sixteen, digging coal with a pick at a mine near Wenona, Illinois. He worked at a Peabody Coal Company mine close to Springfield for eight years beginning in 1900. During that time, he served as president of the UMWA local. In 1908, Medill took the first supervisory position in a career of executive work in the mining industry that lasted almost forty years. He served as superintendent of Dering Coal Company at Westville and West Frankfort. He went to Harrisburg in 1919 as general superintendent of ten mines for O'Gara Coal Company.[12]

Medill held the position of superintendent of the Dowell mine near Carbondale for Union Collieries Company when Republican governor Frank Lowden convinced him to join the state administration as director of the Department of Mines and Minerals in June 1920. Medill explained who influenced the appointment. "When the civil administrative code was set up in 1917 by Gov. Frank O. Lowden, he set up 10 departments, and when he set up the coal mining department, at that time we had no department pertaining to oil and gas. He gave the coal operators of the State of Illinois the prerogative of naming the director and the coal mine union the prerogative of naming the assistant director." He said the UMWA also recommended him for the position.[13]

From his appointment by Lowden until his retirement in 1947, Medill's work experience explains why he referred to himself as a "GOP pet." He served briefly, until the end of Lowden's single term as governor. Republican Len Small became governor in 1921, and Medill continued to head the department until 1924. For two years, he promoted a coal company in Verona, Illinois, and then sold his stock in the firm and went to western Canada as vice president of the Leland Coal Company at Taber, Alberta. He returned to the

United States in 1927 and became general superintendent of the Moffat Coal Company at Oak Creek, Colorado. In 1934, he joined the Rocky Mountain Fuel Company of Denver as superintendent of mines. His tenure of two short years in 1934–35 ended in a discharge, for undisclosed reasons.[14]

The Denver fuel company had struggled since 1927, when Josephine Roche inherited the firm from her father. A liberal activist, Roche experimented with improved working conditions and pay for miners. Her policies, fierce competition from other mining companies, and the Depression put the company in financial jeopardy. Medill's problems with top management may also have reflected Colorado Democratic politics. Roche ran against incumbent governor Edwin C. Johnson in the 1934 primary and lost.[15]

Governor Johnson, a conservative Democrat often considered by party members as acting more like a Republican, hired Medill to make a complete survey of all Colorado mines after an explosion at the Monarch mine at Broomfield, north of Denver. Coal dust and gas were involved in the explosion that killed eight miners. In six months, Medill completed the survey and drafted safety recommendations for the governor.

Returning to Illinois in 1938, Medill lived at Roanoke, in Woodford County. He worked on Green's campaign in 1940 and was reappointed director of the Department of Mines and Minerals on January 20, 1941, at age fifty-nine. Medill said, "I was very fortunate in that both miners organizations [UMWA and PMW], on their own free will, wrote the governor letters endorsing me." Four years later, when Medill's term expired, the UMWA opposed his reappointment.

An assistant director headed the department's mining division. From 1941 to 1947, Robert Weir, who had extensive experience in the mining field, was responsible for the division's administrative business. Before his appointment, Weir had worked as a foreman at the Bell and Zoller mine at Zeigler. He received the blessings of the UMWA and PMW unions. Medill inherited Weir in the position, after Governor Green's decision to appoint people recommended by the mining unions. Medill referred to Weir as "the miners' man."[16] In department documents and testimony by officials, Weir is pictured mostly as a functionary who protected Medill from paperwork and complaints.

Anyone who worked in a southern Illinois coal mine had the book on every other mine. This reflected the close network of miners and the miners' unions, but also it was an indication of how often miners changed jobs and moved to different locations. Miners were known to drive long distances from home every day for better pay or better working conditions. Consequently, there were few secrets among miners.

Scanlan, whose family owned a mine at Venedy, about thirty minutes from No. 5, knew the men who worked at Centralia, the reputation of the mine operator, and the mine's history. When he walked into the mine as an inspector for the first time, Scanlan was not surprised to find dry and dusty conditions. His job was to make sure everyone who worked at the mine and all who had responsibilities for the mine understood the situation and what should be done about it. Every report by Scanlan was posted at the mine for all to read.

For the first two years of his tenure, Scanlan inspected No. 5 every six months, as required by department regulations. In 1943, state law changed the requirement to every three months. His first report, dated February 7, 1942, recommended cleaning and sprinkling the roads used to haul coal in the mine. He also criticized the use of coal dust to tamp the explosive shots at the mine faces, pointing out that the practice violated state law. Because of the volatility of coal dust, he recommended a substitute for tamping that was not combustible, such as clay.[17]

From 1942 to 1944, Scanlan made thirteen inspections and reports. He sent the reports to the Department of Mines and Minerals, where each was date-stamped by a secretary to Medill. The director did not actually see the reports, however. They were sent by secretaries to Weir, who read them as time permitted. All reports went from Weir to the typing pool, where the inspector's recommendations were edited for grammar and spelling. A form letter was attached, containing a version of this final paragraph: "The Department endorses the recommendations made by Inspector Scanlan and requests that you comply with same. Will you please advise the Department upon completion of the recommendations set forth above? Thanking you."[18]

The report and cover letter went to mine officials in Centralia and Chicago. That routine, but cursory treatment by Weir might have worked if company officials had taken the reports seriously, followed the recommendations, and filed an answer. They did not. The official state file of documents for No. 5 contains less than a handful of letters from operators to state officials commenting on reports from 1941 to 1947.[19]

Presumably, this pattern of distributing inspector reports could have continued indefinitely, except for Scanlan and some miners at No. 5. One of the first expressions of concern came in a letter dated November 4, 1944, to the department director from Local 52 of the UMWA. Over the signature of William E. Rowekamp, recording secretary, the letter to Director Medill stated:

> Local Union #52, located at Centralia, Ill., at their last regular meeting instructed Rec. Secy. by a motion to notify the Department of Mines

and Minerals. That the roadways at Centralia Coal Company No. 5 Mine are in need to be cleaned & sprinkled. At the present the condition of those roadways are very dirty and dusty that they are getting dangerous. Mr. Scanlan, State Mine Inspector has recommended in his last inspection to clean roadways and sprinkle same, but the coal company has ignored his request. And we beg your prompt action on this matter.[20]

Medill responded by prompting Assistant Director Weir in Springfield to send a terse note to Scanlan on November 10: "Attached is a letter from Local Union #52, which is self-explanatory. Please investigate this complaint and report your findings to this office." In a separate note, Weir wrote Rowekamp that the complaint had been referred to Scanlan.[21]

Scanlan wasted no time talking about the complaint and mine conditions with No. 5 superintendent Norman Prudent, who was the top official at the mine. In a response to Weir on November 13, 1944, Scanlan reviewed the conversation and made it plain to Weir that conditions needed attention. "The haulage roads in the mine are awful dusty, and much dust is kept in suspension all day by the haulage operations. The dust is very irritating to the respiratory passages and eyes of the men employed on the haulage. Also curtailing the visibility of the Motormen." The inspector also covered the matter of union concern, establishing that he had talked with miners before the letters were written. "The Miners have complained to me about the dust on the last several inspections and I have wrote it up pretty strong on my inspection reports and recommended each time that the haulage roads be adequately sprinkled. But to date they have not done any adequate sprinkling."

Scanlan acknowledged that Prudent had made some improvements based on the inspector's recommendations. "Mr. Prudent the Supt. Has done considerable work at this mine since he has been in charge, he cleaned approximately one mile of air course to where you can run a motor thru it and has sealed off all of the abandoned north working off of the air course that go toward the old abandoned No. 2 mine, as I had recommended in several inspections." Scanlan mentioned that Prudent left an impression he would take action to sprinkle the haulage roads. "I visited the mine to day [November 13] and Mr. Prudent said that he would fix the water tank and sprinkle the roads within a week, said that he would have had this work done sooner, but that they have 20 to 30 men absent each day."[22]

That same day, Scanlan left a note for Rowekamp about Prudent's promise. "Mr. Prudent agreed to bring the water tank on top and fix it and said that he would sprinkle the haulage roads within a week. Said that he wanted to put new wheels on the tank and attach a pipe to it that will spray to out-side of rails." Two weeks later, Weir wrote Rowekamp stating essentially the same information.[23]

Rowekamp and the union local expressed their thanks to Scanlan for taking the issue to Prudent and working with state officials to get results. "Your letter received some time ago in regard to the dusty roads at No. 5 Mine. Well I am proud to tell you that they have sprinkled the 18th North Entry & 21st So. Entry and the main haulage road. . . . The main haulage road is dusty yet but nothing like it was. Myself and the Members of Local, Union #52 appreciate it very much what you have done for us."[24]

The issues of dust in the mine and the need for steps to minimize risk remained a primary concern of the inspector. Scanlan's routine inspection on December 19–20, 1944, found improvements in haulage road conditions, presumably the result of earlier sprinkling. The approval by Scanlan stopped there, however, and his report went into considerable detail pointing out neglect, lack of supervision by officials, and risky working conditions. His report included the following observations and recommendations:

- Blackdamp (carbon monoxide) leaking into motor room from sev-eral bad seals and into the return air current and onto the motor road from abandoned sections of the mine. Recommendation: Repair or rebuild seals in the motor room; seal abandoned sections of the mine.
- Dust in suspension. Recommendation: Continue cleaning haulage roads and sprinkle frequently.
- Loose and dangerous roof conditions on haulage roads ("Loose and dangerous roof conditions are being neglected by both the mine examiner and mine management"). Recommendation: Repair roof; discontinue having men work under dangerous roof.
- Mine is not sufficiently rock dusted, and no rock dusting has been done for more than a year. Recommendation: Mine must be rock dusted.
- Machine and buggy cables have poor splices, and wires are ex-posed. Recommendation: Make better splices in the cables and tape them so wires will not be exposed. Make all electrical connections tight.[25]

Weir sent a letter and a copy of the report to William H. Brown, who as mine manager supervised operations below ground. The state official said, in a parenthetical comment, "These recommendations must be complied with and if necessary the mine should discontinue hoisting coal for a few days until the work can be done. Younger men and those physically able should work steadily and work on idle days when requested by the manager. You all owe it to yourselves and the war effort to keep a clean, safe and efficient mine."[26] The pressure to keep working, even with safety at issue, is evident in Weir's pleading.

This might have been just another exchange of correspondence, even with Weir's admonition, but Scanlan and union local officials prepared to escalate the subject. After reading the December report, workers talked about filing charges against the mine manager and asking that his certificate of competence be revoked for not cleaning the workplace. They planned to inform the mine manager of a complaint to be filed with the State Mining Board, in hopes that action would follow. Hearing of this, Scanlan urged the local not to follow through. "I talked them out of it and told them I thought we could get them to clean up the mine."[27]

None of the recommendations received management attention. Scanlan returned to the mine for an inspection in February 1945 and saw that nothing had been done to correct the problems he had identified in December. He realized that inaction by mine operators could trigger a revolt of miners. Instead of following the usual procedure of filing his report and waiting for Weir to read it and send it on to mine managers, Scanlan mailed a copy of the report with a strongly worded cover letter to Director Medill. He stated:

> The haulage roads in this mine are in a terrible condition. If a person did not see it he would not belief [*sic*] that any one would let a mine get in such condition. In places you can not see the rails and the motors are dragging, one swing motor went by me and at times his lights would go out for the want of a return circuit and it would jump like a rabbit. . . . On this inspection I find that practically nothing has been done toward complying with my recommendations of Dec. 19th and 20th. . . . Mr. Prudent the Supt. advises me that he can not clean up the mine and hoist coal six days a week. The mine should discontinue hoisting coal for awhile and work their men at cleaning roads, taking down loose top, timbering, rock dusting, etc. until the mine is placed in a safe condition. . . . The coal dust in this mine is highly explosive.[28]

Director Medill stepped into the issue of Centralia No. 5 for the first time on record in a February 1945 letter to William Young of Bell and Zoller, which included a copy of Scanlan's report. Medill asked for no specific action. Young replied that the company had been "working under a very severe handicap for the past months. The war demand for coal has required that we operate every possible day and at the same time we are short of men practically every day. This is particularly true at Centralia where the average age of our employees is quite high." He made no promise of action, saying only that he hoped the situation would change and the recommendations could be met.[29]

At about the same time as this exchange, Medill received a mine dust analysis conducted by the department, based on samples collected by Scanlan. One sample showed the dust to be 66 percent combustible, and a second indicated 82 percent combustibility. Anything over 35 percent combustibility was considered dangerous. Scanlan sent the results in a letter to Superintendent Prudent.[30]

Scanlan once again aired grievances of the union local in a letter to Medill dated April 6, 1945. At a meeting with union representatives, Scanlan heard a complaint about the firing of dynamite shots in the mine while men were still working, contrary to law. Scanlan added, "The L.U. [local union] complained to me that practically nothing has been done toward complying with the recommendations of my last inspection. That the roads are as dirty and dusty as usual, that Motormen are still required to pull coal under loose roof, man trips [motor cars] are still pulled under loose roof, places are still being worked 200 ft. or more ahead of air, etc." There is no written response from Medill on record.

A day later, union officials—William Rowekamp, Jake (Jacob) Schmidt, Elmer Moss, Joe H. Vancil, and Thomas Bush—filed charges against mine manager William H. Brown for allowing violation of the Shot Firers Law on March 26 and 27. The statement said, "He [Brown] causes all Men working to breath[e] the Fumes of said shots. And being the Mine is so dry and dusty it could [have] caused an explosion. And endangered the Life of all Men working below on those two days." The men requested a hearing by the Department of Mines and Minerals.[31]

Medill said he had a personal discussion in this time frame with Scanlan about a partial shutdown of the mine so that three days a week could be devoted to dust cleanup and improved ventilation. Testifying before U.S. senators two years later, Medill said, "Scanlan did use his authority at one time to close the mine down. He discussed that with me before he did it and I told him to go ahead. He said, 'Let them work 4 days and 3 days cleanup.'"[32]

During an inspection of No. 5 a week later, Scanlan found that none of his recommendations for lowering risk had been implemented. This resulted in a meeting with Superintendent Prudent. The inspector said he recommended putting the mine on a four-day-per-week production schedule, with three days for cleanup. The alternative, Scanlan said, was to shut down the mine completely. Scanlan provided this version of the conversation:

> I said, "Now Norman, you claim Chicago won't give you the time to shut your mine down and clean it up. Now, I am going to get you some time. I am going to shut your mine down, and there is a war on, and I don't want to hamper the war effort any more than I have to, and what do you think you would want to do? Shut your mine down or use 3 days a week to clean up, and operate the other 4 days?" He told me, "I will have to contact Chicago." Well, I told him, "I can't possibly wait for you to contact Chicago. It is about time that you fellows who operate the mines get big enough to operate your mines without contacting Chicago."[33]

Scanlan never officially closed the mine. Seeing the writing on the wall and presumably learning that Director Medill gave his approval, Prudent accepted Scanlan's recommendation to mine coal four days and clean the mine three days each week. Under this routine, it took about three weeks to clean and rock dust much of No. 5 mine. Scanlan made another inspection when work was concluded and expressed satisfaction. "They did a very good job at that time," Scanlan stated later.[34] This constituted the only time in the six years of Scanlan's tenure as an inspector that he forced management to minimize the dust risk.

Meanwhile, Medill gave Weir the responsibility for resolving union charges filed against mine manager Brown. Weir met with people at the mine on April 27 to investigate charges that Brown had permitted one of his foremen to fire shots during the day shift. Officials admitted the episode occurred as charged by the miners but said it was done under emergency conditions to accommodate a planned April 1 work stoppage to make repairs to the ventilation system. Weir concluded, "The demands of the Local Union that the mine manager's certificates be revoked is in my opinion too severe and I recommend that these demands be not granted."[35]

Rock dusting is, at best, a temporary measure and succeeds in reducing explosion risk only when repeated frequently. On his June 25 inspection, Scanlan observed that dust again needed attention. By July, the dust problem had returned full measure. Federal inspector Perz, making one of his semiannual inspections of No. 5, wrote in his report: "Heavy accumulations of fine coal and coal dust were noted on most of the haulage roads and in the working places. Extremely heavy accumulations of fine coal dust were noted on the roadways in the shuttle-car sections, and at the shuttle-car dumping points. . . . An excessive amount of dust is in suspension during cutting, loading, transferring coal from shuttle cars into mine cars, and transportation operations. No means are used to allay the dust." In the "Summary of Safety Improvements" section, Perz acknowledged, "The main haulageways and most of the room entries have been rock-dusted" since his previous inspection.[36]

Perz's July 1945 report is worth study as an example of the level of detail he provided. Perz said he spent as many as five days on inspections of mines in his district, depending on the mine's size and the issues present. In a twenty-one-page, single-spaced report, he presented more than eighty-five recommendations for improvements at No. 5. The categories of the report and the number of recommendations included: surface structures, nine; hoisting, cages, and shafts, four; methods of mining and timbering, seven; explosives and detonators, six; ventilation, sixteen; control of coal dust, seven; haulage, twelve; electricity, fourteen; and general safety conditions, ten. The recommendations ranged from the seemingly mundane to the serious.

In the report, Perz focused on issues of increasing importance to safety at No. 5. On the subject of dust, he wrote, "The accumulations of loose coal and dust on the haulage roads should be loaded into cars and removed from the mine as soon as possible, and a regular cleaning schedule should be arranged to prevent dust accumulations in the future." Lack of attention by mine operators to safety concerns prompted this statement: "The company does not employ a safety director or safety engineer. No safety organization or safety committee was maintained. . . . Safety bulletins are posted on the bulletin board, but the bulletins in back of the glass cover are not visible due to a heavy coating of coal dust. . . . A safety meeting is held once a month by the officials of the mine, but the employees are not included in these meetings."[37]

Scanlan and members of the UMWA local had learned their lessons well during the first half of 1945 in terms of getting the attention of state officials. They realized responses from mine operators could be obtained only if Medill or the governor's office was aroused. For years, routine letters from Weir had not worked. Once again, Scanlan and the UMWA members elevated issues of mine safety to the state capital in December 1945.

Writing to the director, Scanlan said he and UMWA officials talked after he heard complaints from the miners. "One of the complaints is the dusty conditions at the working faces during cutting and loading operations. The coal at this mine is exceptionally dry and the dust is so dense during loading operations that it is indeed deplorable that men are required to work in it. Visibility at the loading machines is practically nil and work around the machine is a hazard due to poor vision." Scanlan said several men were sick from working in the dust.[38]

After that comment, Scanlan mentioned an issue sure to get the attention of mine operators. "The Local Union has requested that I recommend water sprinklers on the cutting and loading machines and that the falls of coal be sprinkled before loading out." According to mine operators and managers, installing water sprinklers meant a substantial outlay of capital, downtime in the mines, and added maintenance costs. Experts in the coal mine business generally agreed on the effectiveness of sprinkling. Scanlan later said his letter caused a negative reaction among state mining officials and mine operators.

Scanlan's idea for sprinkling was to equip machines on wheels with tanks that held water, place a water pump and hose on the machine, and then run two nozzles on the cutting machines and loading machines. The pumps would throw a spray of water to kill the dust. He said this did not require new equipment. "Just some tanks and some hose, and the tanks could have been made at the mines."

Scanlan couldn't contain himself in this letter and in the last paragraph told of an incident that cast Superintendent Prudent in a poor light. "I tried to discuss this with Supt. Prudent yesterday, but he would not talk to me about it, walked away and left me standing. The miners also complained that some one has taken down my inspection reports at this mine, I am sure that this was done by some one connected with the Management."[39] Although the letter was stamped "Received" on December 10, Scanlan never heard about it from Medill.

With no word from Springfield, Scanlan returned to No. 5 for his routine inspection on December 13–14, 1945. His report echoed previous comments about unsatisfactory conditions. Timbering was insufficient, and roof conditions in the mine remained dangerous, he said. Ventilation problems needed attention. Finally, he summarized the dust situation:

> The coal in this mine is extremely dry, an excessive amount of dust is in suspension during cutting and loading operations. The dust is an explosion hazard, also injurious to the health and safety of the men working around the machines. The dust is very injurious and irritating to the eyes, lungs and respiratory passages. At the loading machine in 13 & 14 North, visibility was absolutely nil, the men are unable to see the roof, ribs, face, the large lumps of coal traveling over the conveyor or the car under the boom, motorman and triprider are unable to see the boom of the loading machine. Work around the machine is extremely hazardous.

His last recommendation: "The mine be adequately rock dusted."[40]

With all relationships strained, miners at No. 5 again wrote to Director Medill. In a letter dated December 17, 1945, and received two days later in Springfield, members of Local 52 filed charges against Superintendent Prudent and Manager Brown for not complying with Scanlan's timbering and ventilation recommendations. The letter also claimed that Brown did not visit the working places every two weeks, as prescribed by law. Union officials asked for revocation of certificates for Prudent and Brown and dismissal from their jobs pending a hearing. On the next day, twenty-eight miners scrawled their signatures on a handwritten statement to Medill that included complaints such as "the dust is so bad you can not see anything at times."[41]

This time, Medill and the State Mining Board took action. They named a committee to inspect conditions at the mine on December 28. Medill sent letters with the announcement to Young at Bell and Zoller and to UMWA member Rowekamp. Prudent received a copy. Members of the committee were Weir; two state inspectors, John Golden of DuQuoin and Charles Blakeney of Danville; and two members of the State Mining Board, B. H. Schull and Murrell Reak, a miner representing the UMWA. Miners at No. 5 and Scanlan were suspicious of this committee, fearing the members were friendly to the mine operators and would not conduct a thorough investigation.

A few days after being notified of the investigation, Prudent and Brown issued a lengthy report to the committee with a cover letter regarding absenteeism at the mine and its impact on the ability to fulfill Scanlan's recommendations. The officials criticized the UMWA local for not cooperating to reduce absenteeism and provided examples of situations where workers thwarted efforts to rock dust and clean haulage roads. Prudent and Brown stated the average age of miners at No. 5 was 59.3 years and said that contributed to absenteeism. Finally, the officials issued a veiled threat to close the mine. "It is the policy of this company to do everything economically possible to improve the safety and health condition at this mine. However, this being a mine that is 38 years old, and requiring at least 90 minutes travel time both ways, including vertical time, together with having an abnormal top condition, it will require a lot of good sound judgment, and thought, by everyone concerned, in order to keep it in operation."[42]

In a report dated January 2, 1946, investigators presented brief remarks on their observations and then made a number of recommendations:

> That not more than 100 men be on one split of air to comply with the General Mining Laws. A light be placed on front of each trip. All loose rock on haulage road be timbered or taken down. That rooms be turned according to law. Generator rooms be fireproof and sufficient quantity of rock dust or sand be kept near generator room to comply with the law. Telephones be installed to comply with the

General Mining Law. Mine be adequately rock dusted. All examiners be equipped with an electric cap lamp.

In many respects, the report confirmed complaints by miners and repeated recommendations made by Perz and Scanlan. However, there were omissions. The report ignored a recommendation by Scanlan for sprinkling. Also, the investigators did not comment on the request to pull certificates and temporarily dismiss Prudent and Brown.[43]

UMWA members sent up a howl over the report. They complained that committee members did not get out of the buggy in which they rode and took little time to explore any conditions off the mainline. They noted the tour was conducted by Prudent, the object of the complaint. On February 26, Rowekamp sent a letter to Medill officially complaining about the inadequacies of the investigation. "Members of Local Union 52 are dissatisfied with the report of the Special Investigation Commission concerning the dusty conditions at Centralia Coal Co. Mine No. 5. Also dirty roadways and for not complying with State Mine Inspectors recommendations."[44] Medill did not respond.

Miners had run out of patience in trying to get official attention for working conditions. They decided to write a letter to Governor Green. UMWA officers commissioned Rowekamp to draft the letter. Afterward, he admitted being nervous and excited. He wanted the letter to be written perfectly, without mistakes, and he took his time. Elmer Moss, a member of the union committee, became impatient and pressed Rowekamp for results. Rowekamp said, "I'd tell him, 'Elmer, that'll take me a while.'" He wrote a draft in pencil for a few to see. After their approval, he carefully typed the two-page letter on official UMWA stationery.[45]

Rowekamp never wrote a more important letter in his life. To this day, phrases from it are etched in the minds of the survivors and of all those who lost loved ones in the disaster. Rowekamp considered it his legacy of a life in the mines, and he shared a copy frequently with his relatives and told them the story of how it came about. The letter, dated March 3, 1946, said:

Dear Governor Green:

We the officers of Local, Union No. 52, U. M. W. of A. have been instructed by the members of Local, Union No. 52 to write a letter to you in protest against the negligence and unfair practices of your Department of Mines and Minerals. But before we go any further, we want you to know that this is not a protest against Mr. Driscoll Scanlan, the State Mine Inspector in this district. Mr. Scanlan is the best inspector that ever came to our mine, he is honest, of good character and a good mining man, he writes his reports just as he finds the mine. But your Mining Board will not let him enforce the law or take the necessary action to protect our lives and health. This protest is against the men above Mr. Scanlan in your Department of Mines and Minerals.

In fact, Governor Green this is a plea to you, to please save our lives, to please make the Department of Mines and Minerals enforce the laws at No. 5 mine of the Centralia Coal Company at Centralia, Illinois, at which mine we are employed, before we have a dust explosion at this mine like just happened in Kentucky and West VA.

For the last couple of years the policy of the Dept. of Mines and Minerals toward us, has been one of ignoring us, when we write complaints to Springfield, it will sometimes be several weeks before we hear from them and then some times we have to write the second letter to them before they will answer us.

In December 1945 we preferred charges before the Mining Board against the Mine Manager and the Superintendent of our mine and requested that their certificates be revoked for operating the mine in violation of the State Mining Laws and for ignoring the recommendations of the State Mine Inspector.

A special investigation commission was sent to the mine, they were very unfair towards us, on the commission was Robert Weir a Boss for our Coal Company. The commission did not inspect all of the mine, they did not stay at the machine that our main complaint was on long enough to fairly see the actual conditions at this machine. They let the Superintendent of the mine lead them around the mine. They rode out of the mine in a mine car, so could not see the dirty and dusty and unsafe conditions on the main haulage roads. And they ignored the Officers of this Local Union, they did not talk to us or give us a chance to call their attentions to unsafe conditions or listen to our complaints.

If we understand the law right, the Mining Board should have held a hearing and we should have been allowed to come before the board and press our charges. After the commission went through our mine we waited several weeks and did not hear from them and then we wrote the Director a letter, he then wrote us that the commission found insufficient evidence to revoke the certificates of the Mine Manager and Mine Superintend[ent]. Then a few days later a report of the commission was posted at the mine making eight recommendations. Any one of these recommendations should be sufficient to revoke the certificates of the Manager and Superintendent to remove them from the mine.

For your information as to the condition at this mine, we are sending you copies of the State Mine Inspectors reports, also a copy of the report of the investigation commission, which you can check against the State Inspectors report and see the unfairness of the commission. Then please check these reports with the last Federal inspection report of July 1945, which you can get from the Director of your Dept. or from our District President Hugh White. After reading these reports, if you doubt our word and the reports of the State and Federal inspectors, we kindly invite you to make a personal inspection of this mine yourself.

We are writing you Governor Green, because we believe you want to give the people an honest administration and that you do not know how unfair our Mining Dept. is toward the men in this mine. Several years ago after a disaster at Gillespie we seen your pictures in the papers going down in the mine to make a personal investigation of the accident. We are giving you a chance to correct the condition at this mine that may cause a much worse disaster than the one at Gillespie or the one in Kentucky. If your Mining Board does not enforce the laws at this mine and back the State Mine Inspector, then we are going to the State's Attorney and to the Public and News Papers.

We will appreciate an early personal reply from you, stating your position in regards to the above and the enforcement of the State Mining Laws.[46]

This became known as the "please save our lives" letter. Four members of the UMWA committee signed the letter: Jake Schmidt, president; William Rowekamp, recording secretary; and two members, Thomas Bush and Elmer Moss. Of the four signers, only Rowekamp lived to tell federal investigators his story.

The letter arrived and was stamped "received" on March 9. It came to the attention of John W. Chapman, one of the governor's three secretaries. Two days later, he wrote a memo to Medill, saying in part:

I have read the letter and the report of the State Mine Inspector very carefully and it is my opinion that the Governor may be subjected to very severe criticism in the event that the facts complained of are true and that as a result of this condition some serious accident occurs at the mine. Will you kindly have this complaint carefully investigated so I can call the report of the investigation to the Governor's attention at the same time I show him this letter?[47]

Caught in the crossfire and now exposed to his boss, Medill responded to Chapman on March 13 with the names of the investigating committee and the wording of a motion passed by the State Mining Board saying there was insufficient evidence to revoke the certificates of competency of the two mining officials. Medill concluded:

While there were some conditions in the mine which should have been corrected, and which are being corrected at the present time, it was because of war-time conditions, shortage of help, and the government demanding every ton of coal that could be produced, that it was not possible to keep the mine in as good condition as it would have been during normal times. The complaint sounds a good deal worse than it really is. The present condition at the mine is not any different than it has been during the past ten or fifteen years. In fact, in spite of the war conditions, the management has made a great number of improvements.

Medill recommended that the governor tell UMWA Local 52 officials that he was referring the matter to the State Mining Board "with instructions that it be given full and complete consideration at their next meeting."[48]

That is exactly what the governor did, or what Chapman did with the governor's signature. A formal letter to Schmidt and Rowekamp, without comment on the complaint, used the precise words suggested by Medill and then thanked the officials for calling the matter to his attention. No evidence exists that the matter came before the State Mining Board. The district office of the UMWA received a copy of the "please save our lives" letter but probably forwarded it to the Department of Mines and Minerals. Neither Chapman nor any people in the department contacted Scanlan or Perz for their comments on mine conditions. The letters and memos became available to newspaper reporters a little more than a year later.

By the beginning of March 1946, every party to complaints about, and recommendations for, No. 5 felt abused. UMWA officials and miners believed they were shown no respect by the State Mining Board and Director Medill. Scanlan fumed because the State Mining Board rejected his recommendation for sprinkling water in the mine. Medill and the State Mining Board suspected collusion at the mine between Scanlan and the UMWA. They did not appreciate having the governor brought into the disagreement.

During the exchange of letters and memos in March, Scanlan and Perz made inspections of No. 5 together. Perz made eighteen new recommendations and repeated eighty-four that remained unchanged. He noted improvements in timbering the work areas but continued to criticize ventilation operations, adding five recommendations and repeating thirteen. Regarding dust conditions, Perz wrote, "No rock dusting has been done in this mine since the July 1945 inspection. The results of the analyses of dust samples collected from the ribs, roof, and road . . . indicate that the mine is in need of generalized dusting."[49]

Perz identified a number of problems under the heading "Explosives, Detonators, and Blasting." He found the supply of explosives and blasting caps more than needed for a thirty-six-hour supply. He also discovered explosives stored too close to power wires and boxes that were not locked. These findings resulted in new recommendations to place the storage boxes further from the roadways and power wires and to maintain no more than a thirty-six-hour supply of explosives and detonators.

Scanlan continued to upbraid mine management for not following earlier recommendations. Regarding general roof conditions, he wrote, "Bad roof conditions, bad rock, poor grade of slate, slips and boulders. Dangerous roof conditions are neglected by the Management." He repeated comments about the dry and dusty conditions in the mine, reporting that "an excessive amount of combustible dust is in suspension during cutting and loading operations. The dust is an explosion hazard, also injurious to the health and safety of the men working around the machines." Refusing to accept the earlier rebuff by the State Mining Board, Scanlan again recommended using water or wetting solutions on cutting machines, on loading machines, and on the falls of coal.[50] He must have known the mention of water would raise the ire of officials in Springfield.

Scanlan reserved some of his strongest criticism for inadequate examination of the mine for safety on each shift, claiming practices were not in compliance with the state mining law. Observing that the mine was being only partially examined on a regular basis, he called for an additional certified mine examiner to work prior to arrival of the day shift. He again recommended adequate rock dusting.

After this report and the UMWA letter to Governor Green, Medill must have had his fill of Scanlan and No. 5 mine. He called the inspector to Springfield for a dressing down. Medill criticized Scanlan's reports as being too long and verbose and instructed him to write briefly and with fewer references to previous recommendations. Medill also issued the same order to all inspectors.

Not surprisingly, Scanlan saw this as an attempt to silence him and reduce the effectiveness of his inspection reports. But Scanlan was a subordinate, and he followed direct orders. His next report, in June 1946, eliminated specific references to previous recommendations and condensed comments about mine conditions. He said later, "If you can't go into a coal mine and report every hazardous condition in there, then your report is curtailed, and it is the same thing as ordering you to pass up certain things."[51]

In his Senate testimony, Scanlan said conditions at No. 5 had reached the point of no return and the mine should have been shut down. The issue of who had authority to shut down a mine and for what reasons became a serious public matter. According to Medill and the State Mining Board, Scanlan had full authority for a shutdown and could exercise it without approval from supervisors. Scanlan contended the State Mining Board and Medill also had such authority under state law. Scanlan claimed that his own unilateral action would have been countermanded and that he would have been fired.

While these matters simmered in Illinois, ominous clouds hovered over labor relations at the national level between the UMWA and John L. Lewis on the one hand and the bituminous coal operators on the other. Unable to reach agreement on a new contract, Lewis ordered union members to strike. In order to avert the strike and continue the production of badly needed coal for the nation, President Harry S. Truman on May 21, 1946, ordered seizure of the mines. Federal seizure meant the mine operators still owned and operated the mines, but the UMWA had a work contract with the government. An agreement signed by Lewis and Secretary of the Interior Julius A. Krug outlined regulations for government operation of the mines, including a federal safety code.[52]

Under the code, the federal government through inspectors from the U.S. Department of Mines could for the first time exercise police power over coal mine safety. This meant inspections by Frank Perz took on new meaning in terms of compliance by operators. Presumably, Bell and Zoller, owners of the Centralia Coal Company, could no longer ignore recommendations without the expectation of penalties. Technically, a federal inspector could shut down a mine by recommending it to the Coal Mines Administration (CMA) established by the seizure order. In such a case, the inspector had to make the declaration of "imminent danger" before a shutdown could occur. Perz did not inspect No. 5 under the new regulations until November 1946.

Scanlan made his first inspection under Medill's revised order for a shorter report on June 25. While Scanlan's report was just one page shorter than usual, he reduced the comments by half, concluding with a sentence designed to cover all previous recommendations: "That the recommendations of the previous inspection that have not been complied with, be complied with." On this occasion, Scanlan mentioned improvements in mine conditions and compliance with several of his March recommendations. "Some of the haulage roads have been cleaned, the mine partly rock dusted, rear trip signal boards painted white, generator room fire proofed, boiler inspected and examiners doing a little better examining." Overall, however, Scanlan offered little comfort to mine operators, concluding his comments, "But nothing has been done toward eliminating the other hazardous conditions reported in that inspection." He again called for improved ventilation, repairs on the roofs, and sprinkling of haulage roads.[53] As with all previous reports he received, Weir attached a form letter and sent the reports to operators at the mine and in Chicago.

Back again for an inspection in September 1946, Scanlan stuck with his abbreviated report but repeated many of the earlier recommendations. He called again for adding one examiner, improving ventilation, and sealing abandoned parts of the mine to prevent seeping of carbon monoxide. He mentioned sprinkling haulage roads, and his final recommendation called for "rock dusting of the mine until the mine is adequately rock dusted."[54]

Perz and Scanlan both made mine inspections in November 1946, but not together. By this time, a change in officials at No. 5 had occurred. Norman Prudent had left to work at another coal company, resulting in the appointment of Walter J. Johnson as general superintendent, and Harry (Cotton) Niermann, a longtime employee of No. 5, as superintendent. Brown continued as mine manager. Perz noted in his report that a total of 266 men were employed at the mine, with 160 on the day shift and 48 on the night shift. Average daily production was 2,159 tons of coal, which was consistent with longtime production records.[55]

Perz added fifty-six items to the long list of previous federal recommendations. But this time, he noted thirteen violations of the recently enacted federal safety code. He joined Scanlan in commenting on the inadequacy of daily mine examinations, pointing out that "the mine examiner for the night shift was not certified." He mentioned ten minor problems that officials had corrected.

In previous reports, Perz discussed the need for rock dusting but did not go into detail about dusty conditions or the need for action. This time, he got specific about the problems. After the explosion, he described dust conditions found in November as "much worse because there had been no rock dust applied since the previous inspection." These were among his observations in the report:

Excessive accumulations of coal dust were present on the 4 west south main haulage road, all intermediate haulage roads, and on the roadways of most of the working places.

The mine was very dry and dusty and an excessive amount of coal dust was raised into suspension during cutting, loading, transferring coal from the shuttle cars into mine cars, and during transportation operations.

Four of the dust samples collected during inspection indicate that the road samples were lower in incombustible content than was recommended for this mine.

Still, Perz did not determine that No. 5 was in "imminent danger." He knew that dust conditions in the mine had existed for decades.[56]

A copy of Perz's preliminary report was posted at the mine and was received by the federal CMA on November 14, 1946. The Bureau of Mines distributed Perz's final report on November 26. Prior to government seizure of the mines, the report trail would have ended at that point. However, because of the seizure, officials in the CMA reviewed inspection reports routinely for violations of the mine safety code. On November 29, Captain N. H. Collisson, coal mines administrator, wrote the Centralia Coal Company demanding prompt attention to the violations and a report of action taken. On November 30, Acting Superintendent Niermann told the CMA that work had been started on correcting violations but was halted due to a strike at the mine. Niermann promised the work would continue when the strike ended.[57]

The CMA sent a letter on January 29, 1947, to N. F. McDonald, president of the Bell and Zoller Coal Company, sales agent and parent company of the Centralia Coal Company. While McDonald held the title of president, he was not involved in operations decisions regarding Centralia. Young had that responsibility. The CMA repeated its order for prompt correction of all violations and reminded the coal company of its responsibility. After calling attention to the lack of response by the company, the letter requested a reply no later than February 14. The UMWA office in Washington received copies of the correspondence. McDonald replied in a letter on February 10, assuring the CMA that action was being taken, but provided no details. Washington officials considered the response inadequate, and on February 21, the CMA directed McDonald to provide more information.

McDonald responded in a letter dated February 24, enclosing a detailed report dated February 7 from General Superintendent Johnson describing the corrections made. McDonald promised even more information later.

Collisson acknowledged receipt of McDonald's letter on March 7, noting his promise that a balance of the report would be forthcoming. No further communication occurred before March 25.

Scanlan's inspection two weeks after the November 1946 federal checkup did not vary in observations or specific recommendations from recent reports, with one exception. He noted that some of the drillers for shot firing at the mine faces used coal dust in tamping explosive charges, in violation of state law and safety regulations. He recommended "all shots be tamped with incombustible material."[58]

Although both inspectors within weeks of each other had commented on the lack of certified examiners in the mine before every shift, they received no response from officials in Springfield or at the mine. The silence, not unusual, made a situation that occurred in December all the more curious and cast doubts over the confidence officials had in the inspectors and their reports. Joe W. Rafby, a night shift employee at the mine, wrote a letter to Director Medill on December 8, 1946, in which he called safety conditions at the mine "deplorable." More specifically, Rafby addressed the examiner issue:

> The Examiner who examines the mine for the second shift has not worked at the face and is not in possession of second and first class miner's certificates. He has been on this job for approximately two years while there are mine examiners in possession of certificates available. These conditions have been brought to the attention of the State mine inspector. The regular mine examiner is riding a motor in and out. The entry and air course has never been examined. The territory is examined every ten or fifteen days. The recommendation of federal and state inspectors have been ignored altogether.[59]

Medill responded by sending a department investigator, James Sneddon, to Centralia with orders to look into the examiner matter. Medill offered no explanation nor would say why he was unwilling to accept the reports of inspectors at face value. Sneddon and Scanlan investigated the charges and found them to be accurate. They confronted mine manager Brown with the information, and Sneddon wrote in his report, "He seemed to know what was going on and did not have much to say." Brown told the inspectors to talk with Niermann.

At the meeting, Sneddon reported, Niermann "seemed to know what was going on and asked what we wanted him to do. I told him all we wanted them to do was have the mine examined to comply with mining laws." Niermann agreed and said he would talk with Young at Bell and Zoller in Chicago and recommend putting on one more examiner in the next few days.

Sneddon wrote by hand a lengthy report to Medill, and Weir sent a letter on December 19 to Brown, stating, "The Mine Examiner is not examining according to law and the man being used as examiner on the night shift does not quality for this job under the law." As Weir so often did with other reports, he asked Brown to "remedy these conditions and notify this office when you have done so."[60]

If officials at the mine had ignored the letter, it would have come as no surprise. This time, however, Niermann responded to Weir in writing that No. 5 "is now being examined as recommended by Inspectors Driscoll Scanlan and James Sneddon." He did not mention rock dusting.[61]

Changes in management of Centralia No. 5 begun in October were completed as of January 1, 1947, with Johnson taking over as general superintendent. The changes appeared to signal an adjustment of attitudes toward improving safety conditions and responding to inspection reports. The first sign came from the letter Niermann sent in December regarding mine examiners. The second resulted from Scanlan's inspection on January 21–22, 1947.

In the state inspector's report of November 1946, Scanlan had expressed concern for adequate ventilation and had made a recommendation to correct the problem. He repeated the recommendation in January because nothing had been done. At that point, Niermann and Scanlan talked about the problem, and Niermann suggested an alternative solution that Scanlan accepted. Niermann then wrote a letter to Weir in which he explained how the two had worked out a solution. Such a level of communication had been rare, or nonexistent, with previous superintendents.[62]

Johnson and Niermann also took action on Perz's recommendations for the establishment of a safety committee and the education of miners about safety issues. They named a committee of three miners. Officials began safety meetings with subordinates and went over observations and recommendations from inspectors. After the meetings, orders were posted for all employees to read. The three-man miner safety committee conducted one inspection of the mine before March 25. That occurred on February 24 and resulted in a written report that was sent to mine manager Brown. It called dust the "biggest grievance." Members of the UMWA local met on the evening of February 25 to discuss the inspection and decided to wait until about April 1 to see if the mine operators would take action on the complaint.

Inspectors Scanlan and Perz arrived at Centralia No. 5 on Tuesday, March 18, for a periodic inspection. Perz's last visit had been in November 1946, and Scanlan had been on site in January. They had followed this routine numerous times since the early 1940s. For the two-day inspection, they were joined by Harry Berger, assistant mine manager, and Paul Comper, a member of the newly formed safety committee.

Given results of the previous inspections, Perz and Scanlan might have expected to sound the same warnings and issue essentially the identical recommendations that had filled their reports for years. To the contrary, in spite of the battles with state officials and mine operators over pleadings to improve mine safety, the two inspectors treated each appearance at the mine as the first. They took as much time as needed to make a thorough inspection, even if they knew the recommendations might be ignored. Surprisingly, conversations during the inspection of No. 5 would turn out to be the most optimistic in years.

In meetings with the two men who accompanied them and later in discussions with Johnson and Niermann, Scanlan and Perz learned more about efforts by local mine officials to comply with earlier recommendations. After Johnson's arrival as the top resident official in late December, he had directed supervisors to discuss inspection reports and how recommendations might be implemented. Two such meetings had been held before the March inspection. On those agendas were rock dusting and a water sprinkler system to dampen coal dust.[63]

Impetus for these discussions came from Young, the boss of Johnson and Niermann. Young had seen the November inspection report from Perz, the first under federal seizure of the mines. He knew Perz and his supervisors had authority to close the mine, and Young read the report with a new sense of urgency. Young might be able to pick up the phone and call officials in Springfield to talk about state inspections, but federal authorities were another matter. He wanted the record to show that Centralia Coal Company had made progress on Perz's recommendations.

Scanlan and Perz learned that a carload of pipe had been ordered earlier for use in a sprinkling system at No. 5. Actually, the order was placed in August 1946, well before Johnson took over as general superintendent. The pipe was ordered for another mine operation but had not arrived or been committed to a project when Johnson first appeared in Centralia. He talked with Young about using the pipe for a sprinkler system, and Young encouraged Johnson to study the issue. Johnson and Niermann talked with other mine operators who were using sprinklers and consulted with engineers about structuring a system for No. 5. No decision had been made. Final approval rested with Young.[64]

The inspectors also discovered a load of rock dust stored along the haulage road, ready for application to dusty areas. Johnson said rock dusting would occur as soon as they had time and manpower. He emphasized the problem with absenteeism and illness that prevented maintenance work in the mine. Scanlan said later, "I don't know when it was delivered but it was delivered and was to be put on immediately. [That was] the understanding we had when we left the mine."[65]

The action and intent of Johnson, so different from former superintendent Norman Prudent, impressed the inspectors. Perz said, "I was very well pleased with Mr. Johnson, Mr. Niermann, because it appeared that they were going in the right direction for safety. They had started safety meetings with their officials, giving them instructions in the violations."[66] More cautious, Scanlan nevertheless had positive feelings about meeting with Johnson. "Mr. Johnson talked to me very candidly and seemed to be more qualified than Mr. Prudent . . . and left me with the feeling that something was going to be done." Miners who accompanied the inspectors also made encouraging comments about safety recommendations. "We had understood in making the inspection with the safety committeeman and the assistant mine manager who accompanied us through the mine, that they were going to move forward toward correcting a lot of the hazards," Scanlan said.[67]

Good feelings about Johnson did not carry over to comments in the official report, however. Scanlan later said he found the mine in better condition "generally speaking," although the dust situation persisted. During testimony before a legislative committee in April, Scanlan said, "On my inspection on March 18 and 19, 1947, I found the mine in better condition than I had found it in a long time." In the federal report, Perz commented on the dust, saying, "The rock-dusting conditions were much worse because there had been no rock dust applied since the previous inspection."[68]

Mine officials had differing opinions about the urgency of rock dusting. Asked why rock dust material had not been applied immediately upon arrival at the mine, Johnson said later, "We did not consider the dust condition down there an imminent hazard. If we had, we certainly would have dropped everything and dusted the mine right up to the faces." In other words, officials claimed that had Perz labeled dust an "imminent danger," they would have heeded his words and fulfilled the recommendations. Scanlan long ago had pronounced the dust situation "explosive." Johnson actually believed ventilation was a more serious problem than dust. "We were in the process of correcting our ventilation setup and we could not do that overnight."[69]

Perz's report cited seventeen hazards that had been corrected, the longest such list since he started making inspections at No. 5. However, he included fifty-two recommendations, including many made in the November report.

He finished writing the report on Saturday, March 22, and mailed it to the federal office in Vincennes, Indiana, starting the lengthy process of review and mailing to people responsible for mine safety. It arrived March 28 at offices of the Bureau of Mines in Washington.

Scanlan's report sounded much the same as before. He recommended that ventilation be increased in places where it was reported to be inadequate; that the dirty haulage roads be cleaned and sprinkled; that the loose roof on the haulage roads be taken down or securely timbered; and that the mine be adequately rock dusted. Scanlan completed his inspection report and mailed it to Springfield. Upon receiving the report, Assistant Director Weir went through the usual processes and signed a letter with Scanlan's recommendations. He mailed it to mine supervisors on March 25.

Illinois law prescribed that mine examiners, with proper credentials, must inspect the mine before each shift of workers to determine whether the mine is safe and make a report. After midnight on March 25, two examiners employed at the mine, Charles Ford and Fred Lichtenfield, began their work. Each examiner inspected one-half of the mine, concluding about 4:00 AM. The two examiners returned to the surface and went to the company office, where they entered a report in a book kept for that purpose. They considered the mine safe for workers on March 25 and stated so in the report.[70] No mention was made of dusty conditions. They testified later that the mine was no dustier than it had been for a long time.

3

Day of Reckoning

TUESDAY, MARCH 25, 1947, BEGAN LIKE ALMOST any other day at No. 5 mine. Nothing unusual happened until the end of the day shift. The workforce was concentrated in the west and northwest sections of the mine, identified as 1 West, 2 West, 4 West, 13–23 North, and 23–24 South, as many as four miles from the hoisting shaft that took miners down and back to the top. Others worked in southwestern areas of the mine. In each, workers took coal from the faces of the mine, hauled it to the shaft bottom, and hoisted it to the surface. Many worked in groups in rooms spread out for thousands of feet, feeding coal onto haulage roads where it was moved in cars on rails, or in buggies where no rails existed. Others worked on the surface, handling coal and assisting operations underground.

The 540-foot hoisting shaft provided the means for reaching the surface. About 1,200 feet south of the hoisting shaft was a double-compartment airshaft 537 feet deep. A seven-foot airplane-type ventilating fan, located underground about 100 feet from the bottom of the intake airshaft, kept air moving throughout the work areas.

During the day shift, men called *drillers* and *shot firers* worked in the mine to prepare for the moment at the end of the shift when explosives would be detonated to blast coal from the faces. Into the drilled holes, workers placed packages of explosive charges containing explosives "permitted by law." No. 5 mine used Black Diamond No. 15 dynamite in eight-ounce cartridges. They were detonated with No. 6 blasting caps and orange wax fuses. Explosives, coal cuttings, and surface clay were wrapped in packages called *dummies*, each about fourteen inches long. These were to be placed in holes and tamped firmly with nonexplosive materials.[1]

Law required that no charges could be detonated until all normal face operations had ended and the men were headed toward the hoisting shaft or were already on top. Firers received a signal to light the shots after safety requirements had been met. Just before 3:26 PM, operations ended, and men started to the surface. Knowing they had up to ten minutes to get away from the blasts, shot firers lighted fuses to the explosive charges.

On March 25, at 3:26 PM, an explosion occurred deep in the Centralia No. 5 mine, where workers had been hauling coal from the mine faces all day. Below ground, 142 miners either had begun the day-ending journey to the mine shaft or were poised to take the cage to the top. Days later, after countless rescue missions and endless hours of sorrowful waiting by relatives and friends, officials announced the death toll was 111. Eight men were rescued, and 23 escaped on their own. Investigators estimated that 65 miners died almost immediately from the explosion shock. The remaining 46 died hours later of carbon monoxide poisoning, after deadly gases filled the working rooms and passageways. Included among the dead were 15 of the 28 men who sent a statement in December 1945 to state officials referring to "bad dust" in the mine. Also killed were 3 of the 4 men who signed the "please save our lives" letter to Governor Dwight Green. Investigators agreed the explosion occurred in the area known as 1 West, one of the working faces most distant from the shaft. The explosion ignited accumulated coal dust, and that spread the blast to other parts of the mine.

They might have called them "the Glenridge Seven," the kind of identification given bands of men who shared extraordinary experiences. The seven men who rode in a car together from north of Centralia to Wamac, site of No. 5 mine, had much more in common than riding to work.

Pete Piasse, George Evans, Earl "Blink" Wilkinson, Joe Bryant and his son Harold "Jack" Bryant, Forrest Rhodes, and Henry Niepoetter made their homes not far from the site of the old Glenridge mine, in an area north of Centralia now called Junction City. They shared a common bond of work at the mine, some for most of their adult lives. Wilkinson took a job in the mine at age sixteen, sometime in 1922. Joe Bryant, born near the Glenridge mine, began labors in 1913 at age fourteen. Evans had been a nearby resident for thirty years. There wasn't much they didn't know about each other and about each other's family.

On the morning of March 25, under cloudy skies with a brisk wind blowing and temperatures near freezing, six of the seven, all in their forties, crammed into Wilkinson's car for the ride to work in nearby Wamac, just as they had done scores of times before. Jack Bryant, youngest of the group at twenty-three and married just six months, drove his own V-8 Ford coupe that day.

Ironically, none of the seven was a longtime employee of Centralia Coal Company. In fact, they had all worked at No. 5 less than a year and did not intend to work there much longer: Centralia No. 5 was a temporary assignment. The reason for this arrangement was their attachment and commitment to the Glenridge mine, which was a cooperative venture owned by the miners. Cash flow at Glenridge often did not meet payroll demands, resulting in payment of only 10 to 30 percent or so of the wages earned. In spite of this financial squeeze, the miners did not want to leave Glenridge permanently. Periodically they took other jobs that paid enough for them to pad their savings accounts or catch up on paying bills. When they had enough money saved to fill the gaps in their Glenridge pay, they returned to work there. Centralia No. 5 served as a means to that end. Niepoetter, for one, planned to return to Glenridge in about a week.[2]

When an explosion rumbled through Centralia No. 5 just as the work shift ended, all seven were below ground. Those close to the source of the explosion died immediately. Other miners hung on, gasping for breath in far corners of the mine. A few, including Joe Bryant, lived long enough to scribble notes for loved ones on old envelopes and pages torn from a time book. In the darkness of the mine, hugging the ground where good air remained, Bryant wrote notes to his wife and several of his eleven children. "Sammie Raymond Be good Boys Jackie [his son who also died in the explosion] Melvin Help Mom Please your father Joe Bryant O Lord Help me." To his wife, Bryant wrote, "My Dear wife good By. Name Baby Joe so you will have a Joe love all dad."[3] The twelfth child, a baby girl, was born three months later. Mrs. Bryant named her Joedy.

Wilkinson was the lone survivor among the Glenridge Seven. He escaped injury and spent several hours after the explosion rescuing survivors and identifying the dead. Years later, he remembered that day and his friends and neighbors: "I started for home in my car and suddenly I realized I was going home alone. It made me sick. I had left for work with the Glenridge men, all of whom worked with me in the mines for years. . . . I was the only one to come home."[4]

The flu kept miner Gus Hohman home from work at No. 5 for a week. Finally recovered, he decided to go back to the mine on March 25. He wanted to be present for an important meeting of the mine safety committee with state inspector Scanlan. Committee members, concerned about problems with coal dust and ventilation, were applying pressure on the mine operator to improve working conditions.

Hohman told his daughter, Elvera Kirkland, "We've got a big meeting at 3:30, a safety meeting, and we're going to get this straightened out." In a report to mine officials on February 24, 1947, the union safety committee had complained of poor timbering and said, "The biggest grievance is dust."[5] Two of the three members of the committee died underground.

Mining was the heritage of Gustave (Gus) Hohman. His father started work in southern Illinois mines before 1900. Father and son worked together at a mine in Zeigler. For years, they drove sixty-five miles south to Zeigler from Centralia every Sunday, worked there all week and stayed in an apartment, and then returned to Centralia for the weekends. When his father died in 1925 as the result of a nonmining accident, Gus started work at No. 5.

As Elvera's father prepared for work on March 25, she argued with his decision to go back to the mine. "Dad, if it's that bad [safety conditions in the mine] why do you even want to go back down there?" Hohman responded, "What else can I do?" She answered, "You've got such a wonderful personality, you could get a job anywhere." Hohman then delivered his valedictory. "If the good Lord wants me, he's going to get me. He may let me get hit on Broadway [Street] with a truck or down there in the mine or wherever he wants me, if it's God's will." At 3:26 PM, the full force of an explosion hit Hohman. He was among the first to die. Three months later, workers cleaning up debris in the mine found his pocket watch 300 feet from where he worked.

An only child, Elvera remembered her father in the fondest terms. His death at age fifty-four took away her idol. But Gus Hohman left a legacy. When Elvera's husband, Donald Kirkland, returned from World War II, he thought first of going to the coal mines, like his father-in-law, where the money looked good compared with other job opportunities. Hohman counseled his daughter's husband to avoid the mines, to find another career even if it paid less, but one with less risk to life and limb. Kirkland took the advice and found work away from the mines at the local Sears Roebuck store.

August Holzhauer, a swing motorman who started work at No. 5 in 1913, worked with a crew of twelve near the bottom of the airshaft, in an area known as 4 West. His partner was Jack Pick Jr. Holzhauer described the moment he realized something was wrong: "We happened to notice a kind of puff of wind . . . and the fan seemed to stop at that time, so then I said, 'Well, there must be an explosion or something.' A few seconds later we seen the dirt and smoke and powder smoke coming out. I didn't hear any blast but I knew what had happened."

On his way to the shaft, Holzhauer found John Lorenzini, a brakeman who worked on the motor cars, staggering and obviously suffering from a lack of good air. Lorenzini had escaped injury or death by ripping off his sweatshirt, soaking it in a pail of water, and holding it against his nose for protection against deadly fumes as he ran for the main shaft. Holzhauer told his fellow workers, "I believe we had better get this man out." He picked Lorenzini up, helped place him on the motor car, and held him so he would not fall off. They got in the hoist cage together, with Holzhauer supporting Lorenzini. Holzhauer said, "When I hit about 10 foot from the top, when the air hit me, I went out. I was conscious but my legs wouldn't carry me, so they had to grab me on the cage there and hold me just as they did him. So they took me first to the engine room and then the wash house and then to the hospital." He remained there until Thursday. Lorenzini survived, although he could not recall much of his rescue.[6]

That morning, Jack Pick Sr., and his son, Jack Jr., parted at the bottom of the shaft. Lugging his lunchbox, the father yelled, "So long, Jack. See you at quittin' time." As the day shift neared an end, Jack Jr. looked at his watch, which read 3:30. "We started up [the shaft], laughing like we always do, and thinking of that fresh air we would be getting in a few minutes. We were about 500 feet underground when all of a sudden there was a rumbling explosion that rocked everything. You could just feel old man death rolling through the tunnels and corridors. There was terrible confusion, enough to make a man crazy. I felt sick all over." Jack Jr. could smell death, "that awful gas, the stuff we are scared of all day and have nightmares about all night." He first thought of his father, much further back in the mine. As late as the next day, the son still held hope that Jack Sr. would make a miraculous appearance. He had worked that day on 1 West, fairly close the point of the explosion, and died in the initial blast.[7]

In the first minutes, men acted instinctively, in spite of growing chaos and danger. Those closest to the hoisting shaft felt little or no impact from the explosion. Then dust and smoke rolled through the passages and compromised clean air. Quick thinking saved a number of lives, but at least one death occurred when a normal human reaction proved fatal. Clifford Copple, forty-two, a motorman working with Lorenzini, immediately feared for his brother Frank, who worked in 1 West. Clifford ran away from the hoisting shaft in search of his brother, and he died. Frank had been killed in the initial explosion.

Henry Goforth, a twenty-nine-year mining veteran, whose father had died on February 23, 1921, in an explosion at No. 5, was working as a motorman on the mainline, about 500 feet from the shaft bottom, when the power went off and the motor he drove stopped. He let the motor coast to the shaft. After about thirty seconds, smoke and dust "began to boil out." Goforth made it out unscathed.[8]

Don Soper, a repairman helper working in the motor room, about 300 feet from the shaft bottom, said, "The first that I knew that anything was wrong was when a cloud of smoke billowed up. The man with me said, 'Don, I think there has been an explosion. Come on.' We ran to the main entrance and got on the first trip up the shaft." He worked with rescue crews for days.[9]

Deep in the mine, the explosion caused extreme destruction and fire, burning to death as many as sixty-five men almost instantly. Near the point of origin in 1 West, the force of the explosion demolished doors, bent and twisted rails, wiped out communications, blew open abandoned workings that had been sealed, damaged locomotives, disabled shuttle cars, and caused timbering in roofs to fall on machinery and tear down electrical lines. The blast maimed men's bodies so terribly that they could be identified only from papers in the pockets of their clothing. In rooms containing workers away from the point of origin, death came slower, from a lack of fresh air and encroaching carbon monoxide, known by miners as *blackdamp*. One group of seventeen workers was found holding onto their lunchboxes, as if they had fallen asleep on their way to the hoist. As miners breathed the gases, life slipped away. Officials concluded that forty-four men working in sections not affected by flame or the violence of the explosion might have saved themselves if they had erected barricades and conserved good air.[10]

At a point distant from the hoisting shaft in 4 West, a group of about twenty-five miners had worked all day near faces of the mine. When it was close to quitting time, they prepared to load up in cars for the ride to the cage. The blast killed some of the men instantly, and their watches stopped at 3:25 and 3:27 PM. Some fourteen survivors scrambled for safety in the dark, staying together for comfort and hope. They wanted to get far from what they believed was the source of the explosion. The men crawled and moved cautiously in the debris and darkness to Room 8 of 23 South, some 1,320 feet from Room 30, where they had stopped working.

Huddling in the room, wishing to avoid the inevitable, the group hoped rescuers might find them. Eventually realizing their fate and growing weaker, those still able decided to write notes to loved ones with words of encouragement and advice for their children. Unable to see what they were writing and weakened by blackdamp, they wrote notes that were brief but affectionate. The men began writing about an hour after the explosion. One man timed his note "6:30 AM" in a moment of forgetfulness, unable to correct it in the dark.

Ned Jackson, a motorman from Odin, put his message on a slab of slate with a piece of chalk. "D. T., take care of Elva and Dickie. Ned." Raymond

Buehne, at age thirty one of the youngest in No. 5 and the father of three small children, addressed his wife by her nickname, "Chub." He wrote, "God bless you all, Beanie, 4:30." Many of the writers did not sign their names. One wrote, "To my wife: It looks like the end for me. I love you, honey, more than life itself. If I don't make it, please do the best you can and always remember and love me, honey. You are the sweetest wife in the world. Goodbye, honey, and Dickey."

Others wrote: "Dear Wife: Please take care of the children. Leave all to my wife. Love." "Dear Wife: Goodbye. Forgive me. Take care of all the children. Love." "Dear Wife: God bless you and the baby." One was addressed to two boys: "Be good boys. Please your father. O Lord help me." Writing to "sweetheart and sons," one miner said, "If I don't make it, sell the house and go live with your folks. Your mom and dad will take care of you and the boys. Please pray for me and join the church for me. Tell dad to quit the mine and take care of mom. Well, baby and my loving boys, good-bye as I am feeling weak. Lots of Love."

In a futile effort to find good air, one man removed his helmet and scooped a hole in the coal wall at the far side of the room. He was found with his face pressed against this hole and his back to the other miners. Most of those in the room had formed a kind of circle as death came. By 7:00 PM, all the notes were written. A last act for one man was to write a message on the rock face above where the men were scattered in the room. It directed rescuers to "look in everybody's pockets. We all have notes. Give them to our wives."[11]

Rescuers found these names written in a time book: Fred Gutzler, Louis Piazzi, Bruno Gaertner, Carl Rohde, Joe Ballantini, Anton Tillman, Leo R. Dehn, Edward Hofstetter, Celso Biagi, Joseph Cerutti, Joe Altadonna, Tony Giovannini, Raymond Buehne, Joe Bryant, Joseph H. Peiler, Joseph Koch Sr., Luther Frazier, Dominick Lenzini, Ned Jackson, Walter H. Fetgatter, John Placek, John Mazeka, Charles Kraus, Martin Freeman Jr., and John W. Gutzler. All died in the first hours after the explosion.

Found several days later, the notes were reviewed by mine authorities and given to survivors of the men. State inspector Scanlan said when releasing information to reporters, "Apparently they were retreating out of the mine. They would have been better off had they remained where they were and built a barricade."[12]

Harry "Cotton" Niermann, the mine superintendent who worked on top, was standing in the engine room talking to a hoisting engineer who had applied for a different position, when the fuse on the mine fan blew about

3:25 PM. Because the fan circulated fresh air to the mine, Niermann moved quickly to change the fuse. "Immediately up came the chief electrician, by the name of Fred Hellmeyer, and about the same time somebody came in—I don't remember—and he said, 'There is something wrong, as there is a terrific amount of powder smoke coming out,'" Niermann recalled. Niermann picked up the telephone and called the home of state inspector Driscoll Scanlan in nearby Nashville. Scanlan was not available, and Niermann left a message with the inspector's wife. Scanlan said later he was notified at 3:50 PM.

Niermann headed quickly for the bottom of the mine shaft. He found a chaotic scene, with miners who did not know what to do and others who went looking for survivors without directions or knowledge of what danger they might encounter. The superintendent met with William Brown, the mine manager who worked below ground. They attempted to organize workers for searches and sent injured and dazed men to the top.[13]

A few men with Niermann and Brown got aboard a motor car and pushed toward 1 West until debris stopped them. They found the body of Mark Watson, a pumper, who became the first known fatality. The rescuers discovered twenty men, sixteen dead on the clay floor, and four living. The four were out of their minds due to the poisonous fumes, and the rescuers had to manhandle them to a safer part of the mine.

After Niermann called, Scanlan's wife found him at the family's mine in Venedy. Scanlan left instructions with a clerk in the Department of Mines and Minerals to alert rescue crews and inform top officials of the department. He hurried the forty miles to Centralia, as did an increasing number of individuals, rescue teams, service providers, and inevitably, relatives and spouses of those under ground. Arriving about 4:40 PM, Scanlan took over rescue operations and went into the mine. He emphasized the need to rescue miners and delay the removal of bodies, if necessary, and ordered everyone out of the mine. Trained rescue crews headed to Centralia from Belleville, West Frankfort, Herrin, Benld, DuQuoin, Eldorado, and other southern Illinois mining towns.

The first rescue teams arrived about 7:45 PM. Scanlan stated in a press conference on March 31 that the bodies of those killed could have been removed from the mine forty-eight hours earlier than they were if he had received full and prompt cooperation from the state mining department's rescue officials. Specifically, he claimed William Williams, the state mine rescue superintendent, was unresponsive to his first requests for rescue teams.[14]

Although everyone lost track of time in the melee, survivors later estimated that after about thirty minutes to an hour below ground—it might have been longer—the tainted air took effect on Niermann. He looked and acted like a wild man, out of control and dangerous to others. Goforth tried to help him. "Mr. Niermann came out screaming and hollering and he fell. I tried to drag him to the cage and he knocked me down and he got up and ran north to the north side of the shaft bottom, and he fell again. I went and tried to get him again and he is a big man and he knocked me down again. I began to feel my head go round and needed some help. So I went on top and told Mr. Scanlan to get three or four men and get him away, and they did."[15]

Over the next twelve to twenty-four hours, calls for relief brought fifty ambulances to the scene. Cots arrived from Scott Field Army Air Base near Belleville, and Red Cross workers came from St. Louis with special equipment for resuscitating gas victims. Rescuers brought blood plasma and pulmonary equipment. Nuns from the Felician Nursing Order and priests with windbreakers over their cassocks offered care to the injured and gave last rites to the dying. Governor Green, suffering from a severe cold, said every state resource was being made available to Centralia. Director Medill hurriedly left southeastern Kansas by automobile.[16]

Thirteen federal Bureau of Mines officials assisted in rescue operations along with thirteen members of the state mining department. Also at the scene were seven state mine rescue teams and one rescue team from the Bell and Zoller Company. Political reactions came quickly, too. State Representative Paul Powell of Vienna, in Springfield for the legislative session, said a day after the explosion that Democrats would demand an investigation by Governor Green to discover whether the explosion could have been prevented.[17]

Meanwhile, rescuers at the scene had no idea how many died or were injured. Eventually, they knew that twenty-four escaped unaided, and eight, including one man who died later, were rescued in the first hours. Mine officials and people in charge of operations could provide no information to families waiting in the cold, damp Wamac weather. An emergency hospital was set up at the Community Center to care for the injured. Scanlan moved cautiously to organize rescue teams, hoping to avoid further injuries and sickness and to minimize threats to safety.

Each rescue crew consisted of two mine rescue teams plus other individuals. Rescue crews were organized in four shifts under the direction of Medill. The first fully equipped and trained rescue team, including Scanlan, made its entry into the mine about 8:00 PM, almost four and a half hours after the explosion. They brought survivors out on stretchers. The second rescue crew entered the mine at midnight with federal and state inspectors. Their work was hindered by carbon monoxide and severe physical damage in many parts of the mine.[18]

Era Boles joined the first rescuers. "I went down with the first crew about 7:00 PM. We were down about two and a half hours. We brought out four men, all which were alive out of a group of twenty. I carried a stretcher from the point where we picked the men up in the south passage to within about fifty feet of the shaft. I had taken off my mask in the good air, but I must have had a snoot full, because suddenly I couldn't stand up anymore." Boles did not hold out much hope for more survivors.[19] All who survived were out of the mine by 10:30 PM.

After participating in the earliest rescue efforts, Henry Goforth went home, arriving there about 7:45 PM. He cleaned up and rested; then he returned to the mine and joined a rescue crew a little before midnight. "We went to the thirteenth and fourteenth north, and we found sixteen bodies there. Our time was up. We agreed we would be back in three hours. We got back on top, it was about 3:30 [AM], and the next crew went down."[20] Goforth's experience mirrored efforts by countless rescue workers in the first hours after the disaster.

A crowd estimated at five hundred persons or more collected at the mine site by evening.[21] Wives, sons, and daughters remained through the night, stoically waiting for word, rarely showing signs of emotion or talking. Occasionally, a woman wiped a tear from her face. Reporter Harry Wilensky of the *St. Louis Post-Dispatch* wrote of one poignant scene: "After darkness fell, many of the relatives retired to a wash house where they sat on the benches the miners had used in changing their clothes. Overhead, suspended on chains and pulleys, hung the street clothing of the men who had failed to come up. In some cases wives recognized their husbands' garments and selected their places for the long vigil."[22] Volunteers of the Red Cross and Salvation Army from throughout southern Illinois set up canteens and served coffee and sandwiches.

The *Centralia Sentinel* became the first newspaper on the streets with news of the explosion in an extra edition that night. Precious little information was available. Rumors about conditions underground spread quickly as survivors came to the top and commented to reporters or talked with mine officials and bystanders. Published reports about the number of bodies brought out of the mine and their identities varied widely in the first days, providing little comfort to those waiting for encouraging words. Scanlan did his best to minimize unfounded statements, but he could not control speculation by mine officials and state authorities.

Sentinel reporters talked with some of those waiting for word of their relatives. Most of those who kept vigil at the mine site expressed hope, punctuated by the word *if*. Among those waiting was Adolf Lenzini, son of miner Pete Lenzini. "I'm sure they have retreated and sealed themselves off. . . . I just feel that he'll be okay. If his crew wasn't caught in the first blast. . . . if they had a chance . . . if."[23]

The gruesome task of bringing the dead to the surface began on Wednesday, March 26. Miners loaded bodies into ambulances that took them to a temporary morgue in a nearby garage. As each group of bodies came up in the miners' cage, a hush fell over the crowd. Families held onto hopes that survivors could still be found. Scanlan refused to speculate, other than to say rescue operations continued in earnest.

As the first shock of the tragedy began to ebb, emotion took over. That happened most often where relatives of miners gathered, in Centralia and nearby communities. It also occurred to a less personal extent on the editorial pages of St. Louis newspapers, little more than an hour away. They asked questions that would rattle the mine operator, the Department of Mines and Minerals, the UMWA, and most assuredly those directly affected by death and injury.

The *Post-Dispatch*, the most vocal media critic of mine operators and state officials leading up to the explosion, pulled no punches in an editorial the day after the explosion:

> The blood of the men who lost their lives in the mine disaster at Centralia is on the hands of the mine operators who continued to run the mine in the face of repeated warnings of an "explosion hazard." It is also on the Illinois State Department of Mines whose inspectors have authority to close mines that do not comply with safety requirements. . . . Why was this mine permitted to operate in the face of these warnings? The Centralia Coal Co. knew the hazard existed. . . . Gov. Green cannot bring back the lives of the entombed. He cannot comfort the grief-stricken survivors. But there is one thing he can do: He can find out why this mine was not closed in accordance with repeated warnings.[24]

Across the city, at the *St. Louis Globe-Democrat*, editorialists took a somewhat softer approach but made pertinent points just the same:

> Had the warnings been heeded, the disaster might easily have been averted. . . . A prompt investigation should, and doubtless will, be launched to determine why the safety recommendations were not carried out and why the state mine inspectors did not insist on compliance with the orders. Not only should the responsibility be fixed for the Centralia explosion, but the state should take the necessary steps to prevent a similar disaster in the future.[25]

As might be expected, elected officials in Congress from Illinois went to work almost immediately on resolutions calling for investigations. Senator C. Wayland Brooks of Illinois and Senator Styles Bridges of New Hampshire, both Republicans, on March 27 sponsored a resolution demanding an inquiry into the failure of federal officials to enforce safety regulations at No. 5. This obviously partisan approach aimed at President Truman and federal officials who had seized the mines brought objections from Democratic senators and turned a routine procedural vote into a melee.[26]

Brooks said the federal government "has become so all-powerful in the last 15 years" that it should be held accountable for the loss of life. Bridges called Interior Secretary Julius A. Krug "the man directly responsible for the disaster." Senator Scott Lucas, Democrat of Illinois, said safety violations were nothing new. "I undertake to say that they were going on at the Centralia mine long before the government took over." Before the vote, Senator Alben Barkley of Kentucky offered an amendment to include state and local officials and the federal inspection service as objects of the investigation. The resolution passed on a voice vote.

A day later, March 28, Representative Charles W. Vursell, Republican of Salem, Illinois, introduced a House resolution to appoint a five-member committee to investigate the explosion. The House approved the resolution but eventually deferred to hearings by a special Senate subcommittee that would hold sessions in Centralia.

In Illinois, while rescue missions continued at No. 5, politicians opened fire, with Governor Green a target. State Representative Carl Preihs, Democrat of Pana, announced two days after the explosion that he would seek the impeachment of Green if it was determined that the governor "neglected or refused to act." His comments came after public release of the letter miners sent to Green a year earlier asking him to "please save our lives." Green, sick in Chicago, said he turned the miners' letter over to the Department of Mines and Minerals and "as far as my office was concerned, that seemed to end it right there."[27]

Meanwhile, the dirty, tiring, emotional job of searching for bodies and hoping for survivors continued in the labyrinth of No. 5. As each group of fatalities became known and bodies were brought to the top, the crowd of relatives dwindled and hope drained from the bystanders. Each day's newspapers gave the latest count and ran lists of the dead. Rumors continued, forcing Scanlan, who had barely slept since arriving at the scene, to address one of them publicly. He acknowledged stories that tapping sounds had been heard within the mine, indicating some miners might still be alive below ground. He responded: "I have investigated all of these rumors thoroughly and found absolutely nothing." Periodically, fresh rescue workers, leaning forward with the weight of oxygen tanks on their backs and wearing helmets with lights shining brilliantly, took the cage into the mine for yet another search.[28]

Frayed nerves among rescuers and an order from Director Medill produced a near revolt and a public clash after two days and nights of searching. Medill told Scanlan to turn on the power in the mine to speed work. The inspector and the workers objected, fearing the danger of another explosion. Medill ordered a chemical test of the air to determine the level of danger. Results indicated deadly gases were present, and Scanlan said the potential for a spark setting off another blast remained high. The ruckus caused a delay of about two hours in rescue operations and angered the workers. They demanded the removal of Medill from responsibilities at the site. Federal officials took no action but said they would watch for further signs of hostility. Throughout the disagreement, workers vocally announced their support for Scanlan.[29]

On Friday, the death toll reached 111 with the discovery of bodies in the far reaches of the south passage. A rescue crew boss announced over a communication tube, "General search completed—all bodies recovered but one." Rescuers knew the location of Clifford Copple's body but had not been able to reach it because of debris. With that announcement, William Young, top official of the mining company, said, "All found, all dead." Rescuers brought the last body to the surface on Sunday. After ventilation was restored to the mine, officials closed No. 5 for two days to permit the clearing of carbon monoxide. On Wednesday, April 2, rescue operations ended officially, and the mine was declared safe for visits by investigators.

Rescue work had been exhausting, emotional, and nerve-racking. Most of the bodies were located in areas of the mine that received the greatest damage. Crews had to negotiate smashed timbers, damaged mine equipment, and falling chunks of coal. Bodies were badly broken and bruised. Many of the dead, blown against sidewalls, had crushed ribs. Others had injuries caused when they were blown against mine cars by the blast. After completing a rescue assignment, crew members looked like they had been underground for weeks.

Among the most miserable work for rescuers was identifying the bodies badly mutilated by the explosion. Unable to identify men by their appearance, rescuers questioned families of miners concerning personal effects their loved ones carried. The *Centralia Sentinel* explained the process in the edition of March 28. "The brand of cigarettes, a pipe, a tobacco pouch . . . perhaps a pocket knife or pair of pliers . . . all clues were carefully noted down and returned to the morgue. Meanwhile, morticians had listed the items found on the dead. The lists were matched and if they proved similar, a relative or friend was called."

When all the bodies were located, the cleanup of debris from the rescue effort began. The Red Cross and the Salvation Army closed their food and drink services. Railroad sleeping cars where rescuers had slept between shifts were pulled away. The miners' wash house where spouses and children had waited for word of their loved ones was closed.

For several days, funerals and wakes consumed residents of Centralia and nearby communities. There were multiple services and burials for members of the same family, and in one case, for four friends: Frank Paulauskis, Dominick Lenzini, Celso Biagi, and Stanley Teckus. The newspapers said twelve funerals were held on Saturday, March 29, eleven on Sunday—Palm Sunday—and twenty-one on Monday, the day of official mourning for Centralia and surrounding communities. Holy Week leading to Easter held special meaning and sorrow and provided unforgettable, lifelong impressions for thousands of residents. Every church in the vicinity scheduled funerals back-to-back, and streets were clogged with processions and traffic, while families waited their turn. Elvera Kirkland, whose father, Gus Hohman, died in the explosion, remembers that nine members of Trinity Lutheran Church died. Throughout neighborhoods with churches, "cars were everywhere, so we walked to the church."[30]

With churches crowded, some families used funeral homes for services. Friends and relatives honored Harry Berger, who worked thirty-five years for Centralia Coal Company, at the Garnier Funeral Home, formerly a private home. Friends and relatives of the miner jammed the building, sat on steps leading to the second floor, and crowded the entrance hallway, listening over a public address system to services conducted by the Reverend E. B. Beaty, a Methodist minister. People, including surviving miners, filed silently past the open casket. Harry Berger was the first of the 111 to be buried in Centralia area cemeteries.[31]

On Monday, March 31, residents of Centralia and the four adjoining communities where victims of the disaster lived mourned at two general memorial services: a community gathering in the high school conducted by eleven pastors, and a requiem High Mass at St. Mary's Catholic Church. Most businesses in Wamac, Central City, Sandoval, Centralia, and Glenridge closed, while funeral processions followed one another through the streets and church bells rang.

That day's edition of the *Sentinel* offered a solemn presentation for its readers. Column rules were turned so that black lines of mourning separated columns of type, and the paper showed palm leaves and floral wreaths at the top of the front page. A complete list of the dead was printed in black boldface type. Centralia mayor O. W. Wright called the day "Black Monday." The fund for the needy, begun earlier and directed by the mayor, had grown to $20,000 in just a few days. The disaster left ninety-nine widows and seventy-eight dependent children under age eighteen.[32]

4

Years of Strife

AS SURVIVORS COUNTED THE CASUALTIES and assessed destruction at No. 5 and contemplated the changed world about them, a bitter feud between two powerful men in Illinois mining circles erupted in headlines across the state, revealing for the first time much of what had led up to the explosion. Behind the scenes, few people outside the coal mining business knew of the internal quarrels that hindered efforts to improve working conditions at No. 5. Once the parties went public to protect their reputations, people across the state had a look at animosities that colored public testimony and news accounts and influenced the lasting impressions of those involved.

The primary contestants were Robert M. Medill, director of the Department of Mines and Minerals, and Driscoll O. Scanlan, state mine inspector. At first glance, the reasons for compatibility between the two outnumbered the points at issue between them. Both had extensive experience in Illinois mines. They proudly served as active members of the Republican Party. When applying for state jobs, they received the backing of the UMWA. In public utterances, each swore allegiance to tough safety standards for coal mines and protections for those who worked below ground. However impressive, those similarities formed only a small piece of the picture.

Tension between the two men had grown steadily from 1941 to 1947. At the peak of their quarrels, private and public, each accused the other of being responsible for the mine explosion and the death of 111 men. This clash caused one person close to both to observe, "There has been, I would say, a hatred existing between Scanlan and Medill for a good long time."[1] He said *hatred*, not "dislike" or "unpleasantness." The record speaks for itself.

There is little reason to believe Medill and Scanlan knew each other before their appointments early in 1941, although both had lengthy experience in Illinois mines. Medill, while possessing a high profile in state administrations of the early 1920s, had worked outside Illinois for fifteen years. They became acquainted formally when newly elected governor Green appointed Medill to head the department at the outset of the new administration, a job Medill had held under two previous governors. Scanlan wanted work as a state mine inspector in the Republican administration, a position for which he felt qualified. Nothing in the background of either presaged a fight.

Scanlan told everyone who asked, "I was raised in a coal mine." As a child, his idea of a delightful Sunday outing was to visit the mine with his father, Patrick Scanlan, who served as foreman at the Mt. Olive and Staunton Coal Company, Mine No. 2. Scanlan's father did not choose him for special treatment. Four of Driscoll's brothers also made careers in mining. With parental encouragement, it was only a matter of time before Driscoll went to work in the mines. In 1920, at age sixteen, Driscoll—called "Dris" by family members—got his first mine job helping surveyors map the Breese-Trenton mine at Beckemeyer. He worked about six years in mining jobs before he was hired as a mine examiner at Clarkson Coal and Mining in Nashville, Illinois, his longtime home.[2]

Scanlan campaigned for Dwight Green in 1940, and when the new governor took office, he applied for the position of state mine inspector. After the screening of applicants and upon the recommendation of Republican House members throughout the state, Green hired sixteen state inspectors, including Scanlan. Reaching out to various constituencies, Green accepted union recommendations for all positions in the mining division of the department, including clerical and inspection jobs. Whether an applicant received the UMWA or PMW endorsement depended on which organization had the majority of members in the legislative district.

Scanlan had the necessary Republican credentials, and the UMWA recommended his appointment. Among the papers accompanying his application, Scanlan included a form that asked a series of political questions about party affiliation, campaign experience, party activities, and how he voted. He also submitted letters of recommendation. One concluded, "He is a great believer in safety first."[3]

While all the recommendations counted, the one that counted more than all the others belonged to State Representative R. J. Branson, Republican of Centralia. In the political terms of the day, Branson was Scanlan's "sponsor." From 1925 to 1956, Branson served in the Illinois House of Representatives from District 42, which included Marion County and Centralia. With that kind of seniority, Branson's word to a new Republican governor was golden. As it turned out, Branson had a role in the conflict that developed between Medill and Scanlan.

Testifying after the explosion, Scanlan laid out the political realities of being appointed a state mine inspector: "Your job is an appointive job, and your mining board is an appointive job, and every time an administration changes you are kicked out and somebody else comes in, and if some coal operator has a lot of influence all he has to do is to get to the county chairman or to some other politician and bring pressure on him."[4]

By 1941, Scanlan and Medill had climbed to positions they would hold for six years, until after the disaster at Centralia No. 5. For three years after their appointments, business between Scanlan and officials in the Department of Mines and Minerals appeared routine and without personal rancor. In these early years of World War II, everyone concentrated on production of coal for the war effort. Scanlan made his periodic inspections and dutifully filed reports.

Scanlan did not allow external matters to influence his observations below ground. From the beginning, he found major safety issues, and he noted them for mine owners, miners, and state officials, along with recommendations for correcting the problems. Officials in Springfield treated the reports routinely, and everyone remained noncombative. Communication, if any, remained cordial and through the normal chain of command. As issues flared after 1944, documents in state files reveal, Scanlan and Medill communicated by letter, in telephone calls, and at private meetings, depending on the issue at hand and the desire to avoid time delays in the bureaucracy. Some of the unofficial contacts inevitably gave rise to disputed accounts of who spoke when and what was said.[5]

What transpired between Scanlan and Medill from late 1944 through the explosion and investigations might have been put down to just another bureaucratic disagreement and quietly forgotten. However, documents preserved by Scanlan and UMWA officials identified the personal nature of the disagreements. As mentioned previously, the first controversy involving Medill at No. 5 mine, according to documents, occurred in November 1944 and continued into February 1945, when Scanlan informed Medill that Centralia miners were about to file charges against mine officials.

This appears to be the first sign of tensions among parties involved at No. 5, although there was little hint of how far the matters would go. In an effort to calm the situation, Medill wrote to William Young, vice president of the Centralia Coal Company. Addressing Young "Dear Bill," Medill sent a copy of Scanlan's report and letter, meekly asking for comments. He did not request an answer to Scanlan's claims about mine management, and he did not order any changes made at the mine.

Young, writing immediately to "Dear Bob," said the war demand had created pressures for productivity at the mine, and there wasn't time to take any action on Scanlan's recommendations. When their correspondence was made public in the days after the explosion, Medill's soft handling of the issue with Young drew considerable criticism.[6]

Medill discussed the matter face-to-face with Scanlan in Benton on March 1–3, 1945, and followed that with a letter a few days later, enclosed with copies of the Young correspondence. Medill said he had talked with Young on the telephone, and "I feel quite sure that he is ready and willing to do the things incorporated in your report as soon as time will permit." Medill also gave Scanlan a bit of advice. "I would suggest that you ask the Mine Committee to be patient a little longer, inasmuch as the coal is badly needed at this time."[7]

If anything, Scanlan agreed with the miners' complaints; however, he considered Medill's request an order, and he spoke to the miners. In later testimony, he quoted one miner at the meeting as saying in essence, "'Scanlan, we are willing to do anything that is right and we will wait until the 1st of April but it is the duty of the Department of Mines and Minerals to enforce the mining laws and take care of us miners, and when the 1st of April comes we want something done.'"[8]

Scanlan continued the conversation with Medill on March 14 in Belleville at a meeting of bituminous coal operators. Scanlan said of the discussion, "I begged Medill to permit me to shut this mine down. I told him that the mine was in such a dirty, dusty and hazardous condition that if the dust became ignited, a dust explosion would spread through the entire mine and probably kill every man in the mine." Scanlan quoted Medill as saying, "'We will just have to take that chance.'" Later Medill acknowledged the meeting and added, "I don't remember what was said."[9]

Eventually during April, after more conversations between Medill and Scanlan, a compromise was reached, and rock dusting occurred without shutting down the mine. This crisis having been avoided, exchanges and meetings on record between Scanlan and Medill subsided. The lull did not signal any new respect among the parties, however. The truce lasted until December 1945, when old issues and tempers flared again over Scanlan's repeated recommendations for water sprinklers in the mine. Medill may have concluded that the only time Scanlan communicated directly was to complain or to raise a controversial issue. The report prompted Medill to call Scanlan on December 20 and order him to Springfield for a meeting with B. H. Schull, a member of the State Mining Board who lived in Indiana, ahead of a scheduled board meeting. Scanlan showed up at the Leland Hotel for the talk with Schull.

Medill sent Schull to dress down the mine inspector and possibly intimidate him.[10] Scanlan said Schull "told me I had no legal right to make hardly any of the recommendations." Scanlan disagreed with Schull and refused to change his recommendation for sprinklers. "Schull and I entered into quite an argument," Scanlan said. Then the two went to the Department of Mines and Minerals, with the expectation that Scanlan would meet with board members. But Scanlan never met with the board. He remained at the offices all day while the board met privately. Medill told Scanlan after the meeting that the board had appointed a commission to inspect the mine and to follow up on charges that were filed against mine officials by Local 52, "and for me to stay out of the picture and away from the mine while the commission was at the mine."[11]

The investigating commission filed its report after an inspection of the mine on December 28. It stated, "The mine is not adequately rock dusted" and noted that ventilation problems existed, but it offered no support for Scanlan's recommendations to wet the dusty areas. "They didn't concur with me on the dust hazard," Scanlan said.[12] Scanlan did not receive a copy of the report for almost three weeks.

The relationship between Medill and Scanlan had reached the point of no return, and the events of March 1946 pushed it over the edge. In his report of the routine inspection on March 6–7, Scanlan repeated his recommendation for sprinklers to control dust. He said, "Dust is an explosion hazard." Upset at Scanlan's repeated recommendations, Medill ordered Scanlan to a meeting in Springfield on March 13. Scanlan wrote in a note attached to his report about the meeting, "Called to Springfield about this report. . . . March 3, 1946, letter from miners to Governor on Medill's desk." This was the "please save our lives" letter from the UMWA local. Scanlan said, "The miners had included a picture of a widow and several orphans of a recent mine disaster that they had clipped from the *United Mine Workers Journal*." He said Medill disparaged the union for sending the picture.

Medill upbraided Scanlan—Scanlan said he was "severely reprimanded"—for repeating the sprinkler recommendation, and then he criticized the inspector's lengthy and comprehensive reports. Scanlan quoted Medill as saying at their meeting, "'These damned hunkies [miners] down here wouldn't know the condition of the coal mine'" except for Scanlan's repeated recommendations. Scanlan said later, "I told him that there wasn't a lot of foreigners in the mine, and those that were [were] pretty intelligent people. Most of the miners were of German descent and were Americans and were pretty intelligent sort of miners, so there wasn't anybody kidding them about the hazards of their mine; and he gave me to understand that I must cut down the size of my inspection reports."[13]

Medill had a decidedly different version of the conversation:

I said to Mr. Scanlan, "you can incorporate everything you have put into these records in a good deal less space and cover the situation just as well." I said, "Mr. Scanlan, I am quite sure that there are some men at that mine and"—I didn't say this at the time—"that can't read or write the English language." I didn't mention any nationalities. "And when you post a report as long as this one is at that time, they come out of the mine and they see that report, their first reaction is fear, which I don't believe is a good thing. As I said before you can say all you want to say about the dust and the rock dusting and the other conditions of the mine without covering so much paper." That was the substance of our visit.

When confronted with Scanlan's accusations a year later that he had slurred the miners, Medill added, "I have associated all my life with all the nationalities that have ever worked in a coal mine, and I have always respected them. I have never belittled a man what never had an education, because I didn't get much myself." He believed Scanlan's words were slanderous.[14]

Another incident about this time confirmed Scanlan's worst fears about Medill's intentions. State Representative Branson, Scanlan's sponsor for the mine inspector's job, saw Medill in a corridor at the statehouse during the 1946 legislative session. The director complained about Scanlan and wanted to transfer him out of the Department of Mines and Minerals. Specifically, Medill said Scanlan's inspection reports were long and tedious. Branson told Medill he respected Scanlan and his work and did not want him discharged or transferred. Some time later, Branson spoke with Scanlan about the Medill conversation and the proposal to transfer him out of the department. Scanlan believed Branson saved his job, and Branson, speaking about the subject after the mine disaster, agreed.[15] Medill made no public comment about the matter.

During the next nine months, through the end of 1946 and into 1947, Scanlan continued his inspections and reports calling for improvement in conditions at No. 5. Joining in the recitation and bolstering Scanlan's claims were semiannual reports by federal mine inspector Frank Perz. The department director appeared to devote his attention to other matters for several months. Then the conflict rose again on a scale grander than anything earlier.

For nearly two decades, Democrats had ruled the political roost in Chicago. Mayor Edward J. Kelly, partner with Patrick Nash in a political machine that had held the city in a vise lock since the early 1930s, suffered serious losses in the elections of 1946. The weakened condition of Democrats gave great hope to Republicans in the mayoral and aldermanic elections of 1947. Reports of corruption in city government dogged Kelly, and Democratic Party leaders finally convinced him to step down in 1947. The party gave the mayoral nomination to Martin H. Kennelly, a longtime alderman seen as having a "clean" reputation. Republican Russell W. Root, backed to the hilt by Governor Green and the statewide GOP organization, provided the competition. The governor had much at stake in the April 1, 1947, election.[16]

Longtime-dedicated Republicans such as Medill eagerly joined the governor's efforts in behalf of Root. After the explosion, Medill said, "I was sufficiently interested in the campaign to do whatever I could do to wipe out the Kelly-Nash machine and the New Deal down at Washington, and [felt] that the wiping out of the Kelly-Nash machine, if it could be done, would be a step in that direction." Accordingly, Medill called a meeting of the state mine inspectors and other department employees on January 31, 1947, for the purpose of soliciting contributions for the Republican campaign.[17] They met at the Springfield mine rescue station, property owned by the State of Illinois. Scanlan attended the meeting, as did most of the inspectors. Again, at least two versions of what occurred at the meeting developed. One came from Medill, one from Scanlan.

Medill said he did not want to put any pressure on the inspectors, and any contributions they collected must be voluntary. "I personally am going to contribute to that campaign fund," he said. "If you find anyone sufficiently interested in the campaign in Chicago that are willing to contribute, tell them to send their checks to the 'Root for Mayor' campaign in Chicago, to headquarters, not to me." He told inspectors to contact "anybody that is friendly to the cause."

One inspector from southern Illinois asked Medill, "Would it be all right to see Mr. [R. M.] McPhail, superintendent of the Peabody Coal Co., at West Frankfort?" Medill said, "I'm not telling you whom to see. It is up to you to see anybody you feel like seeing. If you believe that Mr. McPhail will be interested, it is all right with me, but there is nothing to be put on a pressure basis. Everything has to be voluntary." Medill added that McPhail and associates had been friendly to the Republicans. Medill hoped to raise between $15,000 and $25,000 for the campaign but said that was an estimate he reached on his own.[18]

Scanlan told a much different story. He said Medill announced at the meeting that his department had to raise $25,000 for the mayoral campaign—"the boys" gave Medill a quota—and the only way he knew to get that much was to call on coal operators. Medill said he had talked with four operators the previous day, and two of them had already come through with $1,000 each. The director said he would contact the major coal companies and wanted inspectors to solicit independent and small companies. Scanlan asked Medill who would call on Bell and Zoller, parent of the Centralia mine, and Medill said he would make the call. Medill left the impression with Scanlan that operators needed to make contributions to even the score for favors provided by the department and its inspectors.[19]

On March 2, Mark Saunders, director of the Illinois Department of Finance and a close associate of Governor Green, called Medill. According to Medill, Saunders told him, "We have received complaints in the governor's office and I heard the complaints on the floor of the House this morning that you are putting pressure and your inspectors are putting pressure on the coal companies for donations to the campaign fund. If you are doing that I want you to stop it immediately." Medill acknowledged hearing the same reports. He called another meeting of the inspectors for March 7 in Springfield, where he told inspectors to stop soliciting any contributions or discussing the subject with anyone.[20]

It was only a matter of time before newspapers heard about the meetings. In editions of March 19, less than a week before the mine explosion, the *St. Louis Post-Dispatch* published results of an investigation by reporter Harry Wilensky, who would help the *Post-Dispatch* win a Pulitzer prize for coverage of the mine disaster. Wilensky called the efforts by Medill to raise funds a "shakedown" of mine operators by inspectors. He wrote that inspectors suggested donations of $100 for operators of small mines and up to $1,000 for operators of large mines. The article quoted an unidentified inspector as saying Medill instructed him to ask "all friends satisfied with the inspection service" for money.

Contacted by the newspaper, Medill said, "A number of my men voluntarily sent in contributions. I told them, if they found anybody who wanted to kick in, good. You know, many miners in Southern Illinois have relatives in Chicago and are interested in the campaign there. But I've never authorized any solicitation." One inspector who attended the March 7 meeting and had trouble collecting from a mine operator told the newspaper, "Medill said he's heard of some complaints. He told us, don't solicit, just mention it."[21]

Questioned after the mine explosion by a *Post-Dispatch* reporter and at a hearing by U.S. senators, Scanlan said the request to solicit contributions was offensive, and he did not call on anyone for a donation. Scanlan stated, "Medill said the Chicago newspapers had been calling him about the solicitations. He added that anything this big couldn't be pulled off without publicity. Medill told us not to worry about it. He said as long as 'the boss' was satisfied, we had no worries. By 'the boss' he meant Governor Green."[22]

A few days after the explosion, the private confrontations of Scanlan and Medill could no longer be contained. In the emotional aftermath, pressed by reporters many times a day and looking at the list of investigations that soon would begin, the two men could no longer soldier on in silence. All sides in the controversy armed themselves for the testimony to come and the anticipated headlines. They battled publicly through most of April in front of assorted investigations and public hearings. Neither Scanlan nor Medill backed down an inch. More than personal reputations were at stake. Neither man wanted history to show that he was to blame for the deaths of 111 men.

5

A Pox on All Houses

EDITH CARTER TOOK HER PLACE AMONG other widows and friends at the opening of the U.S. Senate hearings in Centralia. During the first week of April 1947, she sat quietly, motionless, and dry-eyed as the first witnesses appeared. Some people wondered whether she should have been in a public place so soon after the death of her husband.

"My neighbors think because I'm not sitting down crying until my nose gets red as a tomato that I'm heartless," she told a newspaper reporter. "But I'm doing just what my husband asked me to. He wanted me to be a good soldier, and a soldier fights. I want to see these investigators do something to prevent this from happening to other miners and their wives."

Arthur H. Carter, a native of Cambridgeshire, England, had worked at No. 5 about ten years, and the couple had been married three years. He returned to work a week before March 25 after being off two weeks because of the flu. In a conversation with his wife days before the explosion, he said, "Tootsie, we're going to have an explosion in that mine if they don't clean it up. The coal dust is so heavy our shoes are full of it all day long. Whenever that explosion comes I want you to hold yourself together and be a good soldier."

Arthur talked with his wife frequently about conditions in the mine. "He talked about the dust in the mine all the time," she said. "He said the top [tunnel roofing] was bad, too, because they wouldn't put in enough timbers to make it safe. One day a fall of rock missed him by inches."

Edith Carter learned that Arthur, a tracklayer, was among the first killed by the explosion. "He wasn't with the group that lived for an hour or two and left notes," she said. Rescuers identified Carter from the rubber pads found in his shoes. Years earlier, he had broken the toes of both feet in a farm accident. He protected his toes at work in the mine by making pads of sponge rubber and putting them in his shoes.[1]

Hardly had the reality of March 25 sunk in for widows, fatherless children, and survivors than back-biting and finger-pointing began among those directly involved in and responsible for the mine disaster. Churches and funeral homes struggled with scheduling services for the 111 dead men. At the same time, the din of accusations grew from Washington, D.C., to Springfield, Illinois, to the grounds just outside the entrance to No. 5.

While people waited for the latest word on retrieval of bodies and hope for survivors from the depths of the mine, union leaders, state officials, national political leaders, mine operators, and mine inspectors wrestled for page one headlines. The sideshow, as it clearly became before a week had passed, captured prime news space in the *New York Times*, daily papers in Chicago and St. Louis, and the hometown *Centralia Sentinel*. After expressions of sympathy and sorrow, attempts were made to place blame on others and dodge political liabilities.

One of the loudest and earliest voices belonged to John L. Lewis, national leader of the UMWA. Already steaming over the seizure of mines by the federal government and vocally unhappy with President Truman and associates, Lewis needed no prompting to claim the high ground and the front-page headlines. Three days after the explosion, Lewis appeared in Washington before a Senate Public Lands subcommittee considering the appointment of James Boyd, dean of the Colorado School of Mines, as director of the federal Bureau of Mines. Lewis did not like Boyd's nomination by Truman and had spoken against it previously. This appearance gave the union leader an opportunity to combine his distaste for Boyd with his anger over the deaths in Centralia. He opened his remarks with these words: "Since I was here to testify last week on behalf of greater safety in the mining industry and in opposition to Mr. Boyd's nomination as Director of the Bureau of Mines, 111 mine workers, more or less, have been murdered by the criminal negligence of [Secretary of the Interior] J. A. Krug."

Lewis said Krug had "failed to enforce the law; he has failed to enforce the safety code of the industry which he negotiated with this witness. . . . There has been too much blood smeared over our coal. Here the disaster is at Centralia, Illinois. Another may come tonight or tomorrow. I suppose we might all be sorry, but that will not help the anguish of the bereaved." His reference to Krug related directly to the seizure and the granting of authority to officials of the Bureau of Mines to shut down mines that posed "imminent danger."[2]

A day later, Lewis took the offensive again, ordering 400,000 bituminous coal miners across the nation to stop work and mourn for those who died at No. 5. Lewis said miners would walk out at midnight Monday, March 31, and return at midnight the following Sunday. He knowingly began the UMWA mourning a day after the official mourning of local and area residents. Anticipating arguments from federal officials, Lewis said the basic agreement with the government stipulated that the UMWA "may designate memorial periods provided it shall give proper notice to each district." Miners taking such time off would lose pay. The union had never before used the provision.

Unable to refrain from jabbing at federal officials, Lewis again charged Krug with "criminal negligence" in the deaths. Krug, Lewis stated, "is responsible for the death of these brave men and the future impoverishment of their families." He called for the resignation of Krug, adding the secretary "had dishonored his word [and] he has brutalized the mine workers."[3]

The UMWA's mourning period actually did not include six full days of work. Tuesday was a holiday, designated "John Mitchell Day" in honor of the man who headed the UMWA years before Lewis. Many miners took off Thursday and Friday for Easter week events and did not work on Saturdays anyway. This meant they were off work officially only on Wednesday.

With bituminous mines idle, Lewis continued his barrage of criticism during an appearance Thursday, April 3, before the U.S. House Subcommittee on Miners' Welfare. He spoke without interruption for most of the morning and took questions after lunch. Early in a statement to the subcommittee, he attacked Krug, denying that the secretary had killed the miners by affirmative act but blaming him for inaction. "He permitted them to die while he withheld from them succor that it was within his power to give," Lewis charged.

The union leader called attention to the Federal Mine Safety Code adopted by the government after seizure of the mines, claiming the code granted the coal mines administrator authority to shut down mines that failed to meet safety standards. Specifically, Lewis said the federal government, especially Secretary Krug, bore responsibility for not stopping work at Centralia No. 5 after a federal mine inspector's report in November 1946. Lewis said:

> It showed that coal dust existed there in excessive quantities. Coal dust is explosive, and is the nearest thing we have to atomic power in the form of explosives. That report also showed that there was insufficient air in the mine; that it was not properly ventilated; that what air was going into the mine did not reach the working places of the men, miles underground, that it was lost in transit; that at the last

breakthrough the anemometer, an instrument used for measuring air, would not register, showing that there was no air in the mine.

With all the evidence provided by Perz's report, Lewis continued:

> Yet, Mr. Krug . . . said that there was no danger imminent, and because the inspector did not report imminent danger, he did not move to enforce the code. Whenever the inspector's report shows those conditions, danger is imminent. It may come at any moment, or it may be deferred, according to the mysteries of nature and the providence of God. But Mr. Krug did nothing.

Summoning the rhetorical skills that marked his career in coal mining, Lewis added:

> May God in Heaven forgive him for not finding those out before 111 men were killed, and for not taking action long before these men died, and in voicing these views, gentlemen of the Congress, I voice the sentiment in the heart of every coal miner in this country, and that sentiment is shared by other people who work for a living in our great productive plants, because they, too, want protection, and they want enforcement of the safety laws in the callings that they follow.

During a question-and-answer session with members of the subcommittee, Lewis was combative and unresponsive, especially when members asked pointed questions. He accused them—including Representative Richard Nixon of California—of being antiunion and engaged in snarling comments about the questions. At one point in a discussion of compulsory arbitration for coal mining unions, Lewis said to a congressman, "Why would you, Congressman, or any Congressman, want to weaken the bargaining power of the workers of this country by putting their unions in restraint?" He referred to the congressman's idea as "your damnable compulsory arbitration."[4]

Lewis would have liked nothing better than to provoke Krug into a public exchange about mine safety and Centralia, but the interior secretary refused to take the bait. President Truman went only so far as to issue a statement in which he supported Krug and said he had no plans to ask for his resignation. Instead of battling with Lewis, Krug took a different route on the day the union leader testified before a House committee. He directed that 518 government-operated bituminous coal mines, out of more than 2,500, remain closed until they could be certified as safe. Among those were 48 in Illinois, big and small, involving about fifteen thousand workers. Krug said the mines would remain closed until certified safe and in no imminent danger by the local union's mine safety committee and operating managers.

Nevertheless, UMWA officials remained on the attack against Krug and the government. In Illinois, Hugh White, president of UMWA District 12, claimed Krug had admitted negligence in operation of the mines. "Through his action Krug has just pleaded guilty to the charges of negligence made by John L. Lewis," White said.[5]

In the first week after the explosion, state and federal officials announced plans for at least three official investigations and a short list of lesser inquiries and reports. Key players in events before and after March 25 testified under oath several times, and the public record was highly repetitive. As each public meeting occurred, reports filled countless columns of newspaper space throughout the month of April. Officials formulated plans for a governor's fact-finding committee, a round of public hearings by a special subcommittee of the U.S. Senate, and a study of issues by a committee of the Illinois General Assembly.

As these probes formed, a few officials who had been at each other's throats behind the scenes for years went public with their accusations. The personalities involved were Driscoll Scanlan, Robert Medill, and Governor Green. Their comments and actions became the center of attractions and the subject of articles and headlines for weeks. As soon as the death toll was confirmed at 111 and rescue operations ceased, Scanlan attacked Medill in an interview published by the *St. Louis Post-Dispatch.*

Scanlan blamed the explosion and loss of life on "the operators of the mine, and the State Mining Board, including Director Medill and his assistant, Robert Weir." In a sweeping interview that included a multitude of accusations against Medill, Scanlan expressed resentment about the use of mine inspectors as political campaign fund-raisers. He accused Medill of mishandling the use of rescue workers after the explosion and repeated his earlier warnings to Medill and the State Mining Board about unsafe conditions at the mine.

To illustrate his disdain for the department director, Scanlan told the newspaper reporter about an incident involving Medill that occurred during a conference at a Mount Vernon, Illinois, hotel. He stated:

> An oil operator wanted to drill a well through the Glenridge mine at Centralia, and I opposed it as a hazard. I was afraid there'd be lives lost, but the chiefs of the oil and gas division who were with Medill wanted to issue a permit. Medill could have overruled me, but he preferred to get my agreement and I wouldn't go along. He told the two chiefs I had a lot of ability and could go places in the industry,

but I was just too damned honest. He wasn't joking either. He was serious; I thought he was going to fire me.[6]

Newspapers across the state used the "I was just too damned honest" statement in headlines, next to stories of continued mourning for the dead. On the defense, Medill said, "I, as a coal miner, have always had the miners' interests at heart and will continue to do so. It has been my policy and instructions to the inspectors to follow the exact letter of the law."[7] Scanlan was already two steps ahead of the director in making his case public.

Events moved lightning fast. No sooner had Scanlan issued his condemnation of superiors in the department than Governor Green entered the picture. On Saturday, March 29, he sent a telegram to Medill directing him to conduct a resurvey of all coal mines in Illinois to determine whether any were violating safety regulations and Illinois law. He said, "In the meantime I direct that you communicate immediately with each mine inspector in the 14 districts of Illinois. If in their judgment there is any mine in their district which is not now operating with proper protection for workers, you will advise the Federal Coal Mines Administration of that fact and request that the federal operators not permit those mines to open Monday."[8]

Looking back at that statement and its official and unfriendly tone, obviously the governor did not look kindly upon the political predicament he faced, and Medill's job was in jeopardy. Sometime over the weekend, the governor decided to fire Medill, but he did not bother to tell the director. Green came to Centralia for the first time after the explosion on Tuesday, April 1, to address the initial session of his fact-finding committee. He told the group to "pull no punches." Green then punched out Medill with a public statement, saying the director had resigned "for the good of the service." Newspapers reported that Green had not conferred with Medill before the announcement. Green appointed Harold L. Walker, head of the Department of Mining and Metallurgical Engineering at the University of Illinois, as the interim replacement for Medill.[9]

Free of restraints and seething at Scanlan's criticism, Medill retaliated, placing blame for the explosion on the inspector. "If Scanlan would have performed his duty as prescribed under the law, the 111 miners killed in the Centralia disaster would be alive today." Medill said Scanlan had personal knowledge of the safety problems and should have used his authority to close the mine.[10] Medill made that claim frequently in the explosion's aftermath.

Refusing to let any matters raised by Medill go without rebuttal, Scanlan worked the media like a public relations professional. In a statement on April 1, after Medill's firing and comments, he said:

I do not propose to engage in controversy with my superior, Robert Medill. All my reports have been completed in detail and sent to him, describing conditions in the Centralia Coal Co.'s mine No. 5, and in other mines in this area. These reports are self-explanatory. . . . It is my suggestion that the miners in this district be interviewed as to the existing conditions in this mine and other mines in the coal fields of Illinois. Let the miners give their reports on all the Illinois mines under the leadership of Mr. Medill.[11]

The head-to-head clash between Medill and Scanlan slipped off the front pages of newspapers with the firing of the director until the principals testified at hearings. However, the charges of responsibility for the disaster remained long after the burying of the dead and the initial efforts of families to function without spouses, fathers, brothers, cousins, and grandfathers. There would be three more rounds of Scanlan versus Medill: once before the fact-finding committee, a second time before U.S. senators, and finally before Illinois legislators.

During the week of April 1, state and federal officials made inspection trips into the mine. The Department of Mines and Minerals sent State Mining Board members, and the U.S. Bureau of Mines dispatched federal inspectors, including Frank Perz. The objective of both inspections was to describe conditions in the mine after the disaster and to attempt to determine the location and cause of the explosion. Scanlan accompanied the federal inspection team.

Reports of the two inspections differed little in their observations of damage, the location of the origin of the explosion, and conclusions. However, the federal report provided considerably more detail, analysis, and explanation. This reflected to some extent the people who made the inspections. State Mining Board members, while familiar with mine operations, were political appointees and had an interest in placing blame on others and in supporting the ousted director, Medill. The four members who made the inspection included individuals who had clashed with state inspector Scanlan and members of the UMWA local at No. 5.

Board members interviewed Medill, mine manager William Brown, mine examiners Charles Ford and Fred Lichtenfield, and William Rowekamp, author of the "please save our lives" letter. They did not speak with Scanlan but went out of their way to declare the inspector had full authority to close the mine before the explosion. There were many references to a state mine inspector, but only one mention of Scanlan by name. In their conversation with Rowekamp, board members asked if the miner "understood that a state mine inspector had the right to close down a mine if management failed to comply with the state mine inspector's recommendations." Rowekamp said yes, he understood the inspector's rights at the time of the interview, but not before the explosion. When asked why he did not understand them before March 25, "He replied that he had heard if a state mine inspector gets too strict he could be ousted from his office and that he had only heard that and did not know. He was asked where he heard that and he replied that he had been told that the state mine inspector in his district had been told to shorten his reports."[12]

In the next paragraph of their report, board members said they asked former director Medill, "Did you ever tell state mine inspector Driscoll Scanlan that he could not close down a mine for law violation without securing your permission?" They recorded Medill's answer as "no." Under the "Comments" portion of the report, board members stated, "We would like to call special attention to page 2 'Evidence Taken' where former Director Robert W. Medill says he never told any state mine inspector that he (State Mine Inspector) could not close down a mine for law violation without securing his (the Director of Mines and Minerals) permission." The State Mining Board report concluded: "Based on the inspection made by the Mining Board in Mine No. 5 of the Centralia Coal Company near Centralia, Illinois, on April 3 and April 10, 1947, it is the unanimous opinion of the board that the point of origin of the explosion in this mine on the afternoon of March 25, 1947, was at the head of the first West main entry. That the violence was created by a dust explosion of an unknown cause."[13]

The federal inspectors reported that in a number of instances coal dust had been used to tamp dynamite in drilled holes instead of noncombustible material such as clay. Their report did not say this caused the explosion but that it could have contributed. "A blown-out shot of explosives that was stemmed with coal dust, or an underburdened shot of explosives could have ignited the coal dust. The dust cloud could have been raised by the shot which ignited the dust, or it could have been raised by preceding shots in the same working place or the adjacent crosscut."

The report stated that permissible explosives such as dynamite would not often produce dust explosions "even if fired in the hazardous manner and under the hazardous dust conditions described in this report. But when such hazardous practices and conditions are continued over a long period of time, the right combination of circumstances, such as a blown-out or open shot and an ignitable dust cloud in the presence of such shot, will likely precipitate an explosion sooner or later." The report stated the explosion originated at the face of 1 West entry, "that it was strictly a coal-dust explosion which was propagated by coal dust throughout four working sections of the mine, and that the coal dust was raised into the air and ignited by explosives fired in a dangerous and nonpermissible manner."

Under "Lessons to Be Learned from the Conditions as They Relate to the Explosion," federal inspectors tackled the issues of dusty and unsafe conditions, the extent of which presumably had been known for years. "The outstanding lesson to be learned from this disaster is that mines which liberate little or no methane are not immune from widespread and tragic explosions if dry and dusty conditions exist therein and adequate measures are not taken to control the dust hazard."

The inspectors admitted it had not been customary for any groups concerned about mine safety to regard dry and dusty conditions in mines as "constituting imminent danger." The Centralia explosion demonstrated the need to reevaluate this premise, the report declared. In order to prevent future disasters in dusty mines, the inspectors said, "It will be necessary to regard dry and dusty conditions in mines as being imminently dangerous . . . until appropriate measures have been taken to remedy such conditions."[14]

M. J. Ankeny, one of the federal inspectors involved in the investigation, reported to members of the U.S. Senate on April 16 as the report was made public. Asked why a driller would use coal dust if he knew the practice was dangerous, Ankeny replied, "He doesn't know the hazards. He doesn't know how dangerous it is." He added, "Of course, it is much easier merely to tamp the holes with coal dust than to walk back to the clay box for clay. The shift boss should have known this practice was going on, but perhaps he didn't understand the danger either."[15]

Governor Green wasted little time in naming a governor's fact-finding committee, in spite of an illness that kept him away from Centralia. State and federal legislative bodies already had wheels turning for their own investigations, and Green considered his credibility to be on the line. One of the most embarrassing revelations in the barrage of newspaper stories was the report of the "please save our lives" letter.

Green named John E. Cassidy, a former Illinois attorney general, as chairman. Others on the committee were Oliver Bishop of Zeigler, representing the UMWA; David H. Devonald of Chicago, vice president in charge of operations at Peabody Coal Company; James Sneddon of Royalton, inspector-at-large for the Department of Mines and Minerals; state's attorney Wilbert J. Hohit of Washington County, where the mine was located; John E. Jones of Benton, representing the Federal Coal Mines Administration; and W. A. Gallagher of Vincennes, Indiana, with the U.S. Bureau of Mines.

The committee and staff met in Springfield and gathered information for ten days, beginning Tuesday, April 1. Members took testimony from thirty-five witnesses and examined dozens of documents.[16] Several members entered the mine for an inspection. Among those appearing before the committee were surviving miners John Lorenzini, Jack Pick Jr., and Henry Goforth. Driscoll Scanlan gave extensive testimony. He stated that one reason he did not shut down the mine for failure to correct safety problems was that he would have been fired and the decision would have been overturned. After one member of the panel expressed dissatisfaction with Scanlan's reasoning, the inspector said, "If I had closed the mine, Director Medill would have sent someone here to reopen it."[17]

Testimony by explosion survivors added sadness to the proceedings. Jack Pick, wearing a leather flight jacket, talked about trying to find his father, who died in the blast. "I was selfish and wanted to see my dad," he said. "I lost the greatest friend I had in that explosion—my dad. If mining laws can be fully enforced, then somebody else won't have to do this again." He said Scanlan's recommendations for sprinkling and rock dusting "would have helped tremendously."

The fact-finding committee heard testimony from all the central characters in the mine disaster. For the first time publicly, William P. Young, head of the mining company, discussed the extent to which he knew of dust problems in the mine. He remembered that Scanlan had recommended rock dusting in 1945 and that it had been done, but he denied knowing much more than that about the problem. "I was not aware of any unusual conditions because of dust," he told members of the panel. He admitted reading federal inspection reports and "one or two" of the state inspector's reports. A veteran of twenty-seven years in the mining business, Young said the first he knew of the "please save our lives" letter was after the explosion.[18]

The committee report, forty-six pages long, discussed Scanlan's testimony, his skill as an inspector, and his relationships with miners. The report said, "State Inspector Scanlan at all times had the legal authority to close this mine if he considered it unsafe. His manner of testifying before this Committee clearly indicated he has skill, knowledge, and a devotedness to his official duties. Other evidence showed that he had the confidence of the miners who worked in this mine. He testified that the mine should have been closed."

After complimenting Scanlan on his abilities, the report addressed the issue of his responsibility to close the mine. "We believe his expressed fear that if he did so he would be discharged or reprimanded by the State Director of Mines and Minerals is not a sufficient excuse for his failure to close the mines. The safety of the miners, according to his own testimony, was in such jeopardy that we believe he should have risked his job, even if his fear about his job as State Inspector was justified."

The report joined the rising chorus of people and organizations identifying coal dust as the villain of the explosion and the cause of the deaths. "The evidence tends to prove that the explosion originated at the face of the 1st west entry, approximately two miles from the bottom of the hoisting shaft." The report identified two causes of the explosion: "(1) an ignition of unknown source; (2) propagation, sweep or projection of combustion on account of a quantity of coal dust in the mine. The propagation produced carbon monoxide gas in deadly quantities and suffocated from forty to fifty of the victims."

The committee reprimanded the mine operators for "insufficient and too infrequent application or installation of rock dust to keep the mine safe from explosion propagation" and concluded that "coal dust was the direct cause of a large number of fatalities." The report added, "It is apparent that the company officers and management did not exercise the proper degree of diligence toward complying with the recommendations of federal and state inspectors for many months prior to the explosion."

Committee members said they were convinced by evidence that public officials in the Department of Mines and Minerals and members of the State Mining Board "followed a weak, ineffectual and indifferent policy toward enforcement of State Mining Laws for at least eighteen months with respect to this mine." Having seen official documents from that period, members concluded that "The enforcement was largely confined to writing a succession of letters to the Company containing mild requests that the complaints from Inspector Scanlan be remedied and his recommendations obeyed." The report did not mention the governor or Medill by name.

The fact-finding committee lifted any blame from federal officials, including inspector Perz, who had authority to close the mine. "About the only result of Federal seizure on mine operation was the imposition of authority in the Federal Coal Administrator to remove the company management in the event of failure to comply with the Federal Safety Code after a report by a Federal coal mine inspector, or to close the mine if an inspector made an emergency report of 'imminent danger.'" The report accepted the explanation of Perz that imminent danger did not exist.

Also exonerated from blame were the miners who worked at No. 5. "We believe it is impractical to obligate working coal miners to assume the general responsibility for safety measures. . . . They should have a right to assume that the company management and official inspectors were sufficiently competent and diligent to provide reasonably secure working conditions."

The report said who should be held responsible for assuring the safety of coal mines. "The state mining inspector who is in the field, and who should know the mines of his district, in our judgment is the most effective instrument for compelling safe working conditions. For a long time, Illinois law has provided legal authority for state inspectors to summarily close a mine when they consider it unsafe. It is difficult to imagine a more prompt and decisive method for the protection of the workman."

Responding to charges that political appointments and involvement in election campaigns had compromised the effectiveness of mine inspectors, the report recommended that inspectors be covered by civil service law "and their appointment be irrevocable until after a hearing and decision by a state court. We believe the state inspectors should have legal authority and security commensurate with their very important duties."[19] Eventually, the legislature did provide state mine inspectors with civil service status.

In contrast to the investigations by Illinois bodies, public sessions of the subcommittee of the U.S. Senate Committee on Public Lands resembled a circus. Jammed into the Centralia City Council meeting chamber were major players from state and federal government agencies, mine operator officials, grieving widows and family members, reporters and photographers, and mine survivors. All converged for the subcommittee hearings on April 3–5 in Centralia, and some of the principals were in Washington, D.C., for sessions on April 10, 16, and 17.

Three committee members attended most of the sessions: Guy Cordon, Republican of Oregon, chairman, serving his first term in the Senate; Henry C. Dworshak, Republican of Idaho, serving his first term; and Joseph C. O'Mahoney, Democrat of Wyoming, in his third term.[20] Frank Sever, a former prosecutor from Portland, Oregon, was counsel to the subcommittee. Their deepest interests, as revealed by testimony, included obtaining information about dust, rock dusting, sprinkling, ventilation, and who had authority to close the mine.

Testimony for the three days in Centralia was staged carefully to focus on federal concerns. Missing from the hearings were any current or past Illinois state officials other than Medill, Scanlan, and Representative Branson. No members of the State Mining Board, current officials in the Department of Mines and Minerals, leaders of the legislature, or officials from the governor's office appeared.

Harry "Cotton" Niermann, mine superintendent, testified early on Thursday, April 3, calling on his long history with No. 5 to provide a tutorial for senators on the layout of the mine, complete with charts and diagrams. He also gave details of his personal experience on March 25, beginning with the explosion and attempt to rescue survivors. Almost incidental to those details, Niermann stuck close to the company line regarding what happened and why. He blamed the miners and put the best light possible on the intentions of Centralia Coal Company. Niermann talked about plans to rock dust and studies of sprinklers but admitted that rock dusting had not been done often.[21]

Inspectors Perz and Scanlan also testified on Thursday, providing details of their inspections and recommendations. Repeating descriptions of the mine from his reports, Perz said that No. 5 was "much drier than any mine in my district," stating dust created a "serious explosion hazard." However, Perz added, the mine was "no more dangerous than on any of the previous inspections." This provided an opportunity for senators to probe the reasons why Perz had not declared No. 5 in "imminent danger" of an explosion:

> SENATOR O'MAHONEY: Did you at any time regard it as an imminent danger of explosion?
> PERZ: No, I did not; because I was always told the same condition had existed for the past 15 or 20 years.
> O'MAHONEY: Then on March 20, when you finished your examination of this mine, did you feel from the conditions that existed there with respect to coal dust that there was imminent danger of explosion?
> PERZ: No, I did not. I just considered it a serious hazard, the same as I always had in my reports.
> O'MAHONEY: Then with respect to any other condition that you found, did you think that the conditions were so serious as to constitute an imminent danger of explosion?
> PERZ: I did not.

Later in the testimony, Senator Cordon continued the questioning of Perz regarding imminent danger.

> SENATOR CORDON: Well, as you have gone about in these inspections since the government seized the mines have you found any case where, in your opinion, after inspection there was a situation of imminent danger?
> PERZ: No, I haven't found any.
> CORDON: Well, what would you have to find in order to make that finding?
> PERZ: Well, if you would find a very gassy, gas reported frequently, and if I found gas myself—that is, methane gas—then I would call it imminent danger.

CORDON: Then, imminent danger in your view, results from the presence of inflammable gas?

PERZ: That is right, the inflammable gas plus your dry dust. That would be an imminent danger.[22]

Perz and others stated repeatedly that Centralia No. 5 contained almost no methane gas. In the case cited by Perz, there could not be a circumstance at No. 5 eligible for determination of "imminent danger." He acknowledged that the extent of the explosion might have been reduced if rock dusting had occurred regularly. "Had this rock dust been applied according to recommendations, probably this explosion wouldn't have extended out as far as it had. It may have been confined more to one spot," he said.

When O'Mahoney resumed his questions, the inspector explained that he wrote a cover letter with each of his reports:

O'MAHONEY: How serious did you consider the conditions that you have described in that letter?

PERZ: I considered them a serious hazard, which I always have in making the recommendation.

O'MAHONEY: But you apparently felt that it was not so serious that it was necessary for you to recommend closing the mine or anything like that?

PERZ: No, I did not, because conditions haven't changed. Conditions have been the same for the 2 years or more that I have been coming here, and they tell me that the same conditions have existed prior to that time.[23]

Testifying a day before his nemesis Medill, Inspector Scanlan explained in detail the difficulties between the two men. He believed Medill and his associates should have been sufficiently convinced of the dangers to initiate a closure of No. 5. His testimony and claims easily took top billing in newspaper headlines.[24]

To underscore his point, Scanlan told of a meeting with Medill in Belleville in which the inspector had pleaded for a mine closure. Scanlan also described how he forced operators of No. 5 to rock dust in 1945 and repeated claims that inaction by his superiors and operators of the mine caused the disaster. Scanlan did not retreat under questioning by senators and continued to mention his recommendations for a method to sprinkle the coal dust.

At great length, Scanlan produced copies of correspondence, his reports, and other documents and had them entered into the record. Scanlan acknowledged that state law gave inspectors specific authority to close a mine if it presented sufficient danger to workers and not to reopen the mine until problems were corrected. He also went to considerable lengths, including the citation of an attorney general's opinion, to demonstrate that the State Mining Board had responsibility for inspectors and therefore had authority to close a mine.[25]

Scanlan called for senators to give federal inspectors authority by law to force compliance with safety laws. He said the only way to clean up the mess at the state level was to remove inspectors from politics and make them civil service employees. For the first time publicly, Scanlan offered accounts of meetings and conversations earlier in 1947 to demonstrate how Medill had used inspectors to collect campaign funds for a Chicago mayoral candidate.

Medill took the stand on Friday. With the mine inspector's testimony fresh in mind, senators bore down on the former director. One questioner said, "There was a condition there, a continuing condition of hazard that should have had the attention of the [mining] board itself as well as the inspector's attention and was of such gravity as to require the board on its own initiative to act, and if necessary direct Mr. Scanlan to take further and more severe action to get the conditions corrected. Why did the board not do something about that?" Medill responded, "The conditions in the mine had been, as your evidence will show, carried on for the past 15 years. That is, the same condition practically existed for the past 15 years."

Medill then recalled Scanlan's testimony before the governor's fact-finding committee. "On the witness stand before the fact-finding commission he was asked why he hadn't shut this mine down if he considered it a hazard and dangerous. He said because if he did he would lose his job. Now, if I were a State mine inspector in any district and there was a condition that I considered hazardous or dangerous to the lives of the men employed at that mine I would shut that mine down and let somebody else take the load, which he should have done."

Throughout his testimony, Medill identified Scanlan as the person responsible for enforcing safety recommendations. Medill dodged the issue of whether he or the State Mining Board should have acted. A senator asked, "By the same token, does not the same obligation rest upon the department of Mines and Minerals of the state of Illinois?" Medill answered, "Well, they were not as close to the situation as Mr. Scanlan was." On another occasion, Medill answered a question, "It was Inspector Scanlan's duty to follow up that report to see that those recommendations were carried out." Later he said, "Inspector Scanlan, our man, should have shut it [the mine] down under the powers vested in him in this law."

In a final shot at the man who obviously caused the former director no end of grief, Medill complained about Scanlan's behavior during rescue operations at the mine. "Inspector Scanlan was interviewing the press nearly every time the shift changed, telling them his story and broadcasting a lot of gossip that he broadcasted here [at the hearing] that had nothing to do with finding the facts as to who was responsible for this explosion."[26]

Following Medill to testify on Friday morning were nine Centralia miners, including some survivors and those who worked the night shift or were off duty the day of the explosion. The audience included their relatives and friends, as well as relatives of those killed. Mostly senators wanted to know about dust and to hear the stories of the explosion and survival. Tentative at times, and obviously uneasy with the setting involving three U.S. senators, miners did their best to describe what happened to them and others nearby and how they rescued survivors. When asked by senators how the explosion happened, most of the workers declined to answer or avoided the subject. In fact, they knew no more about the blast than others who testified.

Some who appeared over the three days wanted mostly to avoid any blame, even if not directly involved in mine operations. State Representative Branson, a resident of Centralia and "sponsor" of Scanlan's appointment as inspector, spent most of his time making sure he was not accused of involvement in activities that had made the mine dangerous. Branson confirmed that Medill had suggested Scanlan be transferred out of the inspection group and that the state representative had told him it was not a good idea and Scanlan should retain his position. Branson believed the comment saved Scanlan's job.[27]

Several witnesses used the opportunity to make personal charges and accusations, without adding much to the record. Hugh White, president of UMWA District 12, spent most of his time attacking Interior Secretary Krug, much as John L. Lewis had done in public statements. White said, "Criminal negligence on the part of Secretary Krug is responsible for this disaster resulting in the death of 111 men. By every standard of decency he should resign his office." White denied the UMWA had any responsibility for what happened. He placed direct blame on Medill and the State Mining Board, although one member of the board represented the UMWA.[28]

Among representatives of the mine operators, mine manager Brown presented the poorest testimony in the eyes of senators. He all but refused to answer questions, offering evasions and generalizations instead. Brown denied having authority or responsibility for any safety concerns. His responses raised the ire of Senator Dworshak, who said, "I don't like your attitude one bit." The senator then turned to Chairman Cordon and stated, "Mr. Chairman, I think we are wasting our time here. Is this man qualified to speak for the operator of Centralia Mine No. 5? If he is, all right, and if he is not I demand that we subpoena somebody who can give us some information. I think we are wasting our time here."[29]

Top executives of the operating company—Young, Walter Johnson, Niermann, and Brown—repeated their testimony given before the governor's fact-finding committee. The impression left was that Centralia Coal Company officials had done little more than what other mine operators did about rock dusting, or trying new ways of controlling dust particles in the air, or taking the lead on safety precautions. They painted a picture of an industry that did the minimum and that was guided by doing no more than others were doing. Dust being a problem for years in No. 5 prompted neither action nor concern. All officials lamented the explosion and said in one way or another that they wished it had been prevented.

Senators and staff heard testimony in Washington on April 10, 16, and 17 and went over the record of hearings in Centralia. M. J. Ankeny, a federal mine inspector who had inspected the mine days after the explosion, testified about effects of the blast, evidence found to support a point of origin, and steps to be taken in the future to assure greater safety in coal mines. During his discussion with senators, Ankeny was asked what might have prevented the disaster. He said the tragedy could have been prevented altogether "if they had been using water in accordance with the best practices in connection with watering methods. They might have had that face region in such a damp condition that the shots could not have put the dust cloud into suspension in the first place, and therefore it could not have ignited it. There must be a dust cloud before you can ignite coal dust, and a damp condition at the face may have prevented putting that cloud into the air."[30]

The subcommittee issued its report of the hearings to the full Senate on June 5. The report said, "In summing up the responsibility, committee members found that almost everyone concerned was guilty of negligence to one degree or another—management, the miners, the mine workers' union, state bureaus and federal bureaus." After spreading the blame, the report dealt specifically with the cause:

> That evidence in this investigation shows that the immediate cause of the explosion at the Centralia mine was the use of explosives in a non-permissible manner.
>
> That the blasting practice in use in this mine was contrary both to the federal mine safety code and to the Illinois statute.
>
> That the men doing the blasting, in some instances at least, contrary to law, used coal dust for stemming their shots; that is to say, coal dust was used to fill in the drill holes after explosives had been

inserted, instead of non-explosive, non-inflammable material as required by law.

The senators called for legislation giving the U.S. Bureau of Mines or some other federal agency "authority, not only to promulgate an adequate safety code, but also authority to enforce it." The report noted that federal seizure of coal mines would end late in June. "Thereafter, unless the Bureau of Mines or other federal agency is given the power to make and enforce a mine safety code, we will return to former practices, and the lesson of the Centralia disaster will have been to no avail."[31] Despite the dire warning, no changes were made in federal law in the months and years immediately after the explosion.

From the beginning to the end of work by an Illinois legislative investigating committee, members quarreled bitterly and turned the process into partisan sniping. Disputes began with the decision to name six Republicans and four Democrats to the committee. Democrats complained about the Republican advantage and said representation needed to be evenly divided to be truly nonpartisan. The decision reflected two factors: the large Republican majority in each house—thirty-seven to fourteen in the Senate, eighty-seven to sixty-six in the House; and the long-standing precedent that the majority does what it pleases.

Named to the committee by their party caucuses were Senate Republicans Ora A. Oldfield of Centralia, D. Logan Giffin of Springfield, and Merritt J. Little of Aurora; Senate Democrats Norman Barry of Chicago and John W. Fribley of Pana; House Republicans Robert H. Allison of Pekin, William Robison of Carlinville, and Will P. Welker of Vandalia; and House Democrats Paul Powell of Vienna and Carl Preihs of Pana. Members elected Little as chairman.[32]

Before the Senate and House approved naming a committee, Powell, the House minority leader, called for the resignation of Robert Weir, assistant director of the Department of Mines and Minerals. A few days earlier, Governor Green had fired Medill. Powell, clearly the vocal leader of minority members, said Weir was as much a part of the problem as Medill. From his earliest public comments, Powell called the process a Republican "whitewash."

Legislators held sessions in Springfield several days after other investigations had started. They first met on April 4 and submitted a report to the full legislature on May 21. A minority report came a few days later. During those weeks, the committee met five times, mixing that business with a regular legislative session in Springfield. To avoid calling witnesses that already had testified two or three times before other bodies, the committee obtained transcripts of testimony from the governor's fact-finding committee and the U.S. Senate subcommittee. Still, the committee heard from twenty-four witnesses, representing a cross-section of interest groups, apparently as a courtesy. Democrats wanted Green to appear, but he ignored the request.[33]

Generally speaking, none of those testifying added substantially to the public record. However, the appearance of Scanlan on April 24 continued the conflict between the inspector and his former boss, Medill. If a higher level of personal animosity between the two men seemed impossible, Scanlan defied the odds. This appearance meant so much to Scanlan that he spent hours at home preparing testimony. His personal files reveal that he researched all records, correspondence, inspection reports, and public statements and added personal notes that he wanted to incorporate in a statement. Scanlan demonstrated his seriousness by having the statement printed and distributed outside the hearing room.

Scanlan's comments dripped with emotion. This was his last stand, and he intended to make the most of it. He declared:

> There is no committee, be it the governor's, or what not, that is going to make the families of the men killed in this explosion, the survivors of the explosion, or the miners in the other mines in my district believe that I am in any way responsible for this disaster. They all knew, and know, that I had done everything in my power to prevent this disaster. And had my recommendations been complied with, and had not the director and Mining Board overruled and over-ridden me rough-shod, these miners would be alive today. . . . The Governor's Committee said that I should have closed the mine down, even if it meant the quitting of my job. What point would I have gained by shutting this mine down and then quitting? The director would have reopened the mine, another inspector would have been appointed, more care would have been taken in the selection of my successor, there would have been only one inspection report on the bulletin board for the scrutiny of the newspaper men and it probably would not have been too actual; no one would have talked to the newspaper men and a real whitewash job could have been done. . . . I have always tried to take care of the miners in my district; and went as far as I was permitted to go by the director. While trying to take care of the miners I have also tried to take care of myself, so I could not be made the goat in case of a disaster of this kind, so always wrote the actual conditions of the mines as I found them showing no partiality to either the coal

company or miners, writing both up when I found them violating the law.

Scanlan concluded the statement with a final jab at Medill. After claiming that coal operators, especially the major companies, "enjoyed immunity from law enforcement," he added that the Centralia Coal Company enjoyed more favoritism than any other company in his district: "Perhaps one reason for this is that when Medill was up for re-appointment in 1945 and the miners were opposed to his re-appointment, the Centralia Coal Company came to his support and endorsed him. . . . In granting this immunity to the coal operators, the director had a definite purpose in mind, which you all know of by now: it was exposed by the *St. Louis Post-Dispatch* on March 19, 1947."[34] He referred to articles about Medill soliciting campaign funds from Illinois mine operators.

In the committee's final report, Scanlan received more attention than any other principal. The clash between Scanlan and Medill drew this statement:

> Evidence clearly indicated the presence of friction between State Mine Inspector D. O. Scanlan and Robert M. Medill, Director of the Department of Mines and Minerals. Mr. Scanlan testified that the director had criticized his reports for being too long. He also testified that he was in danger of being discharged as the state mine inspector. He laid before the committee a long prepared set of charges in defense of his work as a mine inspector and said that he had been requested to make political campaign solicitations. He further testified that he made no such political solicitations, however.

The report attempted to show that after their inspection in mid-March, inspectors Perz and Scanlan considered the mine much safer than ever before. Legislators were stretching a point. While both inspectors cited an improved attitude toward mine safety among company officials, their inspection reports repeated criticisms and recommendations made many times before about mine conditions. The committee offered this conclusion based on testimony of the two inspectors:

> Although the Federal Bureau of Mines and Minerals had authority to close mines in Illinois, their authority was not exclusive. The state mine inspector also had the authority to close a mine. Mr. Scanlan testified that he did not recognize the mine as being in imminent danger at the time of his inspection of March 17–20, 1947. His reports indicated items rated as major hazards but he also testified that the

mine was in ten times better condition by comparison than it had been on former inspections.[35]

Unwittingly, Scanlan also played a minor role in a carefully staged episode by Democrats on the committee. It began at a session earlier in the day, with mine manager Brown on the stand. Representative Preihs began to ask whether the witness had been solicited for contributions to the Republican candidate for mayor of Chicago. Republican members objected, calling the question irrelevant, and the chairman concurred. Incensed by the censure, Democrats stopped proceedings for a caucus. Representative Powell said they came back to the hearing hoping Republicans would realize their mistake and allow the question when asked of another witness.

Scanlan was the next witness. During questioning, Preihs tried to ask him about a meeting in January at which Medill solicited state inspectors to make calls for money. When again ruled out of order by the chairman, the four Democrats prepared to leave the session. However, Preihs and Powell both took the opportunity to make statements condemning the chairman's rulings and accusing Republicans of a whitewash. Powell said, "We should be permitted to find out if politics played a part in this disaster so we can make laws to correct those conditions. If we can't do this I'm walking out." And with that, the Democrats picked up their hats and coats and left the room.[36]

Except for part of one later session of the commission, Democrats stayed away. They refused to sign the committee's report and issued a minority document. In the end, Democrats took issue with only a few of the committee's recommendations for legislation, although they included partisan rhetoric.

The committee made recommendations for legislation under eight different sections of the coal mine law. It called for stricter requirements for preventing the dangers of dust and specifically requested tighter regulations for rock dusting. In a lengthy passage, the committee recommended prohibiting the solicitation or acceptance of any political campaign contributions by inspectors from any coal company, miners, or union officials. It also sought felony penalties for any inspector or employee of the Department of Mines and Minerals caught soliciting or accepting contributions.[37]

Under the recommendations, inspectors were to examine each mine in their districts at least once every month. The legislators called for an increase in the number of state inspectors to accomplish the task. In a controversial proposal, the committee stated, "No explosives shall be detonated or fired while the men are in the mine excepting for such necessary personnel." Coal company officials claimed the proposal would place the state's coal operators at a competitive disadvantage and would cost jobs. Powell replied, "Better have them laid off than laid out dead."[38]

The committee treated the call for extending civil service to state inspectors in one sentence, requesting "that a civil service unit be established, preferably under the jurisdiction of the Department of Mines and Minerals, and that all state mine inspectors be under this civil service unit when so established." The minority report called this approach "passive" and demanded "That laws be enacted whereby the most strict form of civil service be provided for mine inspectors free and clear of any and all forms of political activities or interference."[39]

Republicans tossed a bone to Democrats in the final recommendation of the report, mentioning a minority proposal to abolish the positions of director and assistant director of the department and to establish administration by a board or commission of "three experienced mining men," including one from the minority party.[40] The proposal never made it to consideration by the legislature, although the majority and minority reports appeared in sufficient time for legislators to consider bills before adjournment on June 30.

The flurry of investigations and hearings provided consensus but little in the way of conclusive evidence about the explosion's cause or how the tragedy might have been prevented. The probes frustrated those looking for solid answers. For example, everyone knew about the dust problem and that its seriousness had been ignored for years. Excuses for a lack of action to minimize the risk sounded weak. Newspapers provided the loudest condemnation of inaction and negligence.

Contradictions prevailed. A thorough exploration of issues by U.S. senators yielded nothing in the way of corrective laws. On the other hand, the most fractious and shallow investigation, by members of the Illinois General Assembly, produced changes in state mining laws. Survivors of the disaster and relatives of those killed received little satisfaction or relief from the proceedings.

No one could determine exactly what happened at the moment of ignition. Regarding blame, the easiest way out was to point a finger at everyone, but some received more attention than others. The lack of evidence made it possible to accuse miners of fatal carelessness. Although he mounted a determined and documented defense, Driscoll Scanlan received the harshest judgment for not closing down the mine. Scanlan's persistent criticism of authorities hurt his chances for exoneration. In the end, testimony exposed a lack of courage and stubborn refusal by all parties to do the right thing.

After the investigations, Bell and Zoller sold the Centralia Coal Company to Peabody Coal Company, and Centralia No. 5 Mine was renamed Peabody Mine No. 21. Operations resumed at the mine on July 21, 1947, with sixty employees, including some survivors of the explosion. After a year of operations, Peabody closed the mine, blaming the high cost of mining coal in an old mine.[41]

The disaster at Centralia No. 5 mine ended the public lives of Medill and Scanlan. Governor Green fired Medill. In December 1947, Scanlan resigned from his job as a state mine inspector, claiming his superiors were "riding" him.[42] He worked with family members in the operation of a coal mine at Venedy, Illinois, and bred horses at his home in Nashville. Medill, approaching retirement age, drifted from public life.

The List by Georges Schreiber, depicting widows of the Centralia mine disaster.
Courtesy of the Estate of the Artist and the Susan Teller Gallery, New York.

Bodies of men killed in the Centralia mine are placed in a hearse during rescue
operations at the mine site. Courtesy of the *Centralia Sentinel*.

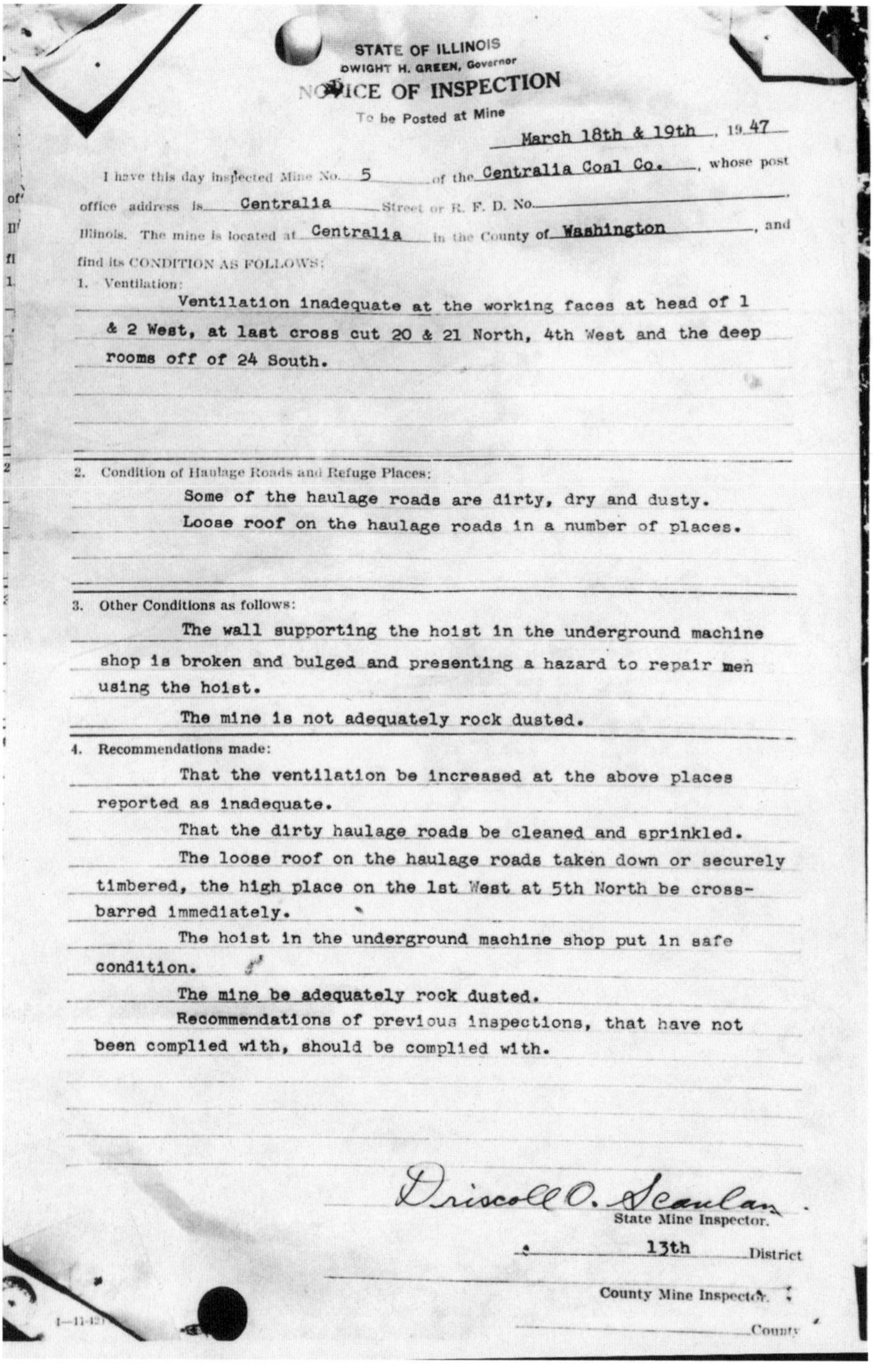

STATE OF ILLINOIS
DWIGHT H. GREEN, Governor

NOTICE OF INSPECTION
To be Posted at Mine

March 18th & 19th, 19 47

I have this day inspected Mine No. 5 of the Centralia Coal Co., whose post office address is Centralia Street or R. F. D. No.

Illinois. The mine is located at Centralia in the County of Washington, and find its CONDITION AS FOLLOWS:

1. Ventilation:

Ventilation inadequate at the working faces at head of 1 & 2 West, at last cross cut 20 & 21 North, 4th West and the deep rooms off of 24 South.

2. Condition of Haulage Roads and Refuge Places:

Some of the haulage roads are dirty, dry and dusty.
Loose roof on the haulage roads in a number of places.

3. Other Conditions as follows:

The wall supporting the hoist in the underground machine shop is broken and bulged and presenting a hazard to repair men using the hoist.
The mine is not adequately rock dusted.

4. Recommendations made:

That the ventilation be increased at the above places reported as inadequate.
That the dirty haulage roads be cleaned and sprinkled.
The loose roof on the haulage roads taken down or securely timbered, the high place on the 1st West at 5th North be cross-barred immediately.
The hoist in the underground machine shop put in safe condition.
The mine be adequately rock dusted.
Recommendations of previous inspections, that have not been complied with, should be complied with.

Driscoll O. Scanlan
State Mine Inspector.

13th District

County Mine Inspector.

County

1—11-42

Copy of the mine inspection report made a week before the Centralia explosion by Driscoll Scanlan, state inspector, which remained posted at the mine during rescue efforts. Courtesy of the *Centralia Sentinel*.

Illinois state legislators on Centralia mine elevator prepare to conduct investigation underground. Courtesy of the *Centralia Sentinel*.

Throngs of citizens gather at Centralia First Methodist Church to mourn mine disaster victims. Courtesy of the *Centralia Sentinel*.

Mourners gather outside St. Mary's Catholic Church in Centralia for memorial services.

Courtesy of the *Centralia Sentinel*.

Governor Dwight Green meets with reporters in Centralia to announce the resignation of Robert Medill, head of the Illinois Department of Mines and Minerals, a week after the explosion. Courtesy of the *Centralia Sentinel*.

U.S. Senate subcommittee holds hearings in Centralia for three days, a little more than a week after the explosion. Courtesy of the *Centralia Sentinel*.

Senator Henry Dworshak of Idaho scans a copy of the *Centralia Sentinel* extra edition published in the first hours after the explosion. Courtesy of the *Centralia Sentinel*.

William P. Young (*left*), vice president of the Centralia Coal Company, puts a friendly hand on Driscoll Scanlan, state mine inspector, at a U.S. Senate hearing. Courtesy of the *Centralia Sentinel*.

John Lorenzini (*right*), who survived the Centralia disaster, sits next to William P. Young during Senate hearing. Courtesy of the *Centralia Sentinel*.

Harry "Cotton" Niermann (*center*), Centralia mine superintendent, speaks with Senator Joseph C. O'Mahoney of Wyoming and Senator Guy Cordon of Oregon, during a recess of the Senate hearing. Courtesy of the *Centralia Sentinel*.

Robert Medill, former head of the Illinois Department of Mines and Minerals, testifies before a Senate subcommittee meeting in Centralia. Courtesy of the *Centralia Sentinel*.

Joe Vancil, last survivor of the Centralia explosion, in 2002. Robert E. Hartley photo.

Fred Bright, one of the Centralia mine survivors at a reunion in 1982 on the thirty-fifth anniversary of the disaster that killed 111 of their fellow workers. Courtesy of the *Centralia Sentinel*.

Fred Hellmeyer, one of the Centralia mine survivors at the 1982 reunion. Courtesy of the *Centralia Sentinel*.

Earl Wilkinson, a survivor of the Centralia mine disaster at the 1982 reunion. Courtesy of the *Centralia Sentinel*.

L. G. Sprehe, another of the Centralia mine survivors at the 1982 reunion. Courtesy of the *Centralia Sentinel*.

Lynn Sharp, a survivor at the 1982 reunion. Courtesy of the *Centralia Sentinel*.

Elvera Kirkland of Centralia looks at a photograph of her father, Gus Hohman, who was killed in the 1947 mine explosion. Courtesy of the *Centralia Sentinel*.

Photograph of Jack Pick Jr., Centralia No. 5 survivor, surrounded by medals and memorabilia of his air force career during World War II. Robert E. Hartley photo.

Classic portrait of John L. Lewis, the man who built and ran the United Mine Workers of America. Photograph by John A. Detwiler. Courtesy of Donald S. Detwiler.

Rescue workers prepare to enter New Orient No. 2 mine at West Frankfort to search for survivors. Courtesy of the Illinois Department of Natural Resources, Office of Mines and Minerals.

A rescue squad, burdened with oxygen tanks and tools, waits to go below at New Orient No. 2. From the *St. Louis Globe-Democrat* Archives of the St. Louis Mercantile Library at the University of Missouri–St. Louis.

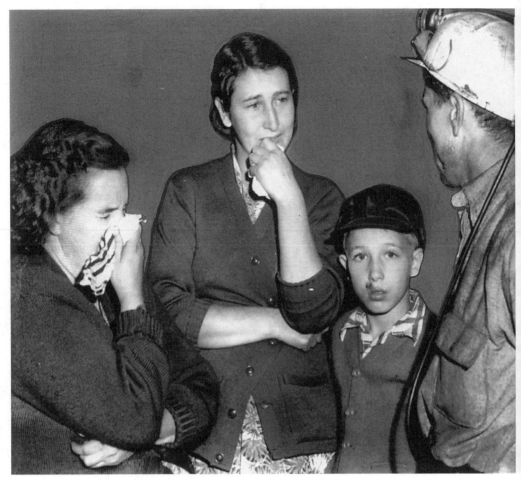

Fearing the worst, miners' wives wait for word of loved ones.

Faces tell the story as another body is brought out of New Orient No. 2.

A victim is carried from the mine before a cluster of rescue workers and officials.

Relatives and friends wait for bodies to be delivered to West Frankfort Junior High School, temporary morgue for New Orient No. 2. From the *St. Louis Globe-Democrat* Archives of the St. Louis Mercantile Library at the University of Missouri–St. Louis.

Omar Lingo, a weary mine inspector, who declared that rock dusting was not adequate at New Orient No. 2. From the *St. Louis Globe-Democrat* Archives of the St. Louis Mercantile Library at the University of Missouri–St. Louis.

6

Miners' Lives

THE CENTRALIA DISASTER AND ITS AFTER-
math—especially for the surviving widows and the fatherless children—gave
birth to nationwide artistic laments in music and artwork. Two specific
works portrayed the depth of futility felt by helpless family members.

Woody Guthrie, a popular songwriter and singer, sympathized with
those left behind in a ballad called "The Dying Miner." It told the heartbreaking tale of miners hopelessly trapped below ground, scrambling in the
dark to write last words for loved ones. The song's verses name individuals—Joe Ballantini, Fred Gutzler, and Joe Bryant—in their final struggles
to find a breath of fresh air. The song is essentially a sad refrain of the coal
mining culture that exposed generations of men—grandfathers, fathers,
sons, brothers—to risks underground.

Artist Georges Schreiber, a native of Brussels, Belgium, moved to New
York in 1928 after studying for years in Berlin, London, Rome, Paris, and
Florence. His works have been exhibited in a number of American muse-
ums, including the Metropolitan Museum of Art. In the 1940s, his style
could be placed in the American Regionalism movement. To commemorate
the Centralia No. 5 deaths, Schreiber prepared a lithograph entitled *The
List* depicting distressed widows and children reaching in anguish toward
a tree on which is nailed the list of dead men.

These contemporary accounts in song and print are a prelude to stories
of men in the mines and of women and children who were affected for decades by the calamity. They are chronicles of lives honoring love, commitment, and loyalty and reflecting happy times tempered by desperation. The
struggles unveiled are about determination and human survival.

For the Joe and Pietro (Pete) Ballantini families, the explosion landed like a bomb, decimating the clan's male leadership. The Ballantini brothers were born in Italy and came to the United States together. Pete, a year older than Joe, worked in Colorado and Missouri mines before settling in Centralia. Joe went to work at No. 5 at age fourteen and remained an employee until his death. He interrupted work in the mine only long enough to serve in World War I. Elaine Ziegler, Joe Ballantini's daughter, told a reporter many years after the explosion, "The last few years he became afraid and fearful of going down in the mines, but he never knew anything else."

Two of Pete Ballantini's nine children, daughter Theresa and son Arthur, reminisced about that fateful day. "I was working at the railroad, and I heard all these ambulance sirens, and I stopped somebody to ask what had happened and was told 'the mine blew up,'" Arthur said. Theresa lived across the street from their brother Angelo, an employee at No. 5 who worked the night shift that started at 4:00 PM. "Angelo was part of the rescue crew," she said. Family members from all over the area converged on the mine to await news of their loved ones.

Theresa and Arthur learned later that their father died after being struck by a trap door. He was one of the first group of sixteen dead miners identified, but it was twenty-seven hours before rescuers brought his body to the surface. His burial at Hillcrest Memorial Park was delayed for ten days. "They were busy burying people whose bodies were in worse shape," Theresa said. "So we just delayed his funeral and burial. He stayed in an open casket in his home until it was time for the funeral. There were so many funerals." Arthur and Theresa have remained close. He retired in 1980 from railroad work, and she held several different jobs until retirement. For many years, they lived in the same block in Centralia.

Elaine Ziegler remembers the difficult times facing her mother, also a native of Italy, who came to the United States at age five. She had been married to Joe for twenty-seven years. "She was a survivor. She was able to survive whatever hardships she had." Ziegler appreciated the comfort given by caring friends. "I still remember the kindness of the people," she said. "How kind and solicitous they were. Our friends came back to see us, and they were so kind." Ziegler and her mother did survive, and together they opened the Helen Kay store in Centralia, a women's sportswear and lingerie shop.

Left with memories of her father, Ziegler recalled the importance of brief, sometimes forgotten moments. "I prefer to remember his life," she said. "He was an Italian. Sometimes I really didn't know if he cared [about me] because he was not a demonstrative man. One year I was in a high school play, and my mother was ill, and my dad came to see the play. That means so much to me. Things that seemed so little at the time mean so much now. We would go walking in the woods hunting mushrooms and picking up walnuts that had fallen on the ground."

In many cases, keepsakes left behind or found at the explosion site provided a special connection to loved ones. It happened to Ziegler. "Someone from the Lions Club [part of the rescue effort] came by and asked if I could identify this ring. I looked at it and said that was my dad's ring. They had taken it off his body; that was the only way they could identify the body."[1]

Mining families congregated in residential neighborhoods throughout Centralia and nearby Wamac. Those quiet enclaves from which miners went to work at No. 5 represented close-knit families, ethnic origins, friendships, car pools, and church membership. On March 25, 1947, and afterward, neighbors wept in each other's homes, walked together to funeral services that seemed to never end, and found comfort as the future unfolded.

The largest geographic cluster of miners' homes was in Centralia's southwest corner, closest to the mine. Twenty-one men in those neighborhoods, including several in what is now Wamac, did not survive on March 25. More than half lived on South Hickory and South Cherry and the cross streets of West Fifteenth, West Sixteenth, and West Seventeenth. Many belonged to the neighborhood church, Trinity Lutheran, the scene of nonstop funeral services for days after the disaster.[2]

On South Cherry and just a few blocks east on South Maple lived families named Gutzler. In the late 1800s, three brothers—Henry, John, and Fred—arrived in the United States from Europe and came to Centralia by way of New Orleans and the Mississippi River. Mining had been a way of life for the family in Europe, and it continued in Illinois with John and Fred working in the mines. Brother Henry found employment as a carpenter.[3]

By 1947, three of John's male children and two of Fred's were working at No. 5. John's sons Harry, fifty-five, John W., fifty-three, and Adolph, forty-eight, had been at No. 5 for decades. Adolph, who started work in coal mines at age sixteen, lived on South Maple, and the other two had homes within a block of each other on South Cherry. Fred's sons John H., sixty-three, and Fred W., fifty-seven, lived across the street from each other on South Cherry.[4]

Seven men in the extended Gutzler family were underground on March 25. In addition to the five Gutzler men, two others were connected to the family by marriage. The husband of John and Fred's sister Clara, Charles Oestreich, was also a miner at No. 5, and the couple lived on South Beech, several blocks north of their relatives. Fred's wife, Linda, had a brother, Edward Bude, who lived on the east side of Centralia and worked at the mine.

As it turned out, of the seven, only Harry, a motorman on the main-line, survived. Like the few others who came out alive, he was near the shaft when the explosion occurred. Harry never went back to work in the mines. He is remembered as quiet and solitary. Unmarried, he lived near the Kaskaskia River, a few miles from Centralia, went to church regularly, and saw the family. He shared next to nothing about his experience or his history as a miner.[5]

On that Tuesday, John W. Gutzler was a supervising face boss on the south side of the mine. His brother Adolph worked near the origin of the blast, where seventeen men died. Their cousin Fred was in the danger zone, drilling holes in the mine faces in which to place explosives for detonation at the end of the shift. His brother John H., a machine man, was in the same vicinity as cousin Adolph. Charles Oestreich, who also drilled holes for explosives, was not far from the origin of the explosion. Edward Bude, a repairman, worked deep in the mine.

After the explosion, a reporter talked with Adolph's widow, Velma, at their home on South Maple. Surrounded by a half-dozen friends and neigh-bors in the living room, she occasionally went to the door, greeted more visitors, and talked in low tones. In response to the reporter's questions, she remembered that Adolph talked frequently about dust in the mine. "He commented on it an awful lot. He was afraid something was going to hap-pen. However, he never talked about it at great length or went into detail about it. I guess he didn't want to worry me."

Velma Gutzler expressed a sentiment shared by many widows about husbands who went underground, always in the shadow of danger. "I didn't like the idea, but I'm the type that tries not to let things like that worry me. He sometimes had a feeling he should have gotten out, but of course he never did."[6]

Wilma Gutzler had been part of the South Cherry neighborhood before she became part of the Gutzler family. She lived across the street from Clyde Gutzler, John W.'s son, who turned away from work in the mine after return-ing from World War II, and they married a year after the explosion. At the time of the disaster, she participated in the mourning of South Cherry's dead. The continuous funeral services made an impression on her. "One hearse would drive away from the church, and another would drive up. The pastor gave virtually the same sermon for each miner. It seemed that every other house on the street had someone who died in the mine," she said.

Saundra Ebbs, a granddaughter of Fred W. Gutzler, recalled, "He is one of those who left a note for his wife." Fred was mentioned by name in one of the notes written in the darkness immediately after the explosion. He apparently survived the initial blast, although the watch found on his body had stopped at 3:25 PM.

One of Fred's last conversations with his wife is well remembered by later generations. Saundra Ebbs's grandmother told the family her husband considered not going to work that day because both husband and wife did not feel well. "But she told him, 'Go ahead, we need the money,'" Ebbs said. Fred's funeral service at Trinity Lutheran was one of the last held. Ebbs said, "I remember my mother saying we moved from the back of the church, when the first funeral was held, to the front when my grandfather's funeral was held. That whole week we did nothing but attend funerals. They were all friends."

The memories of her grandfather are dear. "I remember vividly going to the mine with him one time. He was responsible for driving that day. I don't remember why he didn't go to work, but he picked everyone up and took them to the mine. He took me along, and I was thrilled." Ebbs kept her grandfather's lunch bucket.

Bill Knight had to find some answers. After decades of turning away from learning details surrounding his father's death at No. 5, he visited cemeteries, gathered information about his dad's work underground, and looked through old newspaper accounts in an effort to piece together a lasting memory. A nine-year-old on March 25, 1947, Bill Knight hardly knew his dad, Philip.

Philip was around mining most of his life in Centralia. His father and his father-in-law both worked at the Glenridge mine. He stayed out of the mines for years, finding jobs in nearby oil fields. But irregular work hours kept him away from the family, and his wife, Martha, urged him to find something more stable. Philip went to work below ground, where he died at age forty-five.

Blurred memories were all that remained for Bill Knight from those first days of mourning. Minutes after the explosion, his sister-in-law pulled him aside to say that something had happened at the mine, and his dad would be late coming home. Family members went to the mine site immediately, remaining in or near the wash house where his dad's clothing hung. Rescuers brought the body of Philip Knight to the top four days after the explosion.[7] The funeral was held at the Central City Methodist Church, near the family home. Survivors included an older son and three sisters who lived in the Centralia area.[8]

"Mother was devastated by dad's death," Bill said. Soon she faced fresh challenges. "She'd never worked outside the home and had only an eighth grade education. In those days, women were not prepared for having to earn a living." She found work at a hotel cleaning rooms and at a local dress factory. Eventually Martha, who never remarried, studied for and passed the GED examination to receive the equivalent of a high school diploma. "She got a job with the State of Illinois and moved to Chicago," her son explained.

Bill never was tempted to work in the mines. "I wouldn't go near it," he stated. After eight and a half years in the U.S. Air Force, he worked in the airline industry and retired in 1993. Finally, wishing to postpone the search no longer, he sought answers to decades-old questions about his father and No. 5.

"Happy-go-lucky" was how Betty Pick described her husband, John E. Pick Jr., a survivor of the disaster. That description might explain his exploits during World War II and his decision to be a coal miner.

Jack—his colleagues in the mine called him "Johnny Bull" because of his English ancestors—dated Betty during their years at Centralia High School, and they married in 1945 at the war's end. In high school, Jack was fascinated by airplanes, became a pilot, and owned several planes. When the war began in 1941, he wanted to join the air corps as a pilot. He passed all the tests but learned he needed a college education to be accepted. Rejected by the air corps, he joined the British Royal Air Force, which had a training center at Tulsa, Oklahoma. During a dive-bombing exercise in 1943, Jack damaged a muscle in his eye and had to drop out of training. Disappointed, he returned to Centralia and waited for the draft.

Jack still got his wish to fly, but not in the cockpit. As a radio operator/gunner on a B-17 bomber, he flew nineteen missions from England and thirty-one missions from a base in Italy and "never got scratched," Betty said. He received the air medal with five oak leaf clusters and battle stars for the Eighth and Fifteenth Air Forces. He also participated in the first air raid on Berlin, March 6, 1944. Upon returning from Europe, he ended his service at Scott Air Force Base near Belleville.

At Centralia, Jack discovered jobs were hard to come by. His father, John Pick Sr., had worked in Illinois mines, including No. 5, almost forty years, and it was only natural for Jack to follow in his footsteps. Jack knew the danger. "I learned from him that the dust is always an ever-present hazard," Betty said. "He loved it. It was dangerous work, but he made a good living for us."

Part of the fun, Betty said, was because of Jack's competitiveness. He enjoyed seeing who could mine the most coal and engaged his colleagues in friendly contests. He hunted and fished for recreation and seemed to enjoy living. On the other hand, the life of a coal miner's wife was an adjustment for Betty. "I knew nothing about coal mining. I grew up here and worked with a lot of daughters of miners," she said, but she had little idea of the dangers.

On March 25, Jack came to the end of his day shift. The explosion occurred away from his location, and he suffered no injury. In the confusion of the moment, he joined in rescue efforts, pulling four or more men to safety. Air contamination plagued rescuers and caused a burning in Jack's lungs, but he remained on duty until all survivors had been found and taken to the surface. He searched for his father and listened to reports of men who told of his father's death. Confirmation did not come for several days. Betty said, "Jack was devastated."

Betty made it to the mine and joined others waiting and watching. Eventually, Jack was taken to a makeshift hospital set up at the community center. Betty found him at the center about 10:00 PM, almost seven hours after the explosion. "I had never seen him dirty until that night," she explained. "He always washed up after his shift and came home clean. That night he was covered with black coal dust and grime." Officials wanted Jack to remain overnight, and Betty went home. "I didn't have my clothes off for three days," she said.

Regardless of the trauma, Jack couldn't leave coal mining. When Centralia No. 5 reopened, he returned to work. That lasted only a few months before officials closed the mine permanently. He took a job at Orient No. 4 mine near Waltonville and commuted forty miles a day, for nearly thirty years. Nearing retirement at age sixty-two, Jack was working on a motorboat at a nearby lake when he had a heart attack and died. Betty lives in her pleasing, modest home with a daily reminder of Jack's "happy-go-lucky" days: a wall hanging in the dining room with Jack's military medals and artifacts.[9]

Fathers and sons, brothers, cousins, uncles, and nephews—the combinations jumped out of obituaries that filled pages in the *Centralia Sentinel*. Surviving families were shattered; many would never recover. Others simply went on about the business of living without a loved one.

Brothers Joseph and Andrew Spinner grew up in Central City, on the north side of Centralia, and never lived far from each other. Of their three married sisters, two moved away; the third stayed in Centralia. Their father was German, their mother, Polish. In 1917, Andrew married Marie Graw, who died in 1946, and Joseph married Emma Armstrong in 1919. Through the years, the members of the families grew in number and in closeness.

Andrew was the father of four sons, one of whom was killed in World War II, and a daughter. Joseph had three daughters.

Joseph and Andrew went to work in the mines, first in Glenridge and then at No. 5 in 1940. They did dirty, hard work. Joe had the job classification of cleanup, which meant he went in after the coal was blown down from the face of the mine and cleaned things up. Andrew was a trackman, building tracks for cars that picked up the coal. On March 25, 1947, Joseph worked within 200 feet of the shaft, and his body was recovered immediately. Andrew was almost two and a half miles back in the mine, and it took four days to find his body.

At the time of the explosion, Andrew and his boys lived on a farm near Junction City. His son Ralph remembered life at home as difficult financially for his parents and several children. Because the family needed money, Ralph quit school after the eighth grade and worked in the mine for two years. "I made $105 a week in the coal mines," he recalled. "Dad kept $100 and gave me $5." Ralph got his fill of coal mining during that short stretch. After serving as a radio operator in Europe during World War II, he returned to face a decision about his future work.

Ralph did not want to follow his father and uncle to the mines. He said it was "dirty work, dangerous work." His father agreed. "I said if I'm going to starve to death its going to be on top of the ground." He went to work at Midwest Dairy and later drove a truck for a wine and liquor company. Finally, Ralph went to work for the local Budweiser distributor and retired in 1979. At that point, he started a tool sharpening business at home and retired again in 2003, with no regrets about turning away from coal mining.[10]

As quickly as some survivors and relatives put distance between themselves and the disaster, a few remained closely tied to No. 5 in the eyes and minds of the public. One was Harry "Cotton" Niermann.

Niermann used his special knowledge of No. 5, his familiarity with the miners and mining, his position as a member of mine management, and his dominant personality to cast himself as the resident expert on the mine disaster. Niermann told a consistent story from the hours immediately after the explosion until his death decades later. His very nature—confident and convincing—dared doubters to differ. Whether addressing U.S. senators or a group of friends over coffee, he expressed a definite opinion of how the explosion happened and who made mistakes in the mine.

Niermann's relationship with No. 5 began in December 1917, ten years after the mine opened for business. He described his beginning "as a young boy, starting in the mines." Like so many who worked and who died at the mine, he left briefly for a job at another southern Illinois mine but returned to Centralia. He remained at No. 5 until 1924, when he took a job at Zeigler No. 2 mine, also operated by the Centralia Coal Company. After two years, he came back to Centralia and worked as a miner until 1934. He knew every nook and cranny, corner and tunnel, at the mine.

If Niermann did not see everything that happened at No. 5 from its opening in 1907, he heard about it. That included the story of a man named Charlie Emory who died in an explosion before Niermann started work in 1917. There was more, as he said at the Senate hearings. "Then after my time there was one explosion in the northeast section of No. 5 mine, and the exact year I cannot tell you. . . . It was somewhere along about 1920 or 1921. There were three men lost their lives in that explosion." Others died in incidents underground. One was crushed under falling rock. "As I remember, [there] was a fatal where a car had broken loose and had run down and caught this man against the face." Niermann made the point that death and injury were not unusual occurrences in mining work.

In 1934, Niermann left the ranks of miners and began his climb in supervisory roles. He was promoted to foreman—called "face boss"—and in 1938 was transferred to the sales department, where he traveled and sold coal. Three years later, he returned to No. 5 as superintendent. He remained in that capacity for two years until Norman Prudent relieved him of the responsibility and sent him back to the mine, where he worked "merely helping" until April 1, 1946. He again was superintendent on March 25, 1947.

Media attention in the days immediately after the disaster focused on high-profile individuals with significant responsibilities for safety or those who had a history of involvement in inspection controversies. Those diversions left Niermann on the sidelines. His opportunity to speak came before committees that investigated events at No. 5. He testified before the governor's fact-finding committee and the hearings held by U.S. senators. In these appearances, Niermann had an opportunity to establish his credentials as someone knowledgeable about the mine and its operations who knew the ins and outs of mining.

Niermann spent more time testifying before senators than most other witnesses, at times taking them on a verbal tour of the mine. Using maps, he guided the senators through the complex tunnel system of the mine. He described the ventilation system at length, identified where miners took coal from the faces of the mine, spotted the locations of the teams of workers, and described the acreage of the mine. He claimed then, and countless times later, that the ventilation system worked properly and should not be blamed for deaths. Eventually, the senators got around to asking for Niermann's opinion of the cause of the explosion.

"It is my opinion," he told them, "that there was an excessive amount of powder set off some way, somehow. . . . You will find as you question these men there was an excessive amount of powder smoke that came out on that bottom at that time, early, and that leads me to believe that somewhere, somehow, there was an excessive amount of powder exploded. But how, I don't know." Under further questioning, Niermann said he knew those men exploding dynamite charges on the face of the mine had more powder with them at times than was necessary or safe. Mine officials knew a month earlier that excessive powder had been taken into the mine, and they issued an order to stop the practice, he added. Niermann said when all the factors existed for an explosion, including dust and ignition, the powder accelerated the blast.

Additionally, Niermann cited carelessness by the shot firers as a factor in the explosion. "The shot firers were paid 30 minutes extra a day to shoot [set off explosive charges] after the men were practically out of the mine. . . . They were shooting before the men were through work. We know, because we have a record of when the fan went off. That's when the explosion happened. We had a signal in the engine room. When the fan went off, that signal would tell us. When the fan went off, I went to get it back on. Then we saw the dust and stuff—the back pressure against the fan. It blew the fuses."[11]

Federal investigators declared in their report that the explosion occurred when "an under burdened shot or a blown-out shot stemmed with coal dust ignited dust, and the explosion was propagated by coal dust throughout workings" of the mine. In other words, something happened when explosive shots were fired near the end of the day shift. No mention was made of excessive powder. A report from the Department of Mines and Minerals stated, "The explosion occurred at the end of the working shift, and all operations had ceased at the face excepting for blasting. Blasting was the only operation in progress which could have caused a dust cloud to be raised."[12]

Niermann stated bluntly that the drillers and shot firers had done something wrong and probably caused the dust to ignite. Rarely in reports or public statements did any other individual or investigating group comment as critically on the men working in the mines as Niermann. At the same time, he reluctantly admitted that dust had been a problem and inspectors had repeatedly called it to the attention of mine officials. "Up to a certain extent it was a dusty mine," he said. "I would say that it was dusty because if you have a dry coal, you naturally have some dust."

Putting a good face on the actions of mine operators seemed to be Niermann's mission. At the time of the explosion, he insisted the coal company was innocent. He told senators, "The last time we rock-dusted was in July; I would say it was July of 1946; and after that rock-dusting procedure the state inspector complimented me on the rock-dusting job. He said that was one of the best jobs that he had seen done in that mine for quite some time." A senator asked, "There had been no rock dusting since July 1946?" To which Niermann replied, "I would say not."[13]

In statements through the years, Niermann often returned to comments about the work of miners, their habits, and reasons why they did not survive the explosion. He said miners blasting coal sometimes tamped their shots with combustible coal dust instead of clay, as required. This increased the risk of igniting other dust in the mine. "All the inspectors saw it and everybody else. . . . Every one tamped with coal dust," Niermann stated. "A state inspector came out of the mine one day and came up to me and said, 'Say, Niermann, I caught two of your drillers down there tamping with coal dust.' I said, 'Why didn't you send them out?' The inspector said, 'Oh, what do you mean?' I said, 'That's your duty. That's the law. You're supposed to send them out. They were tamping with coal dust.' 'Aw,' he said, 'I gave them hell. I don't think they'll do it again.' I said, 'You're an ex-coal miner. You know they will.'"

Niermann believed that some of the men killed might have survived if they had known where to look for pockets of fresh air. He acknowledged that the miners' lack of safety information contributed to confusion and may have cost lives. He did not suggest that the coal company had a responsibility for informing the miners. Human nature may have been the cause of the explosion, Niermann mused. "We're all prone to this type of thing [taking chances and breaking rules]. We get by so long with something, we just step over the line a little more all the time. That's human nature. Human nature. They [the drillers] didn't think it was going to happen. Nobody thought it was going to happen." He concluded, "If anybody is to blame, everybody is to blame."[14]

He was known in the mines and outside as "Uncle Bill." He spent a lifetime working at No. 5. As recording secretary of UMWA Local 52, his name is etched forever in history before and after March 25.

William E. Rowekamp, a descendant of German miners, might have lived in relative anonymity except for the Centralia disaster. Instead, his actions before the explosion and his survival on March 25 put him in the public spotlight during a series of investigations. The probes exposed Rowekamp to weeks of personal agony. The quiet, family-loving gentleman farmer preferred to mind his own business.[15]

Rowekamp was born July 17, 1889, in Hoyleton, Illinois. He attended the Lutheran grade school and after graduation worked on a farm for three years. In 1909, he moved to Centralia and worked nights at the Illinois Central Railroad shops. After a few months, he began work at the old Centralia No. 2 mine. Later he took a full-time job at Centralia No. 1. In 1916, he started work at No. 5. Except for periodic shutdowns and a fifteen-month stretch in the army during World War I, he had worked at No. 5 for more than thirty years by 1947. "Practically all my life," he said in testimony.[16]

During his early years at the mine, he lived near Centralia with an older brother, Christ, and his family. Christ also was a veteran of coal mining. In 1929, William married Minnie Siccardi, the widow of a friend whose dying wish was that Bill would look after his widow and two young children.

His avuncular personality made Rowekamp a favorite among colleagues underground. At age fifty-eight, neither old nor young for employees at the mine, he was called "Uncle Bill" out of respect. They honored his experience, modest demeanor, and commitment to the union. As a reward for his loyalty, Local 52 members named him recording secretary in 1942. In that role, he became author or coauthor of communications to mine owners, mine inspectors, the State Mining Board, and the director of the Department of Mines and Minerals during the years of turmoil before 1947. If these officials did not know him personally, they certainly recognized him by "William E. Rowekamp, recording secretary."

During the years leading up to March 25, officials of Local 52 contested decisions by mine operators and complained about unsafe working conditions. They wrote letters to Robert Medill and Robert Weir at the state mines department, and individual members complained directly to Scanlan, the state mine inspector. Most of the correspondence bearing Rowekamp's name was routine and designed to put the issues in writing. While individual letters spelled out the complaints, they were brief and to the point. None of them carried any memorable messages or dramatic statements, with one exception.

That exception was the "please save our lives" letter written by Rowekamp and signed by Local 52 president Jake Schmidt to Governor Dwight Green on March 3, 1946. At the time, few people knew about the letter, but after the disaster, newspapers published it in full, adding an element of high political drama to the sorrow.[17] Reporters and investigators repeatedly asked Rowekamp about the letter, because of the four men who signed it, he was the only survivor. The letter put further emphasis on the Green administration's neglect of warnings and pleadings for improved safety conditions in the mine. Rowekamp's efforts at composing the letter and having others offer advice reached legendary proportions when repeated in newspaper accounts. The family story, as related by Karen Crouse, Rowekamp's great-niece, is that writing the letter took weeks. He consulted a nephew with a college education and typed it himself, "one finger at a time," she related.

As a motorman in the mine, Rowekamp rode a locomotive, or *motor*, and was one of many who took coal in pit cars on rails from distant parts of the mine to a gathering point where the coal was loaded for the trip to the shaft bottom. On March 25, as the day shift ended, he and a few others waited at the bottom of the shaft for the routine ride to the top. One of the men said, "Uncle Bill, turn around and look at that smoke." Instantly, Rowekamp knew that an explosion had occurred, but he did not want to alarm the others. He hesitated to declare an explosion, but the others knew something was amiss by the smoke and smell of powder.

Rowekamp and the group went to the top, where he met Cotton Niermann. The company official sent him down to look for survivors but told him to be careful. One of those who went with Rowekamp was Jack Pick Jr., whose father had been working in a far corner of the mine. In a locomotive, they entered one of the tunnels looking for survivors. Later Rowekamp described the conversation between the two as they moved into the mine darkness.

ROWEKAMP: I see a light down there on the turn.
PICK: No, Uncle Bill, you are seeing things.

They proceeded another 150 feet.

ROWEKAMP: I still see an object there, something wrong down there.
PICK: I think you are seeing things.
ROWEKAMP: I still think I see an object down there.
PICK: Yes, I see it now.

The two men moved closer and recognized a man, identified by Rowekamp as "Brother Lorenzini." Rowekamp said, "[He was] wandering around. So I told one of the boys to grab him so he wouldn't fall and hit his head on a rail and get hurt badly. He was fighting." They took John Lorenzini, forty-one, to the top, where he recovered. The rescuers also suffered ill effects from being in the mine, and Scanlan, who had arrived at the site, sent them to clean up and go home. Rowekamp stayed at the scene until 4:00 AM, having participated in the rescue of eleven men out of thirty-one who survived. The union local appointed him to an emergency committee to look after the immediate needs of the widows and families of the dead miners.[18]

Aside from relating his experience in the moments immediately after the explosion, Rowekamp offered little in testimony to shed light on the cause of the explosion or details of life underground. Apparently, he felt uncomfortable being put on the spot with questions about the actions of others and answered briefly, refusing to speculate. To a question about the explosion's cause, Rowekamp said, "I wouldn't know what to say there. I have nothing to say about it." He offered to provide correspondence files and to cooperate in any other way.[19]

After the investigations, Rowekamp retreated to his farm outside Centralia, where he grew strawberries, raised pigs and chickens, and looked after his wife and stepchildren. Great-niece Karen Crouse remembers times spent at the farm as a youngster after 1947. "I remember going to their farm every spring when the strawberries were ripe. I can remember Uncle Bill wearing an old straw hat and overalls, out to the patch with us and finding us the best spot, then picking hands full to show us what nice berries they were." She remembers him as "pretty quiet," except for one moment that punctuated virtually every visit to the farm.

"Outside the back of the house, Uncle Bill would say, 'There's something I want you to see.' Then Aunt Minnie would say something like 'Oh, no, not again.' But my mother would always assure her that would be just fine. He would read this tattered copy of a letter, holding it with reverence, a tremor in his hands and voice. He would finish and not say much, just a few words about the whole thing not having to happen, how 'they tried to tell them.'"[20] Bill Rowekamp, author of the "please save our lives" letter, died in 1969.

Someone had to be last. In the case of No. 5, the distinction of being the final survivor belongs to Joe Vancil Jr. On March 25, he was twenty years old, the youngest among the survivors.

Mining ran like a coal seam in Vancil's family. His father, Joe H. Vancil Sr., and an uncle, Desmond (Dude) Vancil, both natives of DuQuoin, worked at Centralia No. 5 and died in the explosion. Joe Sr.'s labors took him to a variety of locations in southern Illinois. Joe Jr. attended grade school in DeSoto, and his father worked in mines near Harrisburg. Later they lived in Sparta. Typical of mining families, Joe Jr. started working with coal while attending eighth grade.

"We needed money," he recalled, so as a young boy he sold watermelons to help pay family expenses. On one occasion, he loaded two separate trucks with watermelons and sold them at a roadside. He took the money home and put it on the table. Surprised to see the money, Joe Sr., accused his son of stealing. "Where'd you get this money?" Joe remembers his father asking. The boy took his father to talk to farmers from whom he had bought the watermelons and finally convinced his dad. Joe Sr. decided that if the youngster could sell watermelons, he could sell coal, because people often bought coal for home use from trucks parked along the roads. That was Joe's introduction to coal.

Joe's father and mother moved to Centralia, where Joe Sr. took a job at No. 5. They left their son with his grandmother in Sparta so he could finish school. That was where young Joe met Jean, also a student at Sparta High School. She came from a coal family, too. Her father worked for the railroad, and her grandfather had a seam of coal on the home property. After graduation in 1945, Joe worked a few months at a local mine before the army drafted him. He trained at bases in the United States and then was sent to Europe, where he served among occupation forces in Italy. He was discharged in February 1947.

Joe returned to live with his parents in a four-room house south of Centralia and joined his father and uncle in No. 5. He remembered the night before the explosion as if it were happening as he talked. "It was a stormy night. I'm in the north bedroom, and plaster in the ceiling got wet and fell on my head. I had a vision of Jesus Christ looking at me. [Mother] begged dad not to go to work." That is all he remembered about the time leading up to the explosion.

From conversations with survivors, Joe pieced together some of what happened in the mine. "Dad's crew was working on a second entry to the mine. They were working about a half mile back in the mine," away from where most miners worked. "He heard something and went out of the work area to use the telephone. When he opened the door to a room, it blew in." Joe, working on his dad's crew, was knocked unconscious. "I don't remember what the hell happened," he said fifty-six years after the event. Joe was one of the four men working in that portion of the mine who survived.

A mine rescue team reached Joe about 10:00 PM, more than six hours after the explosion, but passed him by as dead. "They thought we all were dead," he said. A second rescue team arrived soon and paused when Joe gasped. They brought him and the others out of the mine about 12:30 AM. "They gave me oxygen. I came up like a mad man. Someone hauled off and hit me, and like to broke my jaw," he said.

Joe appeared uninjured, and rescue workers sent him home. "I seemed to be all right," he recalled. But looks were deceiving. Over the following six months, he was in and out of the hospital for treatment of various ailments related to the explosion. He missed all the funerals of his colleagues and had little awareness of his surroundings. "Someone laid a newspaper on my bed that had a casualty list, and that is how I found out about my dad."

After recovering, he went back to work at No. 5, and every weekend he went to Sparta to see Jean. They soon married. Joe learned that work in the mines was not the same as before. Officials at first refused to let him go below ground, but he pleaded, "I have got to go back in the mine." They relented and gave him his old job but "watched me like a hawk." The experience unnerved Joe, and he claimed to have visions of those who died in the mine. "I was scared to death," he recalled. He quit coal mining for good and moved to the St. Louis area, where he worked as a welder and pipe fitter. Later he returned to southern Illinois and opened a machine shop in DuQuoin.[21]

On Palm Sunday, March 23, 1997, almost fifty years to the day after the mine disaster, Joe Vancil Jr., the last living survivor, returned to Centralia for a memorial service to commemorate the tragedy and to praise his fellow workers at No. 5. Those gathered honored Joe Vancil with applause.[22]

1

The Reality of Coal Politics

DWIGHT H. GREEN ADDRESSED THE FOLLOW-
ing declaration to the coal miners of Illinois during his 1940 campaign for
governor:

> The lives of you [miners] have been entrusted to the state. The only
> security you have depends upon absolute enforcement of those laws.
> To that end, an investigation of why these laws have not been enforced
> should be made now before a tragedy shocks the nation and before
> we may be called upon again to behold that silent line of loved ones,
> crowded at the mouth of some mine, dreading the evidence of loss
> that will be brought up from below. . . . I pledge to you that all laws
> protecting the health, safety and lives of the men employed in the
> mines will be enforced rigidly and thoroughly. In other words to the
> letter of the law.

The words sounded righteous enough at the time. After the disaster at Centralia No. 5, they sounded hollow and meaningless. Governor Green came
to wish he had never spoken the words, for they formed the introduction to
dozens of campaign speeches made by his opponent, Adlai E. Stevenson,
during the 1948 campaign for governor.[1]

Strikingly handsome—some historians believe him to be the best-looking
governor in Illinois history—Green rode his prosecution and conviction
of gangster Al Capone in 1932 almost straight to the governor's mansion.
After the high-profile Capone case, he posted an enviable record as prosecutor, successful Chicago attorney, and Republican loyalist, making him
the perfect gubernatorial candidate for Colonel Robert McCormick, publisher of the *Chicago Tribune*, who influenced Republican politics across
the Midwest.[2]

In 1939, Republicans persuaded Green to run for mayor of Chicago against Edward J. Kelly, leader of the city's Democratic machine. Green lost but received more than three-fourths of Kelly's vote tally. This showing made Green an odds-on favorite for the Republican gubernatorial nomination a year later. With McCormick's backing, he easily defeated other Republicans and the Democratic nominee to become the second youngest governor of Illinois at age forty-two. He campaigned against the Democratic political machine in Chicago and accused the previous Democratic administration in Springfield of corruption.

Green's victory raised hopes of a reform administration and a new direction for the Republican Party.[3] Instead, he turned out to be a traditional conservative Republican and a central player in a state party dominated by McCormick and the *Tribune*. Beginning with his candidacy in 1940, Green frequently criticized President Franklin D. Roosevelt's domestic policies, while generally supporting the war effort. He successfully sidestepped internal Republican disputes between conservative and moderate forces that kept the party in turmoil. Toughness and new ideas were not his forte. Reporters covering state politics at the time recalled him as quiet and knowledgeable about state government without being brilliant; an organization man, as far as politics went.[4] Despite the 1940 campaign rhetoric, he found ways to cooperate with Chicago Democratic mayor Kelly on major city and state projects.

During the first term, Green used his image as a dashing leader to build his own political organization—opponents called it a *machine*—of loyal Republicans across the state. With GOP prospects improving as the days of Roosevelt dwindled, Green received mention as a possible vice presidential candidate in 1944. Nothing came of it, but his standing on the national level rose, and supporters waited for another opportunity.

Typical of Illinois governors seeking reelection, Green struggled in 1944 and won a second term by only 72,271 votes.[5] He owed the victory to a strong showing in downstate voting precincts, the traditional Republican stronghold that had been eroded by Roosevelt. The *Bloomington Pantagraph* took away some of the glow by stating, "There is no call for the Republican party chieftains in Illinois to congratulate themselves. New and better leadership is called for."[6] Immediately after the election, Green's name surfaced in news accounts and political conversations as a possible presidential candidate in 1948. That might have gone to Green's head except for one fact: the *Tribune*'s McCormick supported the candidacy of Senator Robert Taft of Ohio.

Nonetheless, the national awareness of Green grew, and he gave speeches in places well beyond Illinois. During those years, observers of Green and state government noticed his attention was diverted from watching matters at home. Increasingly, he left details of governing to aides and underlings. Having won two statewide elections, hearing his name mentioned at national levels, and watching as Illinois Republicans won every state office and the legislature in 1946, Green believed he had created a machine that would propel him further at the national level or at least to a third term as governor.

In retrospect, Green may have been mortally wounded before any 1948 campaign officially opened and before his Democratic opponent was known. Two setbacks made him vulnerable. First, he made a serious misstep during the 1947 race for mayor of Chicago. Based on party victories in 1946, McCormick and Green saw an opportunity for a Republican to win the mayoral election. Their optimism came from the party's gain of six congressional seats, five of which were from Chicago districts. Green and supporters believed 1947 could be the year to end Democratic rule in the city and to recognize the governor as kingmaker.[7]

Green set about to raise thousands of campaign dollars for the Republican mayoral candidate, Russell W. Root. Little known in political circles, Root, an attorney, projected a style amenable to Republican orthodoxy. Democrats abandoned Edward J. Kelly and selected Martin H. Kennelly, a businessman and reform candidate. As discussed in chapter 4, the governor targeted coal mine owners and operators throughout Illinois for large contributions, using officials of the Department of Mines and Minerals and state mine inspectors as "bagmen."

In March 1947, the *St. Louis Post-Dispatch* exposed the covert campaign, embarrassing the governor and Robert Medill, director of the department. Feeble excuses and attempts by Medill to shield Green from criticism failed to erase the blemish.[8] A final embarrassment for Green occurred when the Republican candidate, Root, lost badly to Kennelly. These slipups predictably would have been mentioned in the presidential campaign speeches of a Democratic opponent, but Green might have survived if that had been the extent of his troubles. The disaster at No. 5 changed the picture dramatically.

More than one political pundit and editorial writer observed after March 25 that Green's chances of being reelected to a third term died along with the 111 miners. The aftermath of Centralia No. 5 did not help Green, either. He tried to regain political footing on April 1 by firing Medill and issuing public statements that emphasized his grief and sympathy for survivors and families of men killed in the disaster. An investigation by the governor's own task force, testimony at hearings conducted by U.S. senators, and dueling reports from members of the state legislative probe all took aim at either the governor, the Department of Mines and Minerals, or both.

The task force, while avoiding mention of Green by name, blamed the governor's Department of Mines and Minerals for the explosion and loss of life. Later, the legislative investigating committee majority report echoed the charges. The minority report by Democratic members of the committee directed criticism at the governor and complained that Green had declined an invitation to appear before the full investigating committee. Democrats blamed "a clear conspiracy between the Centralia Coal Mine Company, the Administration, the Department of Mines and Minerals and many of the inspectors to permit the mine at Centralia to operate under such hazardous conditions that even a common layman could see that a catastrophe could happen."[9]

Green tried to regain momentum by supporting action taken by the legislature soon after the Centralia explosion. The legislature was in session at the time of the disaster, and before adjourning in July, it adopted changes in state mining laws. These included an increase of six mining inspectors, making a total of twenty-two; improved ventilation of mines; rock dusting closer to the faces; and inspections of all mines every thirty days instead of ninety.[10] Green appeared to get little benefit from the changes in mining law, however. The memory of 111 lost lives hung over the governor like a storm cloud, and his political adversaries would not let him or voters forget.

As the 1948 governor's race approached, other factors influencing Green's future were at work. A number of Republican hopefuls wanted to run for governor in 1948 and did not appreciate Green's interest in a third term. Hoping to dissuade Green, they threatened to contest him in the Republican primary election. Also, Republican officials at the grassroots feared Green's liabilities could doom other Republican candidates in 1948. Complicating the picture was an effort to elevate Green to the national level as the Republican nominee for vice president.[11]

Looking for a way to strengthen the candidacy of Thomas E. Dewey of New York for president, supporters wanted a strong Midwestern vice presidential choice. When they began considering Green, this brought a predictable reaction from the governor's detractors at the *Post-Dispatch*. Weeks before the Republican national convention in June 1948, the paper dredged up the contributions scandal from 1947 and made the connection with the Centralia disaster. An editorial stated:

> His administration is the costliest in Illinois history. It is loaded down with political hacks. The lug is freely used to exact political funds from state employees. . . . The lug was also used by Green to get money from Illinois' coal mine operators and state mine inspectors were forced to neglect their work and jeopardize their standing by

seeking and accepting such money. State laws governing mine safety were not enforced. . . . For these reasons Gov. Green is not fit to be considered for a place on the national ticket.[12]

Backers of the Dewey-Green strategy engineered the selection of the Illinois governor as temporary chairman of the Republican national convention in June, which also made him the keynote speaker. They must have forgotten that Colonel McCormick had no love for Dewey, wanted Taft nominated, and believed Green should stay in Illinois and run for a third term. McCormick's attitude and determination to destroy Green's national ambitions and Green's poor performance as keynoter at the GOP national convention settled the issue. Republicans chose California governor Earl Warren as the vice presidential nominee, and Green turned to his pursuit of a third term.[13]

Early in 1948, Illinois Democratic leaders chose Adlai E. Stevenson as their candidate for governor. Stevenson, often referred to as the "gentleman in politics," had never held an elective position. He worked in Washington, D.C., for the Roosevelt administration, carrying the banner as an internationalist, while a majority of Illinois residents held strong isolationist sentiments. He served as an aide in the Department of the Navy and as Roosevelt's economic missionary in foreign countries, and he worked with two secretaries of state. Periodically, Stevenson practiced law in Chicago.[14] Needless to say, Green and Republican leaders believed Stevenson incapable of challenging the experienced governor for a third term. On the national level, President Truman's prospects for election looked dismal. With the added background of state electoral victories in 1946, Republican confidence soared.

Had Illinois Republicans been watching, however, they might have had second thoughts. In the year since the Centralia disaster, the subject remained embedded in the public consciousness, especially in the southern half of the state. As a political issue, Centralia had ripened, and it took little to bring the memory of the disaster to the surface. Early in the year, Pulitzer prizes for exemplary newspaper work in 1947 were announced. For its coverage of Centralia, the *Post-Dispatch* received the coveted Public Service award. News coverage surrounding the honor reached thousands of households in southern Illinois, carrying with it praise for the reporting team headed by Harry Wilensky that revealed the political story along with the suffering. Not surprisingly, the paper took credit for various government investigations and for the firing of Robert Medill.

At about the same time, a blockbuster article appeared in *Harper's* magazine providing details of political intrigue related to the Centralia episode.[15]

Reader's Digest published a condensed version. Written by John Bartlow Martin, the article restirred the issues that placed Governor Green in a role of primary responsibility. Martin later became a speechwriter for Stevenson and wrote a two-volume biography of the Illinoisan.

Martin's article did Stevenson's work for him and handed the candidate ready-made quotes that condemned the actions of the governor. Speaking in Centralia and vicinity on March 24 and 25, 1948, Stevenson quoted liberally from the article, especially statements about Green. At one point, Stevenson read, "Here lies Green's responsibility—not that, through a secretary's fumble, he failed to act on the miners' appeal to 'save our lives' but rather that his loyal followers were busier building a rich political machine for him than in administering the state for him." He also read from the *Post-Dispatch*:

> To say that the successor of Henry Horner has been a disappointment is to put it mildly—the consequences of political prostitution of the mine inspection service is of course now common knowledge throughout Illinois. It is now widely known that the Green administration carried the political lug further than any other predecessor administration by using mine inspectors to solicit campaign contributions.

Adding his own words to the speech, Stevenson pronounced the theme of his bid for election:

> It is the disease, not only the symptom, that must be eradicated. We must attack that malignant growth on the body politic, the cynical cold-blooded sale of privilege. And I hold that the Governor is responsible for the system whether he personally condones, actively solicits, or passively permits, the sale of governmental favors. There will be no bold or no furtive solicitation of campaign funds for me at the risk of human life in the coal mines or anywhere else.[16]

Green's reaction to Stevenson's thrust was to ridicule the Democrat as a "striped pants" elitist diplomat. No pictures of Stevenson in striped pants could be found. However, Stevenson's aides found one of Green in similar attire. The Democrat smugly agreed to wear a pair, if Green would loan the pants to him.

Refusing to call Stevenson by name, Green referred to the challenger frequently as "the man who has been to London and Paris," or "the man who wasn't here." As was the case with many incumbents of the time, Green could not see the reform tide among the electorate, propelled by returning veterans of World War II who cared little for experienced politicians. They saw only greed and protection of the status quo in those who held positions of power and responsibility. After the war, at the local level across the state, candidates with no background in politics had unseated arrogant officeholders. By 1948, the movement had grown from the grass-roots to Springfield.

While Stevenson loaded his remarks for southern Illinois audiences with Centralia references, he also kept the memory of No. 5 alive across the state. At one location, he said, "A governor who ignores the appeals of miners for protection while his mine inspectors are collecting campaign funds from the operators has, particularly after a tragic disaster, deprived us of any hope for disinterested leadership." He added, "this State should take a vow that there shall be no more 'Centralia tragedies' and that whenever political favoritism has become a contributing cause, none of the guilty will go unpunished, no matter what their station in life or how high their rank or office." In a slightly different version for an audience in Herrin, a town with a long coal mining tradition, Stevenson said, "This barter at the risk of human lives and safety must stop. I ask you here and now to join with me in a vow that there will be no more Centralia tragedies."[17]

During a campaign talk at McLeansboro in April, Stevenson spoke generally about his ideas for the state and mentioned the disaster and "prostitution of the mine inspection services" almost in passing. He made a point, however, of paying his respects to State Representative Paul Powell of Vienna and called for his reelection. "When it comes time to write the obituary of the State House gang next November, Paul Powell will be able to embellish it with all of the sordid details of the Green Gang's more prosperous days," he said, with the representative in the audience.[18]

Powell, without question the most powerful state legislator of either party in southern Illinois, had only begun to form a relationship with Stevenson. The crusty veteran of the legislature, first elected in 1934, looked with suspicion on the Chicago man who had never run for office. Stevenson's wellborn airs and intellectual presence did not mesh comfortably with Powell, the rough-cut deal-maker who rarely talked about or thought of "reform."[19]

Stevenson could see that if he won the election, Powell, the Democratic floor leader, would be a formidable player in Springfield. Furthermore, Powell had a history with the Centralia disaster. He had served on the legislative mine investigating committee that looked into the explosion. Powell and other Democratic members of the committee had rejected the Republican-led majority report and had written their own minority statement that voiced extreme criticism of Governor Green and his administration.

As he carried the Centralia message forward, Stevenson added ideas for legislation that would be responsive to issues raised by the disaster, especially those in the political realm. Speaking during the summer in Salem at a reunion of soldiers and sailors, Stevenson added to his general criticisms of Green:

> What am I going to do to see that Centralia never happens again under any administration, Republican or Democratic? I am going to do my best to take the mine inspectors out of politics. They must be put under civil service and removed from all possibility of political control or influence. . . . And I am going to appoint a director of the Department of Mines and Minerals who is interested in the oil and coal industries and the men who work in them, not politics. Perhaps the present volunteer rescue team organization could be improved by establishing a few permanent full-time rescue teams. Perhaps the Mining Board should be reorganized to diminish the possibility of political interference.[20]

Without benefit of a statewide public opinion poll—a phenomenon of campaigning only widely used in more recent times—Illinois residents had little idea how the competing candidates stood except for insight gained from previous experience. In the fall, as serious campaigning began across the state, Green's chances of gaining a third term looked good, as did Thomas E. Dewey's outlook for defeating President Harry Truman. Stevenson had targeted Green's eight-year record but threatened no mortal wound. Still ahead, however, were Truman's whistle-stop campaign, including swings in Chicago and through central and southern Illinois, and further revelations about Green's behavior in office.

Again, the *Post-Dispatch* delivered the news. In September, articles by investigative reporter Theodore Link revealed deals and payoffs involving hoodlums, officeholders, and contributors to Green's 1944 campaign. Link wrote, "Gamblers, slot machine operators and punchboard distributors in at least six counties were 'shaken down' for nearly $100,000 for Gov. Dwight H. Green's 1944 political campaign." The editorial page, long since fed up with Green, rumbled, "How much longer will Gov. Dwight Green be able to evade or ignore the civic resentment which is sweeping Illinois over commercialized gambling and its attendant gangsterism and graft?"[21]

Even before the latest tales of Green's administration, the challenger used every opportunity to pound away at the mine disaster. On Labor Day, he spoke in Mount Vernon, just down the road from Centralia, choosing to praise Democratic administrations for their social legislation and concern for working people. As in earlier speeches, he applauded the actions of mine inspector Scanlan, who was campaigning in Chicago for the candidate.

An honest, diligent, fearless mine inspector, Driscoll Scanlan, made frequent reports on the dangerous condition of this mine. Nothing was done. Finally, the miners themselves wrote a letter to Governor Green to remind him that for two years his Department of Mines and Minerals had ignored them. "In Fact," the letter said, "this is a plea to you, Governor Green, to please save our lives." But still nothing was done, and a year later the mine blew up, 111 miners died in that tragedy last year, including three of the four who signed that letter for the union.

To a sympathetic southern Illinois crowd, Stevenson again called the disaster "a sorry story of neglect, buck passing and political prostitution of a public service charged with the protection of human life." He mentioned the promises of reform if he was elected and concluded, "It is time Illinois caught up with the procession [of reforms] and if anyone opposes teeth for the mining laws and for their enforcement in Illinois, I am going to expose them, whoever they are."[22]

Green's counterattack with labor was to talk about gains made under the Republican administration. In a radio broadcast late in September, he spoke for several minutes in defense of his record, without mention of mining or workplace safety. A speech before the Illinois Federation of Labor convention in Chicago omitted the subjects. He received the federation's endorsement and stated, "The Illinois Federation of Labor, and other organizations, have praised our labor record, which includes the adoption of prevailing wage law, numerous safety laws, and repeated increases in benefits under the workmen's compensation and unemployment compensation laws."[23]

An exception to the official labor organization support for Green was UMWA Local 52, based in Centralia and representing a number of miners in the region. In an August statement, the local made clear its opposition to the federation's position by withdrawing its membership from the organization:

> We take this method to let the miners and the public of Illinois know that we are against Governor Dwight H. Green for reelection for the following reason: We wrote Governor Dwight H. Green in regard to the dusty condition at Mine Number 5 as we thought the dusty condition was very serious and might cause an explosion. They sent a committee to investigate the dusty condition at Mine Number 5. . . . They reported to the Mining Department that there was not enough dust in the Mine Number 5; also that it was not necessary to put sprinklers on cutting machines to allay the dust.

The statement criticized Green for leaving people in top jobs who were not competent "to look after the safety and welfare of the miners of the State of Illinois." It concluded, "Therefore, we believe if Governor Dwight H. Green had any sympathy for the miners' safety and welfare he would remove them [those officials] from office and put competent men in their place." The statement mentioned for removal "Robert Weir, two state inspectors and two members of the Mining Board." One of those signing the statement was William E. Rowekamp.[24]

Armed with allegations of administrative failures and accusations of unethical behavior by Green in raising campaign funds, Stevenson challenged the governor to come out from hiding. At Bloomington later in September, Stevenson said, "There is still time for Governor Green to tell the people what he thinks about Centralia No. 5, which blew up while his mine inspectors were shaking down the mine operators for campaign funds two years after his Department of Mines and Minerals had been notified by Driscoll Scanlan about the unsafe conditions in that mine and more than a year after the miners themselves had appealed to him to please save their lives."[25]

No one predicted the election outcome. Truman buried the hopes of Dewey. In Illinois, Democrats took the House of Representatives, and candidate Paul Douglas easily won the U.S. Senate seat of Republican Charles Wayland (Curly) Brooks. To complete the sweep and crush the Republican machine of Colonel McCormick and the *Chicago Tribune*, Stevenson not only won the governorship but accumulated a plurality over Green of 572,067 votes, out of more than 2.25 million cast. Even more astonishing, the Democrat carried traditionally Republican downstate Illinois, 863,432 to 837,789. Stevenson won easily in the area surrounding Centralia.[26]

In office, Stevenson faced pressures from labor unions, miners, and the general public to make good on promises and expectations built by the enthusiastic support of newspapers such as the *St. Louis Post-Dispatch* and the *Sun-Times* and *Daily News* in Chicago. One of those expectations included the appointment of Scanlan as director of the Department of Mines and Minerals.

Scanlan had campaigned for Stevenson, especially in the Chicago area, and presumed he would be the choice. Furthermore, Stevenson frequently pointed to Scanlan as the righteous mine inspector whose warnings should have been heeded by his bosses. Scanlan may have carried too much baggage for Stevenson, the former mine inspector having been outspoken in his criticisms and personal attacks. Scanlan never completely shook the accusation of critics that he should have shut down No. 5 before the explosion, and he had been an active Republican. Stevenson finally chose Walter

Eadie, mine manager of the New Orient No. 2 Mine at West Frankfort, after others declined. No wonder Scanlan was disappointed. Not only had Stevenson passed over someone who had specific ideas for changing the Department of Mines and Minerals but he had selected a mine management man instead.[27]

In the aftermath of the Centralia explosion, a clamor arose for federal and state legislation that would improve safety conditions for miners and clarify requirements and responsibilities for mine operators, the Department of Mines and Minerals, the State Mining Board, and mine inspectors. Given the extensive hearings held by U.S. senators and the concerns expressed by federal mining officials, people associated with coal mining, especially members of the unions, expected new national laws. But no new federal laws were approved in the short term.

Federal officials did identify several violations of U.S. codes and serious dangers at Centralia. One of the violations involved blasting practices in the mine. Another was failure to rock dust adequately. Mine operators were informed of the violation of requirements prescribed for use of permissible explosives. However, none of these infractions or oversights constituted "imminent danger" in the eyes of federal inspectors or in their review after the explosion.

In Illinois, pressures for changes in state mining laws developed rapidly. However, reaching agreement required the cooperation of a handful of interested parties, beginning with traditional antagonists, the coal mining unions and the mine operators. Deeply interested in legislation were legislative party leaders, especially those representing parts of the state where coal mines operated. Finally, governmental entities directly involved—the Department of Mines and Minerals, the State Mining Board, and mine inspectors—wanted their say about changes. Historically, these interests rarely agreed on mining law changes and often checkmated each other when it came to obtaining enough votes in the legislature or a governor's signature.

Significant changes in public policy are most likely in the wake of disaster. At the time of the Centralia disaster, the 1947 legislative session was halfway completed. Republicans controlled the legislature and the governor's office, and the majority interests could see the political importance of making changes promptly. The vision of elections in 1948 added pressure, and representatives of mining districts throughout central and southern Illinois pushed for action, regardless of the political party.

In spite of the short time between the disaster and adjournment of the legislature on June 30, legislators and the governor approved a number of changes in mining law. Some ranked as significant, reflecting evidence and opinions highlighted by various investigations. These changes got the most attention:

- Inspections of shipping mines—those sending coal outside the state of Illinois—by state inspectors must be made every thirty days.
- The State Mining Board will appoint state inspectors, instead of the governor.
- No mine inspector may solicit political campaign contributions or gratuities from coal companies or coal sales companies.
- No employee of the Department of Mines and Minerals may solicit or request any mine inspector to solicit political campaign contributions.
- Six state inspector districts were added, bringing the total to twenty-two.
- Mine operators cannot employ miners as face bosses unless they have a certificate of competency as a mine examiner. Mine managers and mine inspectors also must have certificates of competency.
- The ventilation fan must run day and night and must be installed on the surface and housed there. Automatic devices are required to sound an alarm when the fan stops. All fans operated by electricity must be on an independent circuit.
- Operators must spray, sprinkle, or clean areas and roadways where air becomes charged with coal dust. Inspectors can order water or a wetting agent to be used where machines are cutting coal and raising an excessive amount of coal dust in the air.
- The amount of methane present in a mine to classify it as gaseous was reduced.
- In all mines classified as gaseous by state law, workers must use closed lights and avoid smoking.
- No explosives may be detonated or fired when employees are in the mine.
- Three new mine rescue stations were authorized, each with a mobile rescue unit.[28]

Some skeptics questioned whether the new regulations could be monitored effectively, but that did not slow down approval. Nor did action earn the Republican state administration much credit. The campaign for governor and for legislative positions in 1948 went on without much notice of responses by the 1947 legislature.

The 1948 election outcome changed the governing picture dramatically. Stevenson moved into the governor's mansion, and Democrats controlled the House for the first time since 1937 while Republicans remained in charge of the Senate. The House majority gave authority to southern and central Illinois Democrats, represented primarily by Powell, the new Speaker of the House. He moved aggressively to implement Stevenson's program, headed by a reorganization of the Department of Mines and Minerals placing direct responsibility for enforcement of mining laws with the director of the department. The State Mining Board, previously the enforcement authority, was relegated to an advisory capacity.

The legislature in 1949 tweaked mining laws approved in 1947 and stuck to the subjects raised in investigations after Centralia. It added four rescue stations to those already approved, spread among the north, central, and south coalfields, each with a mobile mine rescue unit. On the subject of ventilation, a second shaft, in addition to the hoisting shaft, was required to provide at least two distinct means of leaving the mine for all below ground. Another change required all mines, not just shipping mines, to be inspected every thirty days. Further fine-tuning occurred in the handling of explosives and procedures for firing shots at the mine face. Additional language was added on health and safety issues.[29]

The imprint of Powell's leadership and that of close associates from southern and central Illinois could be seen on each of the bills passed by the legislature and signed by Stevenson. All bills originated in the House. Sponsors included the same names, headed by Clyde Choate of Anna, one of Powell's closest friends. Others represented counties in the southern half of the state, including St. Clair, Vermilion, Effingham, Shelby, Wayne, Sangamon, and Madison. The name of the Republican representative from Centralia, R. J. Branson, did not appear as a sponsor on any coal mining bills, nor did that of any Republicans.

The political picture changed again in the elections of 1950, making Stevenson's initiatives harder to pass. Republicans regained control of the House and maintained a large margin in the Senate. Powell became House minority leader but still played a major role in the introduction and passage of mining legislation. His name appeared first on the bills that eventually became law, followed in each case by Carl Preihs, Powell's legislative cohort from Pana. Nevertheless, the further state officials moved from the Centralia disaster, the more political interest diminished. Four years and two elections had passed since March 25, 1947, and correcting shortcomings in mining safety laws did not seem as important to legislators.

This point became clear during the 1951 legislature. Instead of responding to calls from the governor for sweeping changes in the state mining act, the General Assembly fine-tuned laws passed in previous sessions. One proposal cleaned up language on participation in political campaigns or in contributing to campaigns by making it unlawful for state employees to act directly or indirectly in behalf of a candidate or a political party. Another bill changed the language of the shot firers act to allow for breaking down coal while employees were in the mine if the method used was a "mechanical or chemical-mechanical device."[30]

A major issue arose between Stevenson and the Mine Investigation Commission, a body established many years earlier to advise the General Assembly on mining laws. Commissioners, appointed by the governor, included three representing mining operators, three representing mining unions, and three public members. Stevenson needed the commission's support for his idea to recodify and simplify the mining laws and to have them passed in total by the legislature.[31] This would have opened the mining laws dating to the early 1900s to full review, rather than by amendments, as legislators and mining interests preferred.

Between the 1949 and 1951 legislative sessions, Stevenson asked Harold Walker, head of the University of Illinois Department of Mining and Metallurgical Engineering and director of the state's Department of Mines and Minerals after the removal of Robert Medill in 1947, to lead the recodification project. The governor intended to submit the plan to the 1951 General Assembly. Knowing the protocol for such a sweeping change needed approval of the commission, Stevenson provided members with his plan in January. Mine operators and union representatives recoiled at the thought of taking a serious look at all mining laws. They preferred piecemeal changes, if any. Commission chairman Sam Cape of Harrisburg informed Stevenson of the commission's inability to support the idea, and the governor responded in a letter to the chairman.

Stevenson reiterated his feelings that the mining laws were "ambiguous, obsolete, or both" and needed clarification. He said to Cape, "I am disappointed to hear that the mine unions and the operators have 'unanimously rejected' the draft bill codifying, modernizing and strengthening our laws." Stevenson admitted defeat. "I have conferred with the legislative leaders from the coal mining areas and they advise me that in view of the opposition of both operators and unions, the draft legislation we have so painstakingly prepared for the past year has no chance of passage at this session." He urged the commission to take the initiative in preparing a comprehensive legislative program for the 1953 session, knowing full well that was unlikely, due to the lack of interest by operators and unions.[32]

That was where mining legislation in Illinois stood after the 1951 legislative session and in advance of the next horrific coal mine disaster late that year at West Frankfort.

Part Two

The 1951 West Frankfort Mine Disaster

8

"It's All Blown to Hell"

DOWNTOWN WEST FRANKFORT WAS BRIGHT
with holiday lights. Along the residential streets, lined with modest homes,
decorated evergreen trees glistened from their windows. It was Friday night,
and a sense of holiday filled the air. The following Tuesday would be Christmas Day, 1951, and West Frankfort's New Orient No. 2 coal mine, opened
in 1922 and once said to be the largest shaft mine in the world, would shut
down until Wednesday.

Lying between West Frankfort and Benton, New Orient No. 2's current
output of coal was 9,500 tons a day, against a one-day record of 15,152 set on
November 3, 1926. When the late shift gathered at the shaft head on Friday
evening, it found a message chalked on a blackboard: "MERRY CHRISTMAS
TO THE NIGHT CREW."

Beyond any doubt, West Frankfort was a town that coal built. The place
had been a crossroads store when the railroad line went a bit to the west of
the village of Frankfort. Frontiersmen had built a fort there once, an outpost
against Indian attack called Francis Jordan's Fort, then Frank's Fort, then
Frankfort, and then Frankfort Heights.

When the railroad bypassed Frankfort Heights, business left. The community of West Frankfort started up in 1897, about the time speculators sank
test holes in search of the rich No. 6 seam of coal being mined to the south
between Johnston City and Carterville. The seam was nine feet thick at a
depth of about 500 feet. When a group of local investors started the search
for coal, about one hundred people lived in West Frankfort.

The first shaft was sunk in 1904–5. Mine after mine opened in the vicinity
in the years that followed, and West Frankfort grew mightily, its population
eventually exceeding twenty thousand. The town fattened on coal until

market difficulties began in 1927, and the effects of the Depression lasted until the wartime need for fuel increased in the 1940s.[1]

Even after World War II ended and the market slowed, in December 1951 New Orient No. 2 employed 1,100 workers. Normally, 300 men worked underground on the night shift, but on December 21, the "sick" report included 20 names. Apparently, some began their Christmas break a day early.

Clayton Vaughn, of Benton, stayed away from his scheduled night shift because he "didn't feel right." He had had the same feeling twice before, he said, and had avoided a major explosion each time.[2] The Chicago, Wilmington, and Franklin Coal Company, owner and operator of New Orient No. 2, said 257 were on duty that evening.[3]

On that December night, there was a high school basketball game between Marion and West Frankfort teams. Southern Illinois had long been a basketball hotbed. Storied high school teams from such places as Centralia, Pinckneyville, Mt. Vernon, Johnston City, and Herrin vied successfully for state championship honors. Southern Illinois University had won a national championship in 1946.

When there was little else to feel good about in Egypt's coal-town depression years, there was basketball, often played in gymnasiums built during the period of coal mine prosperity in the early 1920s. Friday night games drew large crowds, and rivalries were keen among teams from places like Benton and West Frankfort in Franklin County, Marion and Carterville in Williamson County, and Harrisburg and Eldorado in Saline County. Coal miners living in and near those towns made the sport a favorite.

On this Friday night, the team from Marion played at West Frankfort before 2,000 fans in the Central High School gymnasium. The game began shortly after 7:00 PM. Before it was half over, the public address system suddenly came alive with a voice calling over and over, "Dr. Barnett, Dr. Andy Barnett, please report to No. 4 portal at New Orient Mine at once—there has been a catastrophe!"[4]

Murmurs of dismay ran through the crowd of spectators who knew Dr. Barnett was the physician at New Orient No. 2. Play at the game continued, but hardly anyone paid attention. Singly, in pairs, and in small groups, the audience began to make its way to the exits. Later estimates were that 750 left the game before it ended, and many went toward the mine. It must have been difficult for members of either team to pay attention to the rest of the game. West Frankfort teammates must have been especially distressed, because friends and relatives worked in the mine. The teams played through to the final whistle, with Marion winning, 56 to 44.

On a bitter cold evening, with the temperature falling toward 10 degrees above zero, the concerned and the curious began arriving at the gate to the mine. They found it blocked by police to all except officials, rescue teams, and journalists. Miners' family members, frantic for information, parked cars along a nearby roadway, climbed a three-strand barbed wire fence, and walked across snow- and ice-covered fields to the pit head. Some of the women, in house slippers, wore coats hastily thrown over robes and gowns. A desperate vigil began.[5]

Trained rescue workers arrived from Belleville, Benld, Benton, Dowell, DuQuoin, Herrin, and Springfield in the age-old ready response of miners rendering assistance to other miners in distress. The cage at portal No. 4 took most rescue workers below, while others used the escape shaft stairway. As the cage returned to the top and opened, clouds of black smoke billowed out.

The scene around the portal was grim, with family members at first hysterical, then in despair, and then resigned. Rescue workers rested prone on the concrete floor, waiting their turn to go below. Red Cross and Salvation Army representatives appeared and handed out coffee, donuts, and sandwiches. Gradually, the large building housing the shaft head and the washroom filled to capacity, with many more waiting outside and in parked automobiles lining the nearby roads.

Word coming up from below indicated there had been a massive explosion approximately two miles northwest of the No. 4 shaft, near the place where an explosion had killed three and injured two in 1947. Rescuers reported that timbers a foot square were snapped in two like straws. The explosion knocked loaded coal cars off their tracks, hurled heavy machinery about, and bent steel rails like fishhooks. The blast force destroyed machines weighing twenty tons.

Omar Lingo, a mine inspector from Nason who participated in rescue operations, said, "There were bodies scattered all over the explosion area. Most were lying face down, some of them badly mangled. Many [were] burned beyond recognition. It appeared as though a fire had sped down the tunnelway like a shot blasting everything in front of it. I saw a 15-ton motor car that had been overturned, and five-ton coal cars twisted and bent and knocked off the track. Railroad ties were pushed together." Lingo said there had not been adequate rock dusting in the mine.[6]

Due to the size of the mine and the distance of the explosion from the shaft, some workers above and below ground heard and felt nothing. Joseph L. Barnett, a foreman working several miles from the explosion, first learned of the explosion when he was told by telephone "to get the men out." Alex Balabos, who came out of the mine unaided, reported, "I didn't hear a thing when all the lights went out. Then all of a sudden there was wind roaring down the tunnel. It was like a cyclone. I had to hold my hat to keep it on. Dust blew all over me. I said to my buddy, 'That's an explosion.' We took hold of each other's hand and followed the railroad track to the shaft opening." Balabos and his buddy were among the lucky ones. Some got out only with great difficulty, and many not at all. Once warned, some men underground escaped from the choking gas that followed the explosion by making their way to the shafts where the cages worked. They also climbed the stairway in the ventilation shaft to safety.[7]

Rescue teams could not remain underground long because of the conditions. They surfaced grim-faced. One who came out "shaking with emotion" declared, "It's all blown to hell, it looks like we lost them all!"[8] Paul McCormick, a veteran of forty years in the mines and twenty-two on a rescue team, had been at Centralia. Later he said, "West Frankfort [was] tore up much worse [than Centralia]."[9] No. 2 was a huge mine, thirteen square miles in extent. At a depth of 500 feet at the main hoisting shaft, it had sixty miles of passageways, some of them three or four miles long. Four shafts were used, two for moving coal and miners and two for ventilation and escape.

Wilfred McDaniels, the night mine manager, was among the first to observe trouble below when smoke and dust came up the No. 4 shaft and power failed in the mine and at the surface. When power returned in approximately five minutes, he went below and diverted intake air to the stairway of the escape shaft. He told workers in all parts of the mine that could be reached by telephone to come to the surface.

Returning to the top, McDaniels joined a group of volunteers that went below without rescue equipment. The rescuers included Arlie Cook, mine manager, Charles Pullum, assistant superintendent, and John Petroff and Les Lappin, timbermen. Holding wet rags to their faces to guard against the dust, smoke, and gas, they rescued Clarence Short of Zeigler, carrying him a long distance on a stretcher, and Paul Donahue of Johnston City, bringing them out at 11:00 PM. Ralph Kent of Marion and Roy Summers of Benton were brought to the top fifteen minutes later. Those who came out unaided began to appear on the surface about the same time.

A frightful suspense enveloped family members waiting for information on who lived and who died. Some men who came out safely went back to the mine as part of rescue teams, while others went home to reassure their families. The difficulty of accounting for everyone prolonged the agony. Safety engineer C. M. "Chalk" Walker, who worked the day shift on Friday, went back into the pit early in the evening and remained until daybreak Saturday leading rescue teams.

Charlene Nicholson, a young mother of two, waited at No. 4 portal from 10:00 PM Friday until 4:00 AM Saturday, not knowing whether her husband Kenneth had survived. He finally emerged "coal grimed" but unhurt. He had stayed below and joined the rescue effort. Relieved at her husband's return, Charlene was still worried because her uncle, Joe Zeboski of West Frankfort, was missing.[10] She later found out he had died in the mine.

The first bodies brought up at 5:55 AM Saturday were those of Hearstel Summers of Benton and William Smith, J. L. Black, and Howard Wall, all of West Frankfort, eliciting hysterical screams and sobs from waiting women.[11] "Tell me the truth!" one woman pleaded of a rescue worker. "I want to know. I must know." He could only shake his head.[12]

Lloyd Dupree, twenty-six, of Pittsburg, who worked in Peabody Mine No. 43 near Harrisburg, came to do rescue work. His father, Clyde, was found dead. Lloyd said of his two small sons, "They can be anything else they want, but not miners." After an accident underground, miners often said, "I won't go back." But many did. One explained, "Maybe it's a state of mind, the way we've been brought up. Often it's the best job we can get. We make pretty good money [$16.35 a day in 1951] when we work. The mine is cool in summer and warm in winter."[13]

Hope dwindled as Saturday wore on. Officials mobilized a National Guard unit to keep order, and a special detail of the state police was on hand. Increasingly contaminated air drove out rescue workers at 9:00 AM, until ventilation of the mine was changed so they could continue. Some were overcome by gas and smoke, and several had to be hospitalized. Approximately thirty women remained at the shaft head in forlorn groups, some sobbing.

One hundred thirty-three workers escaped unaided and unharmed. For many of them, passage out of the mine took several hours, causing great fear for the lives of the men underground among their loved ones above. Paul Donohue worked near the point of the explosion. He heard a massive sound that was followed in four or five minutes by a "terrific" roaring blast of air and dense clouds of smoke. Found by the first rescue party, he walked to the cage, boarded it, and then lost consciousness until reaching the surface. West Frankfort city commissioner August Allen, a repairman, walked four miles to one of the two escape shafts and climbed 500 feet to safety.

Floyd Hall later gave an account of one group's search for safety.

I suppose it isn't for me to reason why things happen as they sometimes do but rather to accept life and death as the certainties they really are.

Thinking back to December 21, I recall that 5:30 PM found me on my way to work with Robert Hines, Paul Taylor, and Cecil Sanders.

Two hours later Taylor and Hines were dead. A last minute change placed me in a nonexplosion area.

The man trips all leave the bottom of No. 4 portal at approximately 6:25 PM transporting the men to various working sections. After alighting from the man trip, I began the coal loading operations. I had just finished loading the fifth car when the power went off at 7:35 PM. After about five minutes I [was] notified that all men were ordered to evacuate the mine. My first thought was that the ventilating fan had stopped running.

I soon learned that my first impression was wrong. Most of the men in the working section were assembled when word came over the phone to proceed to the main north junction, a distance of two and one half miles, and from there via the main air course to the old air shaft located just out of the city limits of West Frankfort[,] a total of almost five miles to walk.

We began our long trek. The purpose of not telling the men what is wrong is to keep down panic. Our exit was in an orderly manner. We took our time[,] stopping to rest and take a drink from our lunch buckets and to talk.

We had traveled about three quarters of a mile when we met a crew of twenty men. We learned that our routing had been changed and we could proceed to No. 4 portal via the air course some two miles from where we were.

This news relieved my mind somewhat. There was an immediate change to banter and jocularity due to our not being informed of what had happened. We gained the entrance door only to find that we couldn't enter the main air course. We backtracked. Frank Smith phoned the office on top and was told the same route we had just explored. Some forty men had gathered around the phone.

We talked the situation over and decided there were two other routes open to us[,] either the main north entry some three hundred feet through choking smoke or directly into the air course through a man door [a door for use by miners but not machines]. Some of us took the one, some the other and we all made it. Both routes joined some three hundred feet distant.

We made our way up the air course entries, there are two, sometimes in one, then the other[,] because of rock falls that had to be climbed or gone around for a distance of a quarter of a mile and finally gained the air shaft steps for the vertical climb six hundred feet to the surface. I'd rather walk six miles than attempt that six hundred feet up those air shaft steps.

Since that was the only way out, we finally made it and gladly this time. We finally reached the surface at 10:25 PM exhausted but very thankful to be alive, for only then did we know what had happened.[14]

Tom Wilson had a different set of experiences in making his torturous way out of the mine.

My buddies and I went to work as usual. There were seven of us[:] Paul Deason, Caesar Bonacorsi, Leo Weaver, Dave McReynolds, Charley Hatfield, Arthur Smith, and I. We arrived at our working places at 6:45 PM.

All of us do not work in the same room but are close enough that we consider we are all working together. At 7:35 PM all of a sudden our ears seemed like they would burst, but we didn't hear any noise. We first thought there had been a fall somewhere close by. The tunnels we work in can almost be compared with a gun barrel as anything that happens in one entry will be heard or felt in all the entries near by. We decided to go out and investigate. While we were talking it began to get hot so we decided there had been an explosion.

In the mine you have three entries that are called intake air courses. That is where the air comes in. . . . The proper way to escape from a mine in case of fire or explosion is to face the air. So we started for the [intake] air course. When we got there, our hopes fell because the smoke and dust was so bad we had to get back on the return air course. We traveled about 1,500 feet when we ran into smoke so we decided [to] build a brattice [diversion of air] at the mouth of one of the entries.

After we had gotten our entry bratticed off we sat down to rest and talk. We had been there about an hour and forty minutes when the air course seemed to have cleared up enough to try again. After a few minutes we looked through a trap door and the sight that met our eyes would be hard to describe. Seeing those big rails twisted, cross bars that support the roof broken, top coal and rock down everywhere, trolley wires down, and no light sure gave us a lost feeling.

We knew by this time things were pretty bad. We were facing the air that kept the smoke and heat from catching up with us. After ages, it seemed, we finally reached the [shaft] bottom where we met some fellows carrying a buddy out on a stretcher. . . .

When the cage landed at the top we didn't get there a minute too soon, because we rode the last cage that ran for several hours other than for rescue workers. After changing clothes, we went home to let our families know we were safe. We returned to the mine and went below again to help remove the 119 fellows that were killed.[15]

Tom Haley told of his group's experience:

On the evening of December 21 I reached the No. 4 portal of New Orient Mine, parked my car, and went to the wash house as usual. Everyone was in a good mood. We talked about Christmas.

When I had finished changing clothes, I went to get my orders from Mr. West, our repair boss. My regular buddy did not show up that night, and I was told to take Ted Thomas as my buddy. When Ted and I reached the shaft bottom we got a mine locomotive and went to the shop to get our tools.

Ted and I went to the 11th North, 1st East, and moved a cutting machine back about 25 yards, and then started to our locomotive to get our tools. Just before we reached our locomotive, the power went off, and I felt a strong concussion that felt like someone had squeezed me and locked my ears. My buddy said "My God! That reminds me of overseas." I said to him, "Ted, there has been an explosion." I rang the Night Mine Manager and told him something terrible had happened. He told me, "Yes get the men together and bring them out on the haulage track."

By then Red Swofford, Elzie Barnfield, "Cowboy" Roberts, and Joe Miller came toward us. We started out the way McDaniels had told us to go. There was a lot of smoke and dust and empty spike kegs and brattice boards on the track there, but we kept going. We all agreed we would not be able to make it out on the haulage way. We would have to take to the air course.

In the air course someone had made a little propeller out of wood and nailed it to a prop. It would turn if the air was moving. When we got there, it was just standing. It was clear to all of us that the air was not moving. The farther north we went, the hotter it got. Heat was coming from the roof and off the ribs. I finally suggested that we best go back. When I had gone about fifty feet, I heard a little noise, and when I got back to the windmill, the little propeller was spinning. I called to the men and told them we had fresh air. You can imagine how good this fresh air felt to us.

We sat there for about five minutes. I just happened to glance to my right, and saw a light. I hollered and walked that way and told them we had fresh air where we were. These were men who were pretty well exhausted. They were Paul Deason, Arthur Smith, Dave McReynolds, Caesar Bonacorsi, Leo Weaver, Charlie Hatfield, and Tom Wilson. That made thirteen of us.

We started out through the 21st West air course and crossed over to the Main North air course. We came upon two men who had been carrying Clarence Short on a stretcher, but they were so exhausted they could go no farther. Ted Thomas, Caesar Bonacorsi, Tom Wilson, and I took over, and we finally got to the cage at No. 4 portal and were hoisted to the surface at approximately 11:15 PM. When we set the stretcher down on the floor of the first aid room, I, too, was completely exhausted. After about fifteen minutes I was able to leave and immediately went home to let my folks know I was all right.[16]

Many others escaped the mine, but at least twenty family members at the pit head kept up a forlorn vigil through the night, and others huddled near the gate in the freezing cold. Marie Thomas, twenty-eight, said her family had exchanged Christmas gifts early, almost as if in anticipation of tragedy. She had given her husband, John, twenty-nine, a new gold wedding ring.[17] When rescuers brought up his body, the wedding band she had given him just hours before was on his finger. Grieving at home with her children, Brenda, nine, and John Jr., six, Marie recalled that as her husband left for work on Friday afternoon, he remarked, "This is my last shift before Christmas. We'll have a good holiday together."[18]

More than five hundred persons took part in the underground rescue effort. They found that many had died instantly in the explosion, hurled by its force against the roof or walls of the passageways or against the heavy machinery. Melvin Melville, one of the rescue workers, reported seeing bodies that "looked like they had been roasted." Others had died more slowly, the victims of carbon monoxide that followed the blast. A group of about a dozen who died from the poisonous air had time to pray and to write notes for loved ones. Seeking to escape the gas, they poured water on the mine floor and buried their faces in it. Still, the gas ended their lives.[19]

Some of the bodies were four miles from the rescue operation shaft and had to be carried out on stretchers, a long, lonely walk in the darkness, with only cap lights for illumination. Three brothers, Albert, Ed, and Paul Yates, searched the mine and found a fourth brother, Zell, dead. One dead miner, Oral Bradley Jr., pastor of two small Baptist churches, had a Bible in his pocket. He left a wife and two small children. Ellis Reach and his son, Ellis Jr., died in the mine. Ellis Jr.'s wife, Jeanette, and four children, the youngest three days old, survived him.

By the end of the day Saturday, twenty-eight of the dead had been brought to the surface, some bodies so mangled and defaced by the explosion they could be identified only by numbers stamped on their mine caps or on metal tags kept in their pockets. Rescuers saw or heard no signs of life below ground. Walter Eadie, director of the Department of Mines and Minerals and former manager of New Orient No. 2, believed all those remaining underground were dead.

The deadly effects of the explosion appeared to have extended for about a mile in each of two passageways. Workers more distant from the point of the blast made their way to the main shaft or one of the escape shafts. Evidence below ground and pressure gauge readings at the ventilating fan suggested there might have been a second explosion approximately three minutes after the first and of almost equal intensity.

On Sunday, women still gathered at the No. 4 portal, expecting the worst but hopeful until the end. Each time a buzzer signaled that the cage was surfacing with more bodies, usually three at a time, women hurried to the stretchers, asking "Is it . . . ?" The answer brought heartbreak to some, while the others returned to wait. When Marie Thomas heard her husband's name called, she collapsed and was taken to the hospital.[20]

By Monday, ninety-one were known dead. For all the effort, rescuers, who brought four men out early on, found only one more alive. His name was Cecil Sanders. Fifty-eight hours after the explosion, a rescue party early Monday morning went into an entry that had not previously been searched and found Sanders lying among a small group of dead miners, some of whose bodies were still warm.

As Sanders recounted it:

> I was at the 14th North, 25th West off the Old Main North when we heard the explosion and realized what had happened. Three of us took off up the north air course. When we got as far as the 3rd and 4th, we met seven others coming toward us. Gas was closing in from both sides. We build [sic] a brattice out of burlap and nailed it on props so that the bad air could go around us. This worked for about two hours, but then the gas began to close in again. We went into the 1st North and bratticed ourselves off there. We could feel the gas closing in again and as the ten of us approached the fate we had resigned ourselves to, we all thought of our families.

Sanders said he wrote a note to his wife on the blank inside of a cough drop box, saying, "May the good Lord bless and keep you, dear wife and kids. Meet me in Heaven. Husband and Dad. Cecil." After that, he "lay down and prayed, then . . . dropped off to sleep."[21]

One of those in Sanders's group who died beside him, Bill Williams, wrote a note to his wife on the inside of a cigarette package. "Laura—I love you all way. If I go tonight tell Charles [their son] and D. [son's wife] I love them too. Williams." The note was badly scribbled, and some read the second sentence as "I go tonight with Christ. I love him too."

Waking some time later, Sanders saw lights and heard his rescuers. "Help me, boys, help me," he called. "My God," he heard one of them say, "There's a man alive." Yellow chalked arrows and the words "men here" made by Joe Revak and Claude Roland, both among the dead found near Sanders, guided a rescue team from Eldorado to him.[22] Aroused, Sanders asked first for a drink of water. "What day is this?" he asked. "The day before Christmas," he was told. "This is a wonderful Christmas eve," he said. The veteran rescue worker Paul McCormick, one of the first to reach Sanders, remembered that the miner said, "'I'm glad you found me. I thought you'd come.'"[23]

Sanders later spoke to a nationwide radio audience from his bed in the West Frankfort UMWA hospital. He said the miners heard a "big crash" and then smelled the carbon monoxide gas coming on. "The gas current was so strong it caught us between two air courses. We knew the only thing to do was find a hole and hope the gas would go over us. We ran back into the rocks just as far as we could go. But it wasn't far enough. The gas seemed to cover us." His group rationed what water it had and passed around a pencil to write notes. Sanders said, "I told the boys 'now we are at the end of the load. This gas is going to take us.'" A deacon for seventeen years in the Benton Baptist Church, Sanders sang "Amazing Grace" from his hospital bed. He did not know if he would return to work in the mine. Sanders's wife said, "We've prayed and prayed for this. It's a miracle." She gave God the credit. Sanders also credited the "hand of Almighty God" with saving him.[24] The Eldorado rescue team deserved some credit, too.

Even the worst news eventually wore itself out, and by January 4, 1952, for the first time in two weeks, the front page of the *Benton Evening News* paid no attention to the New Orient No. 2 disaster. Instead there was a brief item concerning an accident at the Hill Country mine near Carrier Mills in Saline County. No lives were lost.

9

Burying the Dead

GOVERNOR ADLAI E. STEVENSON LEFT
Springfield shortly before 9:00 AM on Saturday, December 22, 1951, in a
small airplane. His annual Christmas party for hundreds of central Illinois
children went on without him in the Springfield Armory. Upon arriving at
the West Frankfort mine, he said, "Do you need more help?" Ironically,
Stevenson had used the fact of the Centralia disaster three and a half years
earlier in his 1948 campaign against then governor Dwight Green. Now he
faced an even more tragic occurrence.[1]

Campaigning in Herrin in March 1948, Stevenson had criticized the
Green administration for ignoring reports of problems at Centralia No. 5
and for accepting election campaign contributions from mine operators.
"This barter at the risk of human lives and safety must stop," he said. "I ask
you . . . to join with me in a vow there will be no more Centralia tragedies."
Stevenson won the election over Governor Green by a huge majority.[2]

Almost at once in West Frankfort on December 22, 1951, Stevenson began
to build a defensive wall around him regarding blame for the New Orient
No. 2 explosion. He "deplored" the fact that a "modern mine safety code"
he had recommended the previous January was rejected by the mine operators, the unions, and the state senators from southern Illinois and was
never introduced in the General Assembly.

Stevenson had tried since June to introduce a mining law reform plan
developed by the Illinois Department of Mines and Minerals and the Department of Mining and Metallurgical Engineering of the University of Illinois.
The Mine Investigation Commission had rejected it. He said the proposal,
if adopted, might have prevented the tragedy at No. 2. Stevenson asked that
a fund be established to receive contributions for the benefit of families of
the dead.

148

Walter Eadie, director of the Department of Mines and Minerals by appointment of the governor, arrived at the scene by 4:30 AM Saturday. Eadie had been a mine manager at No. 2 before entering state government. His appointment illustrated the often close and interlocking relationship of the coal industry and the state department responsible for mining regulation. Eadie stated that the methane gas that commonly builds up in a mine as part of the mining process caused the explosion. Eadie's spin on the cause of the explosion seemed to exonerate his department.

UMWA president John L. Lewis and Secretary of Interior Oscar Chapman arrived together Sunday afternoon, along with John J. Forbes, head of the U.S. Bureau of Mines. Their arrival caused a "buzz of excitement" as they went down into the mine and stayed for twelve minutes. When Lewis emerged from the cage, "his bushy eyebrows and long bushy hair protruded incongruously from the miner's helmet he wore, making it appear much too small." Coal dust streaked his face, almost as if he had been made up for the part.[3] Lewis, entering his fourth decade as the head of the union, at seventy-one was no longer as active and filled with energy as in earlier years. By 1951, he preferred the company of business executives to that of trade unionists, but he still maintained a strong presence in the worlds of organized labor and political action.

Lewis joined the "It's not my fault" chorus by stating that he had favored stricter federal safety rules for many years. "I hope some of those sons of bitches in Congress vote against safety legislation now. I wish they could see this," he said. For years, Lewis had jousted with Congress, the Department of the Interior, and the president over coal mine legislation. The UMWA had warned the management of No. 2 in August that the mine was in an "extremely dangerous" condition and had cited thirty-one points of deficiency noted by federal inspectors. Company officials had replied that some of the defects would be corrected but that the correction of others was "not in Illinois practice."[4] Coal companies often used those words to avoid making safety improvements, implying they were not required by law or regulation in Illinois.

In an editorial entitled "Blame Can Be Fixed" on the Monday following the explosion, the *St. Louis Post-Dispatch* claimed that fault could be found in the Illinois General Assembly, Congress, the Chicago, Wilmington, and Franklin Coal Company, the UMWA and its president, and Eadie. Lewis, the editorial said, had not sought legislation giving the U.S. Bureau of Mines regulatory responsibilities. The editorial did not name Governor Stevenson. The *Post-Dispatch* had been infatuated with Stevenson since his entry into Illinois politics. In short, almost every responsible party could be faulted.

Three days later, a *Post-Dispatch* editorial charged Lewis and the UMWA with obstructing a bill in Congress after the Centralia disaster that would have given the U.S. Bureau of Mines regulatory power. The bill got side-tracked in a dispute over personalities.[5] Some recommendations made by the bureau after the Centralia disaster were not approved, most noticeably that worked-out sections of the mine be sealed off and that only fresh intake air be used at working faces. Federal officials did not have the authority to enforce those actions nor did Illinois mining law require them. Eadie and John Foster, superintendent of No. 2 mine, viewed them as "controversial" and "not in Illinois practice."[6]

Ranking officials of the Bureau of Mines appeared at the mine after the disaster, including M. J. Ankeny, chief of inspections, and James Westfield, head of the accident and health division, in addition to Director Forbes. The stage was set to fix responsibility for a disaster that had taken 119 lives.

While the process of fixing responsibility for the New Orient No. 2 explosion went forward, citizens began to bury their dead. Rescue work ended on Monday, December 24. All but one of the miners who had been underground when the explosion occurred were accounted for, dead or alive. One hundred seventeen bodies had been brought to the surface. Of the five rescued, Ralph Kent died in the hospital. Only James Cantrell, the assistant night manager, still lay on the mine floor, buried under rock. His body was found two days later during an inspection. Although he had been traumatized by falling rock, it appeared he had died from carbon monoxide. Safety engineer "Chalk" Walker reported the finding by telephone from deep inside the mine. In lives lost, it was the greatest coal mine calamity in the United States since 1928 and remains in that position today.

Grief radiated outward from No. 2 in all directions. The dead came from sixteen communities: West Frankfort mourned 49; Benton, 38; Johnston City, 9; and other towns, as many as 3. Eight of the towns were north of the mine and eight south. The death toll left 105 widows, 161 dependent children, and 16 other dependents. Holiday parties were canceled, festive lights turned off, and decorated trees darkened. Funeral wreaths hung at the four major intersections in West Frankfort, while whole communities mourned.

Ambulances carried the injured from the mine to the hospital and the dead to a temporary morgue set up in the gymnasium of West Frankfort Junior High. Each body was laid on burlap on the floor, the face still black. Individual identifications were made by mine lamp or pocket tag number or by family members. Then the faces were covered.

Oscar Chapman and John L. Lewis left the mine on Sunday afternoon for the temporary morgue and walked among the rows of bodies on the floor. Lewis looked at each face. "It just isn't right," he muttered. When Chapman asked him if death had come quickly, "It hits you just like that," Lewis answered, snapping his fingers. For some of the dead, it had not been that fast.

The morgue overflowed. Working in three eight-hour shifts each day, forty funeral directors assisted in identifying the dead and preparing them for burial. The twenty-seven ministers of the West Frankfort Ministerial Alliance also took turns working around the clock. Volunteer grave diggers were recruited and asked to bring their own tools. They worked all night on Christmas Eve, illuminated by automobile headlights, but could not keep up with the demand for freshly dug graves. There were twenty-seven funerals on Monday, forty-five on Tuesday, Christmas Day, and the balance on Wednesday. More than forty of the dead were buried in the Odd Fellows and Masonic Cemetery north of Benton. Funeral processions from West Frankfort passed the buildings of No. 2 mine's No. 4 portal, a grim reminder against the winter sky.

A review of those who died was heartbreaking. The list included two brothers, John and Joseph Quayle, who had served together in the navy. Their late father had been a miner all his working life, beginning in England at the age of twelve. Carl Williams of Benton and his father, James, of Thompsonville were among the dead. Bill McDaniel, nineteen, planned to give Marie Joan Haskell an engagement ring on Christmas Eve. Marie, a "dark-haired blue-eyed brunette," was in the senior class of West Frankfort High School. She and Bill expected to marry after her graduation. His father, Eugene McDaniel, a miner, did rescue work in the mine. After Bill's body was found, Eugene paid the balance due on the engagement and wedding rings and on Christmas Day gave them to Marie.[7]

Among the dead were a son and son-in-law of Mr. and Mrs. Amos Westray, who had lost another son in an earlier disaster in the same mine. Lee Brashear, a reporter from the *St. Louis Globe-Democrat*, wrote before the funerals took place, "It is a long bleak walk from the Sandusky cottage on West Oak Street to the rambling green roofed home on E. St. Louis Street where the Amos L. Westray family lives." That walk took Brashear, in his words, "Across muddy lanes and railroad tracks to Main Street, a long narrow thoroughfare which is the sum and substance of the once bustling mining town." Entering the unlighted parlor of the Westray home, he found Mrs. Westray, "a thin, birdlike little woman," who said, "I gave two sons and a son-in-law to that mine. My husband works for that mine. That's all there is to it."

Her widowed daughter, Betty Ramsey, said, "We haven't got anything to say. They're dead." Of her husband, Alex, she said, "He's worked around the mines all his life." Heather Westray, Mrs. Westray's daughter-in-law, quieted three children and added, "Somebody done something that was wrong. I knew all day Friday there was going to be trouble in that old mine." Brashear wrote that the three figures standing side by side in the dimly lit room "had the sculptured dignity of a Greek frieze."

Heather told the reporter that her "husband Roy was a 36 year old [coal] loader. He made the best record in the mine for years. They wanted him to be a boss, but he liked the job he did. On Friday night, he just got a new set of false teeth, and they were giving him plenty of trouble. He thought he'd go work the night shift to take his mind off those teeth." Heather recalled that on Friday night, "I was just sitting here, feeling that something bad was going to happen."

Mrs. Amos Westray spoke again. "This family's been with the mines 30 years or more." Brashear wrote, "There was a strange, strong pride" in her voice, "a pride that distinguishes miners from ordinary men." She said, "You can't think about the danger all the time, you'd go crazy. But something like this—it just isn't right. It seems like they want to kill off all our fine young men."

Betty Ramsey added, "We wouldn't give up hope right away. We thought maybe they'd brattice themselves off from the gas." Her mother said, "Then on Sunday a neighbor come by. He was a good Christian man; he wouldn't tell a lie. 'Don't have no more hope,' he told us. They found the bodies that night."

"Why don't they do something to stop it?" Heather asked passionately. "There was gas in that mine all day. My husband heard the fellows talking about it. The lights kept going out. Why, that mine was so hot it liked to blow the tipple clear off. . . . They didn't inspect it near good enough."

The older Mrs. Westray spoke again. "One thing . . . you're able to pay your debts and hold your head high. John L. takes care of our people all right. He's a good man. We've all been praying that he can do something to stop these accidents."

Earlier in the day, Brashear visited in the home of Goldie Sandusky, whose second husband, Stanley, lay in the parlor in a shiny gray casket surrounded by flowers. In the warm room, heated by a coal stove that glowed red, their fragrance was heavy in the air. Goldie's first husband, Noah Avery, had died in the same mine twenty years earlier. Brashear noted that she was "a tall, silver haired woman with pain and patience in her eyes." To Brashear, "her white frame house [seemed] exactly like every other house in this drab, wind-swept community."

Later Brashear wrote, "It is hard for outsiders to understand a town like West Frankfort and the people who live there." The widows the reporter talked to blamed no one. Miners' wives, he wrote, have "learned to live with horror" and often hid their sorrow. Goldie Sandusky's twenty-five-year-old daughter, Mrs. Sam Glodich, asked Brashear, "How can we explain? . . . You don't live in a mining town. You can't tell our story unless you have gone through it. The waiting, I mean. The waiting every night, every day. Will they come home safe? And the hoping. We always hope, right up to the last minute. We hoped all last Sunday, when they were still getting the bodies out of the mine. We wouldn't believe it about Stanley until we found out for sure."

Brashear noticed that Mrs. Glodich's "soft spoken southern sounding voice . . . seemed to hover on the edge of tears." She said, "I'll tell you what I can, but I can't tell you much. Mines are always dangerous. . . . You sort of get used to danger after awhile, I guess." Her father, Noah Avery, was killed in a rock fall in No. 2 when she was five years old. Stanley Sandusky, his "best friend," was with Noah when he died, trying to help him. Nine years later, he married Noah's widow. "Sandy [Sandusky] was like a real father to us." Photos of Stanley were handed around. They bore the image of a "tall, stooped [man with a] pleasant, lined face [and] thinning hair." Mrs. Glodich said, "I don't know whose fault it was. You keep wanting to blame somebody." Goldie Sandusky added, "Some of my best friends' husbands [now] are gone."

From the Sandusky home, Lee Brashear visited Mrs. Ellis Reach Jr. Her husband died with his father, Ellis Sr. She was the mother of four. "My husband was a company man, a face boss," she said. "You'd call it a foreman, I guess. I wouldn't want to say I think there was anything wrong with the mine. It was just one of those terrible things." A visiting neighbor spoke up firmly. "If you're going to tell about us, tell it the right way. Most of the time we do pretty well. We're a good, free-hearted people. Our men make money. We're a lot more civilized than you folks up North think we are." Mrs. Reach added, "Like the pastor said in church yesterday, our men go down in the coal mines to keep the machinery going so other people can live."

The cemetery and the mine tipple, Lee Brashear wrote, "Form a bitter boundary line between the bereaved mining town and the uncomprehending outside world." He remembered what Goldie Sandusky had said, "Go ahead and tell them how a miner lives—and how he dies too."[8]

The feature story by Brashear appeared in the *Globe-Democrat* on December 30. It stirred resentment in West Frankfort over the way the reporter characterized the town and its people. An editorial in the *West Frankfort Daily American* on January 2 called the article "sordid, offensive journalism. . . . Those who know the community and its people will realize what a poor job of reporting it is."[9]

Dickson Terry of the *St. Louis Post-Dispatch* visited several miners' homes in Benton during the day before Christmas. It was, he wrote "a day of grief. You could feel it in the air. You could feel it in the grey sky and the cold, icy streets . . . almost bare of traffic." It was not difficult to identify those homes where death had come. Relatives and friends were gathered there. The men sat in the living room talking in hushed tones. Their women were busy in the kitchen and at other household chores. Christmas trees went unlighted. Often a newly made widow sat "with head bowed, perhaps staring blankly at the carpet."

In the Shelby Pauley home, with a coal stove for heat, shades were drawn, and it was dim and close. Mrs. Pauley sat with Laura Lee, nine, Gloria Jean, eight, and Shelby Jr., five. "We had the tree up," she said flatly. "I took it down, and I just went ahead and gave the kids their toys." The tone of her voice seemed to say, "What's the use, what's the use?" Shelby, forty, had been a miner for ten years. He was afraid of the mine, Mrs. Pauley said, and the night before the explosion, he dreamed of being trapped there. Family debt had kept him at work as a miner. Mrs. Pauley said, "All I know now is: I'm going to take what insurance money I get and put a roof over the children's heads. I know I'll be able to get along somehow."

Charles Southern was a widely respected miner who studied and qualified for several responsible positions. At age forty-three and a foreman in No. 2, he had been a miner twenty-seven years. In his house on Christmas Eve, there were still several unopened packages under the tree. His widow sat nearby with her sons Charles, seventeen, and Phillip, thirteen. Friends felt that Charley could have led men out to safety if anyone could. He was that sort of person. Charles Jr. said, "When they found him it looked as though he had been running toward the [underground] fire station."

Mrs. Southern said, "He was never afraid. The day it happened he left the house whistling." The reporter asked, had she ever been afraid? "Me? I've always been afraid. . . . The fear has lived with women of his family for four generations. My husband's great-grandfather and his grandfather both were killed in mines." Charles's father was a miner for fifty years before retirement. Had she made any plans for the future? "I've thought of it—only to dread it." Charles Jr. and Phillip put their arms around her, and the three stood together, crying silently, as their visitor closed the door.

Mrs. Paul (Virgil) Dollins said she hadn't been able to sleep since the explosion. Virgil, she said, was not afraid of the mine. Even if he had been afraid, "mining's about the only thing you can do around here." With their son Paul, sixteen, "we were planning such a big Christmas," she said. "But now, I don't know what we'll do. We don't own our house, he didn't have insurance. . . . I just don't know." Her older son, Ronald, serving in the air force, was on his way to Korea.

Mrs. Harry Gunter sat in a rocking chair in the space that served as both living room and bedroom. Other furnishings included a big four-poster bed, a daybed, two chests, and a small Christmas tree placed on a sewing machine. Her brother, William Sanders, also killed in the mine, had been buried earlier that day. Her husband, thirty-eight years of age and nine years in the mine, would be buried on the day after Christmas. She spoke of her children, Jimmy, eighteen, Sharon, fifteen, and Curtis, eight. Mrs. Gunter had suggested to Harry that he leave the mine for safer work. But "there's just something about the mines. Once they get in . . . they don't ever seem to get out. He was never afraid. The fear was nothing new to me. There was always the dread in my family. For generations the men in my family have been in the mines. I've had uncles and cousins killed. There's always the dread. But that's our life, I guess."[10]

Shared funerals were common. Ellis Reach Sr. and Ellis Reach Jr. were eulogized together in the Central City Methodist Church, as were Sam Montgomery and Rolla Jones, neighbors and close friends, in the Hazel Dell Church. The final rites of brothers Guy and Robert Rice took place in a single service in the Zeigler Baptist Church. The Quayle brothers and their friend Zell Yates shared a service in Johnston City. Brothers-in-law Roy Westray and Alexander Ramsey were memorialized in a single funeral and buried near older brother Wayne Westray, who died in No. 2 mine a decade earlier.

10

Seeking the Cause and Greater Safety

THE SERIOUS BUSINESS OF DECIDING WHAT happened, and why, and how it might have been prevented went on while relatives and friends buried the dead.

Governor Stevenson correctly stated that he had made strong efforts in 1949, 1950, and 1951 to improve mining law. On May 16, 1951, he issued a statement about those efforts and their result, explaining that the mine code was a patchwork of regulations that badly needed improvement. While the safety record was "very good," changes in the code were needed, he said. Working with the legislature after he became governor, Stevenson had rearranged the structure of the Department of Mines and Minerals to correct the problems associated with the Centralia disaster. The legislature had responded to that disaster in 1947 and 1949 with piecemeal changes in the Coal Mining Act that met with approval from the various mining constituencies, but broad reform had not been politically possible.

Beginning in 1950, the governor, Harold L. Walker of the University of Illinois Department of Mining and Metallurgical Engineering, the Illinois Department of Mines and Minerals, and the Labor Relations Board worked together to develop a bill to amend the Coal Mining Act. The Mine Investigation Commission (MIC) reviewed and rejected it, with the concurrence of the mine operators and the UMWA. State senators from the southern districts, predominantly Republicans, agreed with the commission, and the bill was not introduced in the General Assembly. Stevenson offered to assist the mine operators in bringing in an acceptable bill.[1]

In 1942, Edward Wieb of the Russell Sage Foundation wrote "Preventing Fatal Explosions," in which he evaluated Illinois's Mine Investigation Commission. It had been created by the General Assembly in 1909, after the Cherry mine disaster, and had been reauthorized by each General

Assembly since that time. The commission consisted of three representatives of the coal mine operators, three representatives of the union, and three at large members.

The work of the MIC was chiefly to evaluate proposals for greater mine safety. Until Wieb's article, the General Assembly had never accepted a proposal without unanimous approval of the MIC. That meant any one of the nine commission members had an absolute veto over any proposal. There was no appeal process. According to Wieb, that fact "nullifies any resemblance to collective bargaining." Thus the commission was "of little use to miners" and was "virtually nullified" as an instrument for improving mine safety. Wieb felt that the commission had consistently overlooked the concept of greater safety meaning greater economy of operation.[2]

On July 31, 1951, federal inspectors at No. 2 found violations of the U.S. Bureau of Mines safety code regarding the presence of methane gas, inadequate ventilation, and inadequate rock dusting. They recommended sealing worked-out rooms and not using "second-hand air" on the working face that had first been directed past old workings. On August 10, the union warned the Chicago, Wilmington, and Franklin Coal Company that the mine was "extremely hazardous." Operators of the mine agreed to certain changes but not others. The federal bureau had no authority to enforce its recommendations.

Since No. 2 was classified as a "gassy" mine, regulations required examination for safety before each shift. Approximately a dozen mine examiners made the pre–night shift inspection beginning at 3:30 PM each day the night shift worked. On December 21, the mine was rated safe immediately before the explosion, even though methane gas had been found in several places.

Stevenson and Interior Secretary Oscar Chapman agreed that the state and the U.S. Bureau of Mines would collaborate on a disaster investigation. Stevenson said, "These men must not have died in vain, and such a ghastly tragedy must be used to the fullest to enlarge our knowledge. . . . Our purpose will not be to find a scapegoat."[3] His biographer could find no evidence in Stevenson's personal correspondence that he was deeply touched by the West Frankfort disaster.[4]

Stevenson said the investigation would be headed by Walter Eadie, director of the Department of Mines and Minerals and a former employee of the coal company, assisted by Harold Walker of the University of Illinois, who had been director of Mines and Minerals for a time after the Centralia disaster. Secretary Chapman assigned Bureau of Mines personnel to the investigation.

A group that included Eadie, Walker, John L. Lewis, John J. Forbes, director of the Bureau of Mines, H. H. Treadwell, vice president of the

Chicago, Wilmington, and Franklin Coal Company, and thirty-one others inspected the mine for seven and a half hours on December 26. After emerging, Lewis pledged to stay until he was sure the investigation was on the right track. He said he had determined what caused the explosion but did not reveal his conclusion. He also suggested that he might call a ten-day UMWA work stoppage in honor of the dead. The investigation continued on the following day for two and a half hours before ending. Eadie concluded that it had been a methane explosion.[5]

Meeting with the news media, Lewis said management had known for four or five days before the explosion that certain sections of the mine were forcing out unusual quantities of methane. He told of how the men had died. Three-thousand-pound coal carts were "piled up on each other as if they were empty sardine cans," he said. Lewis described coal dust as "the greatest explosive known short of atomic power." He also said that the federal authority should have regulatory power over coal mines.[6]

In speaking of the New Orient No. 2 disaster, Lewis's own words are the best indication of the depth of his feeling and his rhetorical skill:

> The mining industry continues to be a morticians' paradise. I just watched 119 funerals in two days. Can you imagine anything more heart-rending? One hundred nineteen funerals in that little community in two days!
>
> They went to work, the last shift before Christmas. And many of them were brought home to their loved ones in rubber sacks—rubber sacks! Because they were mangled, and shattered, and blown apart, and cooked with gas, until they no longer resembled human beings. And the best the morticians could do was to put them in long rubber sacks with a zipper.
>
> Those men in the Orient mine died in three ways. There were the men who died from "afterdamp," or absence of oxygen, beyond the perimeter of the explosion itself. They just died from carbon monoxide. There were the men who were in the path of the violence of the explosion, who died from violence, from being dismembered, decapitated, hurled against equipment or timber, or having timber driven through their bodies. Then there were the men who died in the path of the flame; cooked, roasted by gas—the explosion of methane, the most volatile, the most insidious, the most powerful, the most terrible of all the known hydrocarbon gases, the very quintessence of refinement in explosives from nature's crucible which it has taken untold millions of years to create and refine, invisible to any of the five senses but terrible in its ravages, having an expansion volume

of 27 times its volume when ignited. These men were cooked in that extreme heat.[7]

UMWA officials arrived in West Frankfort on December 24 to disburse $1,000 to each family that lost a wage earner in No. 2. Within a week, the union had paid over $100,000 and promised that monthly assistance would be provided, with $30 going to each widow and an added $10 for each child. By the end of the first week, at least $4,620 had been paid on that account. The State Industrial Commission stated it would provide lump sums of $6,800 to $9,600 to each family, with the amount depending on family size.

After Stevenson's appeal for contributions to aid the survivors, money came from many sources. The CIO sent $10,000, and the UMWA provided $2,500 to the Benton–West Frankfort fund for emergency use. Other donors included August A. Busch Jr., $1,000; Falstaff Brewing Company, $1,000; A&P Food Stores of St. Louis, $1,000; the two major St. Louis newspapers, $1,000 each; 44th Illinois National Guard Division, $500; and many more contributions from communities, service clubs, churches, and individuals. Children of the Auburn Methodist Sunday school sent $3.87. On January 21, Stevenson reported that $37,410.73 had come to him in contributions and had been turned over to the local fund. Eventually, the amount donated from all sources exceeded $200,000.

The fund was divided among survivors according to the formula established by the Illinois Workmen's Compensation Act. Thirty-one widows without dependents each received $1,397.15. Twenty-six with one child each received $1,540.95. Twenty-one with two children were each given $1,664.23. Fifteen with three children each were given $1,869.69. And twelve with four children each were given $1,972.42. Dependents other than widows and children, such as siblings and parents, were each compensated according to the formula. Sixteen of them received amounts ranging from $290.62 to $1,561.50.[8]

A lengthy letter from Robert E. Howe, chief lobbyist for the UMWA, denied charges by the *St. Louis Post-Dispatch* that John L. Lewis had dragged his feet on improving mine safety after the Centralia disaster. The newspaper alleged that a disagreement between Lewis and Julius Krug, then secretary of the interior, over the appointment of the director of the U.S. Bureau of Mines had been the sticking point. The *Post-Dispatch* published Howe's letter but responded on the same page that the allegation was a matter of opinion, and the important matter was to get on with the business of changing the law to make coal mines safer.[9]

Stevenson said on December 31 he might call a special session of the General Assembly to consider changes in the Coal Mining Act. The next regular session would not begin until early in 1953. He "doubted very much" that changes in the act he proposed a year earlier would have prevented the disaster at West Frankfort.[10]

Eadie quickly prepared his report on the explosion in No. 2 and placed it on the governor's desk January 8. The report began with the known facts of the explosion. Then it stated that from 1923 until the end of November 1951, No. 2 had yielded 51,952,470 tons of coal. On the day of the disaster, the mine employed 1,127 men, who produced an average of 10,000 tons of coal a day. The safety record of No. 2 in 1949, 1950, and 1951 had been excellent, Eadie reported. Only two men were killed during those years until the night of December 21.

Eadie's report stated that the ignition of methane gas, either from an electric arc coming from the motor attached to eight loaded cars or from a cigarette or pipe being lit, caused the explosion. The blast proceeded down the passageways, fired by the rapid burning of coal dust. Smoking materials were found at several places in the mine, the report said.

Eadie offered these recommendations for changes in procedures:

1. State mine inspectors should take dust samples in all areas and send them to the laboratory for testing. If rock dusting appears scanty, the inspectors should call for more dusting to be done at once.

2. All areas should be kept clean of coal and dust.

3. Secondhand air should not be directed across the working face.

4. If doors are used in the ventilating system, they should be used in pairs to form air locks.

5. Tests for methane should be made before taking motorized equipment into working areas and after coal has been drilled, cut, or broken down.

6. Firmer enforcement of the "no smoking" rule is necessary, following evidence of "flagrant violations" of the smoking prohibition in the mine.

7. When coal is releasing more methane than usual, that area should be closed.

Eadie recommended two legislative provisions to the MIC for providing fresh air along haulage areas. He assigned blame to no one, although he pointed to "flagrant violations" of the mining act's ban on smoking.[11] In evaluating his comments, it must be remembered that Eadie's subordinates had responsibility for inspection of the mine and that he had been an employee of the Chicago, Wilmington, and Franklin Coal Company before becoming director of the department.

Stevenson responded immediately to Eadie's report. He was concerned about the "visual" examination of dust in the mine to determine whether it was at or above the level of combustibility. "My attention has been caught," he wrote, "by the references to visual examination of dust conditions in the mine and to your conclusion that '. . . it now becomes apparent that visual examination alone is not adequate in determining the combustible properties of dust found in coal mines.'" The governor asked, is there a better method of testing? If so, why was that method not used? Who determines what method is used?[12]

Eadie replied that No. 2 had sixty miles of passageways, and laboratory testing of dust samples from the entire length was not practicable. While state inspector James Wilson took only 4 samples from the mine for testing in 1951, the seventeen other mine inspectors had taken 2,056 in other mines that year. The implication was that Wilson did not sample often enough. "Mr. Wilson has apparently depended too much upon visual examinations," Eadie stated. He closed by stating that since the explosion, additional dust and air samples had been taken in other mines. He anticipated adding two positions in the laboratory to keep up with the work of analysis.[13] In June 1952, Eadie fired Wilson for "neglect and incompetence." In a complaint reminiscent of charges made about Governor Green in 1947, Wilson said that state mine inspectors had been asked to contribute to Stevenson's campaign fund.[14]

The Department of Mines and Minerals received the final report of the U.S. Bureau of Mines on the explosion on January 23, 1952. It was much more detailed than Eadie's report to Stevenson. For example, tables showed the results of laboratory testing of air and dust samples and the location and condition of pieces of equipment. The report referred to the accumulation of coal dust as "highly explosive." The system of ventilation in use was not adequate to prevent methane gas from "leaking" out of old workings into current work areas. Coal dust had collected excessively along roadways. Rock dusting was not sufficient, and water used to settle the coal dust was not adequately supplied to prevent the spreading of the explosion. The bureau stated that electrical equipment in the area of the explosion was not maintained properly to prevent the ignition of gas by an arc or a spark.

Federal inspectors found "ample evidence as to the cause and probably origin of the explosion."[15] They mentioned that working areas in the blast area were ventilated by return air from old workings that might have been contaminated by methane. Numerous old roofs had caved in and were releasing methane. At the moment of explosion, a door in the mine was open, reducing the air pressure and possibly allowing more gas to escape. The bureau's report stated that an arc or spark from "nonpermissable" electrical equipment caused the explosion. The ignition of coal dust spread the blast and perhaps ignited methane at other worked-out places. In other words, the explosion resulted from an inadequate ventilating system, the use of faulty electrical equipment, and the presence of coal dust not properly rock dusted.[16]

The Bureau of Mines report recommended:

1. Pure intake air should be provided to no more than two and preferably not more than one mechanized unit and should be circulated to ventilate abandoned areas and/or their edges before being exhausted. There should be a movement of air through abandoned and/or caved areas to prevent the accumulation of methane gas. If not ventilated, abandoned areas should be sealed. The ventilating system should be designed to prevent interruption of input air at the working faces.

2. Safety lamp tests for gas should be made before taking electrical equipment into a working area, just before operations at the face, and after coal has been cut or drilled.

3. Examiners' reports should specify locations and conditions accurately, in ink or indelible pencil.

4. Electrical equipment should be operated, and power lines and cables installed, only in pure intake air. Electrical equipment should meet permissible standards. Welding and cutting torches should be used only in pure intake air.

5. No person entering the mine should carry matches, lighters, or smoking materials. Management should install "a regular and systematic search" for such articles, with violators prosecuted.

6. Rock dust should be applied to within forty feet of the working faces in such quantity that the noncombustible content of the dust will be at least 65 percent. The mine should be kept clean of accumulations of loose coal and dust.[17]

Apparently, Eadie saw the report from the Bureau of Mines prior to January 23. On the fourteenth, he wrote Stevenson that he found little difference in the conclusions of his report and that of the bureau. He identified a slight disagreement in the direction of the blast forces. Recognizing that he had identified smoking as a possible source of the ignition, but the bureau had not, Eadie devoted several paragraphs to the bureau's evidence of smoking in the mine. He quoted the portion of the bureau report that called for management to search workers for smoking materials.[18] Eadie's insistence that smoking set off the explosion pointed the finger of blame for the tragedy at the workers rather than management.

Harold Walker wrote to Stevenson on January 24. A native of Benton, he served as the governor's personal representative in the investigation of the No. 2 explosion. He spent three days in the mine in that capacity and interviewed a number of persons. Walker received reports from both the Department of Mines and Minerals and the Bureau of Mines. He informed the governor that he had carefully studied and compared the two and found them to be in "exceptionally good agreement" in almost all respects. Walker described certain differences in the two reports regarding the direction of forces from the explosion. He then turned to the probable cause of the ignition of the methane gas, noting that "the department [of Mines and Minerals] places special emphasis upon the possibility of smoking as the source of ignition." Walker concurred with Eadie, saying "that ignition very probably was caused by personnel smoking." He also recognized the possibility that an arc or spark from a piece of electrical equipment could have been the cause.

Walker said that smoking in coal mines, although common, was difficult to prevent. He recommended legislation to require the search of a representative sample of underground workers each day. If that could not be done, he suggested management set up a "safe smoking place" where workers could smoke during lunch. Those smoking elsewhere should be prosecuted, he said.

The volume of air used to ventilate the mine was adequate, Walker concluded, but was improperly distributed. Methane gas is present in all coal mines, and for the sake of safety, it becomes a matter of diluting and removing the gas by ventilation, he said. In regard to rock dusting, Walker felt that "the Department of Mines and Minerals, the mine inspector, and the Coal Company all acted in good faith." He did not explain what that meant. The coal company's president denied that rock dusting was insufficient. Records of the company, Walker said, revealed that less than one-half of the amount of rock dust bought in the years 1947 and 1948 was purchased in 1951. He acknowledged that rock dusting may have been inadequate in 1951. Although the Mines and Minerals laboratory for testing dust samples was established in 1948, the inspector in No. 2 relied on visual observation. Walker favored legislation to require taking dust samples for laboratory analysis regularly.[19]

With Walker's report, the balance of opinion was two to one in favor of smoking as the cause of igniting the explosion. Additionally, shortcomings of management in regard to ventilation, use of electrical equipment, and rock dusting seemed to be demonstrated facts.

Testifying before the Illinois Mine Investigation Commission on February 26, Walker stated that the lighting of a pipe or a cigarette most likely caused the explosion. He presented slides to illustrate his argument, saying, "The ignition very probably was caused by personnel smoking." He added that the bureau was "positively wrong" in holding that an electric arc or spark touched off the explosion. Eadie, he said, was leaning toward impartiality in stating that the cause might have been electrical equipment when he believed otherwise. Walker, an academician and presumably less subject to political influence, appeared to be on the side of the department in blaming smokers, while the bureau leaned toward blame for management.[20]

Walker told the commission that the "preliminary" bureau report was similar to the department report regarding the cause of the explosion but was later revised to come down on the side of an electric arc or spark. Walker said when he discussed the matter with W. H. Tomlinson, head of the Indiana division of the bureau, Tomlinson said, "You understand my hands are tied and I must make a report my boss will sign." Walker thought "that was bad," but he was "reluctant to conclude" that the bureau was "subject to influence."[21] He said Eadie was a party to that conversation.[22]

Hugh White, UMWA District 12 president, who had been in the mine during the investigation that followed the explosion, told the commission that he "did not see any evidence of cigarettes or matches but did see many electrically operated machines that are capable of making electric sparks that are many times hotter than a match or cigarette." He also said that changes in the mining act proposed by Stevenson early in 1951 would not have prevented the No. 2 explosion. The commission agreed.[23]

The MIC heard testimony for several days in Benton and then in Springfield late in February. In Benton, witnesses mainly were officials of the mine and examiners who had been in the mine shortly before the explosion. Under questioning, safety man "Chalk" Walker and night mine manager Wilfred McDaniels gave detailed descriptions of their lengthy periods of rescue work. Neither was in the mine when the explosion occurred.[24]

McDaniels knew of smoking in the mine but found it difficult to prevent. He assumed that the two dead timbermen found near the ignition point had smoked on the job. In his opinion, "one of the two timbermen decided to light a cigarette. That light caused the explosion. The [electric] cable had never been hooked to the drill which was said to have caused" the trouble.[25] Arlie Cook, the day mine manager, reported difficulty in searching for smoking materials. He denied saying before the explosion that the mine was unsafe.[26]

In 1949, C. A. Herbert of the U.S. Bureau of Mines had stated that "smoking was practiced repetitiously" in underground coal mines. David Clayton, the Franklin County coroner, reported that 60 percent of the men who died in New Orient No. 2 on December 21 had smoking materials in their clothing. In his twenty-five years as coroner, he had "repeatedly found" matches and cigarettes on the bodies of workers killed in mine accidents. The coroner's jury ruled "an explosion" as the cause of death at No. 2.[27]

Members of the Mine Investigation Commission questioned Thomas L. Garwood, chief engineer at No. 2, at length about the location of the ignition point and its possible cause.

> Q: Now, Mr. Garwood . . . where do you place the ignition point?
> A: At the position of the two [dead] timbermen, or in the close vicinity to them.
> Q: Are there any conclusions that you have reached with reference to the nature of the ignition?
> A: To me there was not any conclusive evidence.
> Q: Could it have been from the hydraulic jack or the loading machine?
> A: Personally I do not think so.
> Q: Was there any electric equipment at the zone of origin?
> A: No sir.
> Q: Was there any evidence smoking might have caused it?
> A: These two bodies [of timbermen] that were found by Mr. James Westfield, of the Bureau of Mines, and Lloyd Saylor was with him, and he pointed to the two bodies and pointed to a spot between two pieces of coal and said, there lies the cigarette that was evidence and there was a half a package of cigarettes with the top burned off. It was taken away, that is as far as I know.
> Q: What happened to the evidence?
> A: Westfield said somebody picked up the package of cigarettes. He don't know what happened to it. I was with him and Saylor.[28]

M. J. Ankeny, chief of the Coal Mine Inspection branch of the Bureau of Mines, also appeared before the commission.

> Q: You have read, I take it, the State of Illinois report of the investigation of their disaster?
> A: Yes, sir.

Q: And you are aware of the two possible ignition sources which they mentioned, either electrical or smoking?

A: Yes, I am aware of the possibility.

Q: In the Federal report it only gives electrical ignition as the ignition source. [Was] smoking considered as a possibility in your discussions at the post explosion investigation?

A: Oh, yes, and also, during the investigation on the ground, and we were unable to establish factually, that any one who was at a point where they might have ignited gas, was smoking at the time the gas was ignited. We were able to establish factually that there was open electric equipment operating at the time the explosion occurred at places where the gas very likely could have been. There was evidence found during the investigation that smoking was being done in the mine and, of course, our inspectors had reported it even before the disaster.

Q: That was in your July report?

A: Yes, there were cigarettes, and I saw the partially burned cigarettes that were supposed to have been brought out of the mine. I saw them on the outside after the Orient No. 2 disaster.

Q: Who brought that out, Mr. Ankeny?

A: I believe it was in the possession of one of the inspectors.

Q: He found it down there?

A: He found it but we found no evidence to show that the smoking was actually being done. There was evidence of smoking materials at the point near where those two [dead] timbermen were at the entrance to this caved-in area, but there was not anything found on their bodies of that material. It was found it could very easily have been cached some time in the past, maybe when those entries were developed further.

Q: Is Westfield familiar with that?

A: He is more familiar with that than I am because he was the first man that approached where those bodies were.[29]

When James Westfield, who worked in accident prevention at the bureau, appeared before the commission, he was asked a similar question.

Q: What evidence, if any, did you find of smoking down there?

A: There were, throughout the mine a number of instances where cigarettes had been found, matches had been found. Sometimes whole packages of matches were found near bodies. But in [the ignition area] at the location of the two [dead] timbermen I happened to be with the first group that went into this section and Mr. South, one of our inspectors, picked up a package of cigarettes. [It] was burned down about half. There were parts of three cigarettes lying alongside of these two bodies, possibly off one or two feet. Neither matches nor a lighter could be found in the hands of the two timbermen.[30]

Westfield said that visual inspection was not sufficient for testing coal dust. Regarding the coal dust and loose coal in the mine, he said, "The amount was just enormous for any mine."[31]

Ankeny testified that "one cannot study [the Centralia and West Frankfort mine disasters] without coming to the conclusion that the state mining laws were manifestly inadequate or that the enforcement of such laws had failed."[32] He said that before the Centralia explosion, inadequate rock dusting and the presence of coal dust did not comprise an "imminent danger" to federal inspectors. Such designation was necessary before a mine could be shut down to correct dangerous circumstances. After Centralia, federal officials included dust accumulation among conditions constituting "imminent danger." Ankeny said that modern mechanized mining created far more coal dust than previous methods and produced methane gas at a greater rate, calling for an improved pattern of ventilation and greater attention to keeping the mine clean.[33] Mines in Illinois, he said, were laid out to maximize production, not safety.[34]

"In any well regulated mine," Ankeny said, "the instant you find gas with a flame safety lamp you remove the men and cut off the power from the section that might be affected until the gas can be removed."[35] Of the mine examiners who inspected No. 2 shortly before the explosion, several told the MIC they had detected gas in old ends near the ignition point for some time. Ankeny stated that at the time of the explosion, "a large body of explosive gas [had emerged] from an abandoned and caving area and a short circuit in the ventilating system caused by a mine door left open had reduced pressure and hastened the emergence of the gas."[36]

Thomas Garwood testified that multiple explosions seemed to have occurred. He presented evidence indicating there were five distinct explosions instead of one. Compressed air in what was called an Airdox system was used for blasting the coal down from the working face. The air was delivered to the working faces through lines brought down from the surface. Garwood said the force of the original explosion ruptured the Airdox lines at several places and released air at 12,000 pounds of pressure per square inch, stirring coal dust and causing it to rise above the rock dusted surface so as to cause another explosion of coal dust, not methane gas. He believed rock dust snuffed out the flame at each explosion point, only for another to occur at the next Airdox break. He was questioned by the commission.

> Q: Then, even if that mine were more than adequately rock dusted, your position then is that the break in these Airdox lines took up all this coal dust, the blanket that was on the floor, and took it into the air, and there was an ignition and it touched off another explosion?
>
> A: Yes, sir. Each one of those was subsequently snuffed out by rock dust.

Garwood explained that the explosion was not due to inadequate rock dusting but rather to the rupture of Airdox lines caused by the initial force, lifting coal dust into the air above the rock dust on the mine floor. That coal dust then exploded, with this process repeated several times. Without the Airdox line ruptures, he said, subsequent explosions would not have occurred.[37]

Commissioners asked Ankeny about Garwood's claim. "Do you believe that the severity of this explosion was caused by the bursting of the Airdox lines?" He replied, "In my opinion, it was an increase in the slightest degree."[38] Westfield did not believe that breaking of the Airdox lines contributed to the intensity or duration of the explosions.[39] He said that "there was an excessive amount of dirt in the haulage-way" that contributed to the continuance of the explosive force and flame.[40]

Representatives of the Cardox Corporation that supplied the Airdox lines strongly disagreed with Garwood's opinion. James G. Hesson said breaks in the Airdox lines did not lift coal dust. "Any air from a broken airline would be insignificant compared to the explosion force required to break it."[41] He said the initial explosion ignited the dust. Fred Bailey, director of safety for Cardox, said, "With due respect to Mr. Thomas Garwood, I cannot agree with his theory that four separate coal dust explosions occurred."[42] Garwood appeared to be in the minority.

Sherman Whitlow, president of the No. 2 UMWA Local 1265 for twelve years, told the commission that he heard "no complaints of the mine being unsafe." He knew about smoking in the mine but did not know how to prevent it. Vernon McDaniels, a member of the local's safety committee, reported several "small" complaints during the last six months—of such things as delayed rock dusting, dirty roadways, and coal falling from the ceiling of passageways. He did not know that the mine safety committee could recommend closure to the operator if it found a condition of "immediate danger" and that the operator was obliged to take closure action.[43]

Ankeny stated that the record of the safety committee system set up in 1946 had been "spotty" and "not too successful."[44]

Commissioners confronted John R. Foster, superintendent of No. 2 mine, with the statement in Walker's report that "the rock dusting program [in No. 2] was less than adequate in 1951 as compared to former years." He was asked if that was his conclusion, too. Foster said that in 1947 and 1948, coal was broken from the working face by controlled dynamite shots. Shot firers used rock dust mixed with noncombustible clay to tamp around the fuses in the shot holes. Half of the rock dust purchased in 1948 and 1949 was used for that purpose. The mine operator installed the Airdox system, which used compressed air instead of powder, beginning in 1949, and in 1951, approximately 70 percent of the coal mined was shot down by Airdox. That greatly reduced the amount of rock dust needed for tamping material, he stated.

Foster testified that the mine produced 600,000 tons less coal in 1951 than in 1947 or 1948. He said the amount of rock dust applied in proportion to tons of coal produced was in about the same ratio in 1947, 1948, and 1951. In the earlier years, miners spread rock dust by hand, while in 1951, it was done more efficiently by machines. Questioning followed after Foster summarized his statement.

Q: Mr. Foster, do you have any positive files of how much rock dust was used in 1951?

A: In the year 1947, days worked 263, tonnage 2,581,000. Rock dust spread 852 tons. Year 1951, days worked 168, tonnage 1,894,000, rock dust spread 627 tons.[45]

When commissioners asked Foster for an opinion about the cause of the explosion ignition, he said it was "a spark" that could have come from a cigarette or from a piece of electrical equipment.[46]

U.S. Senator Hubert Humphrey, chairman of the Subcommittee on Labor and Management of the Senate Committee on Labor and Public Welfare, sent a representative to West Frankfort during the underground investigation of the New Orient No. 2 explosion. He expected the subcommittee to hold hearings on the bill introduced by Senator Matthew M. Neely of West Virginia in April 1951, S 1310. The subcommittee had approved a similar bill two years earlier. Humphrey expressed regret that it had not been approved by the full Congress at that time. "I think it will be rather difficult," he said, "for Congress to turn down effective mine safety legislation in view of the disaster at West Frankfort."[47]

The Neely bill, proposing greater authority for federal officials in seeking mine safety, was referred to the Senate Committee on Labor and Public Welfare on January 16, 1952, and the committee referred it to a Special Subcommittee on Mine Safety. The subcommittee held hearings on S 1310 from January 24 to 30. On January 28, Governor Stevenson offered a statement to the subcommittee that in his absence was read by Director Eadie.

Stevenson took the offensive in behalf of states' rights to perform mine inspection so long as it was done properly. Stevenson's statement said he understood that the bills before the subcommittee applied the Federal Mine Safety Code to all coal mines in the United States. He believed the proposals would empower federal mine inspectors to enforce compliance with that code, and the effect would be to replace state inspection with federal inspection.

Stevenson pointed to changes made in Illinois after the 1947 Centralia disaster, most notably separating state mine inspectors from patronage, setting up a merit system, and restructuring the Department of Mines and Minerals. The governor described the efforts he made in 1949 and 1950 to bring about a thorough revision of the Illinois Coal Mining Act that were rejected by the MIC. He said he had then asked the MIC to prepare a revision, and it had agreed to do so for introduction in the General Assembly in January 1953.

Then came the "shattering news," as Stevenson called the disaster at No. 2. "I have never said that the adoption last year of the proposed bill would have prevented the West Frankfort disaster. It is probable that the explosion could have taken place had that bill been adopted." After the West Frankfort disaster, Stevenson said, he asked the MIC to hold a hearing on his plan and to speed up the promised revision of the mining code. If that occurred, he said, a special session of the General Assembly would be called to consider it.

Stevenson informed the subcommittee of efforts in Illinois to bring about better coal mine inspection. He recognized that Congress might view increased federal inspection with greater federal enforcement power as necessary for increasing safety and for leveling the economic playing field for operators throughout the United States. Toward the conclusion of his written testimony, Stevenson said, "I have come to have a new respect for what a state government can do if it has the will to do it. Perhaps will is not enough but Illinois will continue to work towards the goal of maximum safety in its mines."[48]

Stevenson's biographer John Bartlow Martin, comparing the disasters at Centralia and West Frankfort, concluded that "while the Stevenson administration was far less culpable than the Green administration, it deserved at least as much criticism as it received."[49] Martin, who had a personal and working relationship with Stevenson, in general was favorably inclined toward Stevenson in his two-volume biography.

Earlier in the month of January, Stevenson had made known his intention to seek reelection in 1952. Though he had been considered a potential candidate for the presidency of the United States, he disclaimed any interest in that position. Events would prove otherwise.

The star witness before the Subcommittee on Mine Safety was UMWA president John L. Lewis. He was the last to appear, and he spoke at length. He began by saying, "It is a fair statement that the explosion at Orient No. 2 Mine startled and shocked the peoples of the civilized world." He continued by reciting statistics on the lifetime incomes lost when miners were killed in accidents. From 1900 to 1950, he said, 119 lives, the number lost in New Orient No. 2, were snuffed out in mine accidents in the bituminous fields every seventeen workdays, an average of 7.03 each day.

In 1951, Lewis said, 800 men died in coal mines of all kinds. An average of 50,000 were injured annually. From 1930 to 1950 in bituminous mines, an average of 227 miners were injured each day. Wagging his finger at those he believed were at fault for the deaths and injuries, Lewis said mine managers usually were opposed to safety measures. Faulty equipment, in his view, was a prime causative factor in deaths and injuries. Neither the UMWA nor local safety committees had the power to close a mine, he noted. Miners who walked off the job faced dismissal and the loss of unemployment insurance and other benefits.

Then Lewis turned his attention to amendments in the Illinois Coal Mining Act that Stevenson had proposed early in 1951. The governor was "misinformed," Lewis said, in blaming the UMWA for the No. 2 explosion on the ground that it blocked the changes in Illinois law the governor proposed. In fact, Lewis said, the UMWA had not been consulted in the preparation of the proposal. Lewis recited, one by one, a long list of defects in the Stevenson proposal. "In summing up," he said, "this bill was found to be totally inadequate, vague, confusing, and in our opinion, in no way does it solve the problems."[50]

The Special Subcommittee on Mine Safety reported S 1310 favorably to its parent committee. The bill appeared to be on a fast track. The Committee on Labor and Public Welfare essentially rewrote the bill and reported it favorably back to the full Senate. The committee issued Senate Report 1223 on the bill, providing much useful information concerning the condition of coal mine safety in the United States.

The report stated there had been eighty-two disasters in which five or more persons were killed in U.S. coal mines since 1933. In the eighty-two, a total of 1,543 miners died. To provide perspective, the total number of persons killed in coal mine accidents of all kinds during that same period was 21,554. Single fatality accidents took far more lives than did those officially classified as "disasters."

The committee reported that prior to the disaster at West Frankfort, the U.S. Bureau of Mines had found "serious hazards" in 4,380 mines, approximately one-half of all coal mines in the United States. A letter was sent to the owner-operators of those mines. Only 474—11 percent—replied.

In Illinois, an average of twenty violations of the Federal Mine Safety Code occurred in each inspected mine. The violations included such matters as the ventilation of worked-out areas, rock dusting, the use of nonpermissible electrical equipment, the use of nonpermissible explosives, and the manner in which permissible explosives were employed. Of New Orient No. 2, the committee report observed, "It would be difficult for the human mind to conceive of a more perfect death trap."[51]

The Senate committee stated in report 1223 that if the Federal Mine Safety Code had been effective in No. 2, the explosion that took 120 lives would not have occurred. (One man who was injured in the mine died several weeks later, but he had had other physical problems as well.) Following findings of the Bureau of Mines, the report claimed that a spark or arc from a piece of nonpermissible electrical equipment ignited the methane and that the explosion was extended by the rapid burning of coal dust that had not been adequately treated with rock dust. That summary was contrary to the conclusion by the Illinois Department of Mines and Minerals and the chairman of the Department of Mining and Metallurgical Engineering of the University of Illinois that a match or cigarette lighter ignited the methane. While enforcement of the Federal Mine Safety Code would have done much to eliminate nonpermissible electrical equipment, it could not have prevented miners from carrying smoking materials underground. For advocates of greater federal control, it seemed better to assume that the cause of the ignition was an electric arc or spark, something that could be ruled against.

The Senate report stated that from 1942 to 1951 the U.S. Bureau of Mines had inspected New Orient No. 2 sixteen times. Repeatedly it found the ventilation system to be hazardous, the amount of dust and dirt to be excessive and its treatment to be inadequate, and the use of nonpermissible electrical equipment to be dangerous. The bureau saw "serious hazards" in No. 2

and notified the coal company, the union, and the Illinois Department of Mine and Minerals of that conclusion.

Senator Paul Douglas of Illinois was a cosponsor of the Neely bill. U.S. Representative Melvin Price of East St. Louis, Illinois, recalling the companion bill he introduced in 1947 after the Centralia disaster, also backed the Neely bill. U.S. Representative C. W. "Runt" Bishop of Carterville, in the district that included West Frankfort, lost a brother-in-law in No. 2 and favored placing more power in federal hands. U.S. Senator Edward Martin, a Republican from the coal state of Pennsylvania, was among the first to oppose the Neely bill. He refused to support an expansion of federal authority at the expense of the states and felt that state inspectors could do a better job. The UMWA bitterly attacked Martin, charging that he was heavily indebted politically to the mine operators of his state. Douglas felt that Martin was "mistaken."[52] A *St. Louis Globe-Democrat* editorial on January 3 held Senator Martin's objections to be "specious on their face." It did not accept his reasons for opposing the Neely bill.

The bill was debated and extensively amended in the Senate, passed on May 7, 1952, and went to the House. The House amended and passed the bill on July 2, 1952, and President Truman signed it on July 15, 1952. The *St. Louis Post-Dispatch* reported that the president signed S 1310 "with considerable reluctance. While the measure does give federal inspectors authority, on a limited basis, to close mines" on a finding of imminent danger, the newspaper said, "the safety bill was considerably watered down by Congress." Truman's misgivings about the bill included concern for complicated procedures, limitations on the number of mines covered, and exceptions regarding electrical equipment and faulty ventilation that favored mine operators, and he preferred to give the secretary of the interior authority to close mines rather than the director of the U.S. Bureau of Mines.[53]

Before the Democratic national convention ended, only days after Truman signed S 1310, Adlai Stevenson accepted the nomination as the party's candidate for president of the United States. There is no way of knowing how the New Orient No. 2 explosion would have affected his candidacy for governor if he had remained in the state race. It was not an issue in the presidential contest. Stevenson was soundly beaten by General Dwight Eisenhower in November, both in the nation and in Illinois.[54]

The Illinois Coal Mining Act was revised in 1953. Changes dealt with issues that had been sharpened by the explosion in New Orient No. 2. They included uses of electrical equipment, timbering, ventilation, rock dusting, hauling coal, moving personnel within the mine, and maintaining cleanliness of the underground environment. The changes gave the Department of Mines and Minerals greater authority to gather and distribute safety information and to improve mining methods generally. The authority of mine inspectors to close a mine or a section of one in cases of imminent danger was clarified.

11

Affected Lives

WITH 105 WIDOWS AND 161 CHILDREN LEFT TO
mourn, the impact of the 1951 explosion in New Orient No. 2 reverberated
down through the years. Upon the first anniversary of the disaster, a memorial service was held in the West Frankfort Central High School, where
the public first learned of the catastrophe during a basketball game. The
previous day, the *Benton Evening News* published half a page of touching
remembrances of those who perished.[1]

A thousand persons attended the memorial service, many more than
could have been accommodated at any of the area's churches. At the service,
sponsored by the UMWA local, a Catholic priest offered the invocation,
and a respected West Frankfort school administrator, L. Goebel Patton,
slowly read the names of the 119 men who died as a result of the disaster.
Weeping and expressions of grief accompanied the reading. After a song by
the group called the Gospelaires, from Johnston City, the Reverend T. H.
King, pastor of the First Baptist Church in West Frankfort, gave the principal address. His subject was "What Would Jesus Do if He Were Here?" It
was appropriate that he should speak, for more of the victims were Baptist
than any other denomination.

Luther German of Springfield represented John L. Lewis and Hugh
White, president of the UMWA Illinois District 12. Cecil Sanders, the miner
rescued from the mine fifty-eight hours after the explosion occurred, did not
attend. He had moved to Mt. Vernon, Illinois, to escape daily reminders of
his experience. Sanders still could not discuss the explosion and its aftermath. In attempting to testify before the Mine Investigation Commission
the previous February, he had broken down and had been excused.[2]

The tenth anniversary of the New Orient No. 2 disaster passed without
any formal ceremony, but the disaster "was deeply remembered by all of

Franklin County." By that time, Sanders and his wife lived in Rock Falls, Illinois, nearer their children and further from the mine. The same edition of the newspaper containing the report on Sanders noted that the mine operator closed No. 2 on November 30, 1960, after producing coal for thirty-nine years. During that time, it yielded 63 million tons of coal, believed to be a record for a single mine. After the 1951 disaster, the number of miners employed was reduced by three-quarters, to about 300. During the 1920s, a payroll of 1,900 names was not uncommon. When the mine was finally closed, the number was down to 195.[3]

In 1976, the *Benton Evening News* took editorial notice of the twenty-fifth anniversary of the tragedy and termed it "fitting that there should be no public ceremony." Despite much investigation, the newspaper stated, "There is still uncertainty as to the exact cause of the explosion."[4] That undoubtedly was true, but from the perspective of 2006, the weight of evidence points to the careless use of smoking materials. In the many thousands of words written about the No. 2 disaster, the names of the "two dead timbermen" near the ignition point, with cigarette butts scattered around them, never appeared. Such omission could only have been motivated by the desire to spare their families public censure.

Oral Bradley Jr. died in No. 2 mine, his body burned beyond recognition. An uncle died in the mine with him. His grandfather, Lloyd, died in a mine accident near West Frankfort in 1928. Tragedy seemed to stalk the Bradley family.

A small Bible found in Oral's jacket pocket aided in identifying his remains. He mined coal during the week and on Sunday served as pastor of two small Baptist churches. His wife, Ella, was left alone after the explosion to rear their children, Karen, five, and Glenn, three. She, too, lost an uncle in the tragedy.

Oral and Ella grew up in the village of Logan. She played boys' games. One day he looked at her and said, in surprise, "You're a girl!" After that, it was different. Oral—she called him Junior—joined the Marine Corps in 1943 and saw combat in the Pacific. He and Ella married soon after the war ended, and in 1946, they became parents. As the young family struggled to get established, she interested Oral in attending church. In a short while, he said to her, "The Lord's called me to preach." Ella said, "Just about a year before he was killed," Oral became the part-time preacher at both the Bethel Church near Macedonia and the Knob Prairie Church north of Aiken.

More than half a century later, Ella greeted a visitor at the door of her home near Carbondale. It was a stately structure, with four tall columns across its front. Inside was evidence of a well-ordered life. A massive stone fireplace and ceiling beams highlighted the room. Ella brought out faded newspapers and clippings and a small Bible carefully kept in a plastic bag. The Bible still bore marks of coal dust. "That was the worst Christmas," she said. "I don't like Christmas, ever since."

"He always prayed down in the mines," Ella said, and not long before his death brought six miner friends into the church. He was "a good-hearted kid, everybody liked him. Spent every dime he made, gave it away. If he had a dime and you needed it worse than he did, he'd give it to you. He'd bring me a dozen roses when the kids needed shoes. We had a big fight about that."

After the disaster, Ella did stenographic and clerical work in a Benton doctor's office. She also worked at one or two additional other jobs to keep the family going. She became part of a social group of women, widowed by the explosion, with small children. "We'd just get together at one or the other houses," she said, "and let the kids all play, maybe have a wiener roast." One of her friends, Maxine Miller, who had two children, lost her husband, father, brother, and brother-in-law in the mine explosion.

Content with her life, Ella coped with its problems. "I stayed single nine years. So far, I'd done just fine, raising two kids," she said. Then she met Dick Sweet, who came to Benton as a builder and manager of root beer stands. Sweet's wife had died years before. Ella said Dick told his friend who brought them together that he was looking for a woman "who wasn't divorced, wasn't bed hopping, out chasing around." They became friends and married in 1960.

By that time, Sweet had become a professional bird dog trainer who worked with hunting dogs and competed with Brittany spaniels in field trials. Preferring an outdoor life, in 1959 he bought an old farmhouse on a pie-slice-shaped ten acres east of Carbondale, with a barn suitable for the horse he used in working with the dogs.

"Dick had the same principles I did," Ella said. "He was a *decent* person, the straightest guy that ever lived." Success came quickly, and in 1962 he won the national Brittany field championship with a dog named Miller's Desert Dust. He also learned that in the bird dog world he couldn't make the kind of living he wanted for his family. In 1962, their daughter Tammy was born.

Sweet bought property near Carbondale at the right time. Ella said, "It became a gold mine." They sold parts of the property and then put the capital to work building commercial spaces. He was his own designer, architect, laborer, and skilled workman. The location became known as "Sweet's

Corner." Ella helped him all the way. She told her visitor, "Dick wasn't lucky, just diligent. The two were so different," she said. "He and my first husband, as different as night and day. Oral would give away everything he had. Dick wouldn't. He was rather tight, but he wouldn't cheat you."

Sweet died in 1987 in Florida, where the couple had gone for the winter. Ella lives alone with a small dog for company, in the house he remodeled for her. Two of her children, and grandchildren, are near. Karen lives in a small house next door to Ella and teaches in Murphysboro. She has three children. Tammy, lives close by in Herrin. She earned a master's degree in industrial engineering and has two children. Glenn chose a career in the navy and met an untimely death several years later. His son, who resembles Grandfather Oral, is thinking of going into the Baptist ministry.

Asked about the other women who were widowed by the blast in No. 2, Ella said, "A lot of them have remarried." And their children? "So far as I know, they all did alright."[5]

The only memory Robert Hines has of his father is of people standing around a brown casket in the living room of their house in West Frankfort. "I was four years old and it was Christmas Eve 1951," Hines told a reporter. "It would have been our fifth wedding anniversary," his mother Geneva said. "Instead, that was the day he was buried."

"Before he went to work that night he held our little girl," she recalled. "He said she looked just like him. He told me to take good care of her. He didn't say anything about having a bad feeling. There was a lot of miners that didn't show up that day for work, but he did." Later Geneva moved to West City and remarried.

Her son Robert wanted to be a coal miner like his father. She spoke against it, but after high school, Robert went into the mines. He worked at Old Ben No. 9 and No. 24 and then in a mine at Zeigler. When interviewed in 2002, he was thankful for thirty-five years as a miner. "A lot has changed," he said. "Safety-wise it's a lot better." He wished to see greater use made of the coal resource in place of dependence on oil from abroad.[6]

George Dunlop, the father of Sharon Raymond and Georgia Colp, died in No. 2. The girls were twelve and ten years old in 1951. More than fifty years later, they retain vivid memories of the disaster. An uncle came to their home in Freeman Spur on the night of the explosion and took their mother to the mine. Both agree their mother, Lucille, "never recovered" from the death of her husband. She later married George Boyd, a school principal. She often talked of her first husband and "easily became distraught."

The Dunlop family had a hard time in the months following the disaster. Georgia remembers, "We really lived like vagabonds for a while," moving in and out of relatives' homes. Her mother left the house in Freeman Spur and moved the family to West Frankfort. Sharon says she and Georgia could not have survived if "they hadn't leaned on each other." They completed their high school educations, and both became beauticians. Sharon married James Raymond in 1959 and ran her own business successfully for twenty-five years in West Frankfort. She retired at age fifty-four, and James died in 1997. Sharon is a Sunday school teacher in the First Church of God in West Frankfort. The church has been a major force in the life of the Dunlop family. Sharon says it "was essential in sustaining Mother."

Sharon and James had two daughters, Sabrina and Lisa. Sabrina, forty-four, does paralegal work in Seattle, Washington. Her sister Lisa, younger by two years and educated at Bradley University, is an industrial engineer in Morristown, Tennessee. Georgia married Deon Colp, an insurance agent in Marion. They have a son, David, who graduated from Mid-America Bible College and is pastor of a Church of God congregation in Middletown, Ohio. Their daughter, Michelle, a graduate of Southern Illinois University, teaches second grade in Lincoln School in Marion, Illinois.[7]

Charles McDaniel was eight years old when No. 2 blew up. His memory of the disaster is clear and sharp. His father, Verron, worked the day shift and was still at the mine when the explosion occurred. Verron sent a message to his family by a friend that he was going to stay at the mine to do rescue work. In the excitement of the evening, his friend forgot. For three days, while Verron remained on rescue duty, his family did not know whether he was dead or alive.

Verron survived that experience, but, Charles says, he was "like a zombie" for two or three months. It was hard for him to shake the terrible images he had seen. His appetite failed, and "all he could smell was burnt flesh." He lost almost forty pounds before his spirits rose. Verron, who started coal mine work at age fifteen and knew no other trade, returned to the mine until he retired in 1969. He died in 1996.

Charles says that after the disaster, Verron would not recommend anyone for mine work until Charles, at age twenty-four, wanted to become a miner. During his first day underground, he "expected the mine to blow up around him." Charles worked at coal mining in No. 5 and No. 6 for thirty-one years. Injuries from work in the mines took a physical toll. McDaniel and his wife are proud parents of three sons who are police officers in southern Illinois.

Asked about the effects of the disaster on the widows and children of the men who died, he said the blow was greatest to the spouses. "Harder on the widows," he said, even though many of them eventually remarried. "You know, women didn't work in those days," and many of the widows had problems financially. The fatherless children of his generation, he believes, were less affected and in most cases grew up as "normal kids."[8]

Jack Westray's father, Wayne, died earlier in an accident at No. 2 mine in 1941. Jack was fourteen when No. 2 blew up in 1951, claiming two uncles. Tragedy in that mine shaped Jack's life.

Jack was a member of a Boy Scout troop that volunteered for duty at the junior high school gymnasium where the bodies of dead miners were laid out for identification. The scouts directed foot traffic at the door and around the building and helped as they could. Jack looked in the windows and saw bodies bloated far beyond recognition. He wanted nothing to do with work in the mines. After graduation from high school, he served in the air force for eleven years. Military duty left little time for his wife and two young sons, so he left the service and got a job in St. Louis. Westray and his wife divorced, and he married again, acquiring in the process an additional child. He retired at age sixty-five and moved back to West Frankfort to be near his mother, Elva.

While Jack had an aversion to working in the mines, he said that his cousin Lewis, whose father, Roy, died in the 1951 explosion, became a miner. Asked his opinion of the impact on lives of children whose fathers and relatives died in No. 2, he said most grew up in a "fairly normal" way.[9]

Conclusion: After the Disasters

THE STORY OF COAL IN ILLINOIS, AND FOR
that matter in the United States, since the early 1950s in many respects is
depressing. Decline in production and employment has been steady, to a
point where only about 3,500 miners were at work in the state in 2004,
compared with 20,000 in 1979. During peak years after 1951, Illinois mines
produced up to 90 million tons annually. Today the number is a third of
that mark. The outlook for the future is at best hopeful. No new mines are
expected to open in the foreseeable future, and the development of new
technology that could help improve the picture remains speculative.[1]

By most standards, coal miners in the United States work in an environment much safer than during the late 1940s and early 1950s, although accidents do happen. Much of the credit goes to federal and state government
regulations and safety requirements. At the same time, legislation designed
to protect the environment and public health enacted since then also has
made it more difficult to mine and market coal. For example, the Clean Air
Act contains strict limits on emissions of sulfur dioxide for industries burning coal, opening the door to the use of fuels that are competitors of coal.

The UMWA, once one of the nation's strongest and most aggressive
unions, is a shadow of itself fifty years ago. Just as the strength of the UMWA
paralleled the leadership of John L. Lewis, the decline began and accelerated on his watch. In the early years of the twenty-first century, UMWA
members faced stagnation in wages and reduction in benefits as coal companies struggled to stay out of bankruptcy.

After the explosion at Centralia's No. 5 mine in 1947, Lewis spoke before
Congress for five hours. In 1952, following the great loss of life in West
Frankfort's New Orient No. 2 mine explosion the previous year, he contrib-

uted to passage of the first Federal Mine Safety Act. But for the most part during the 1950s, he played a steadily declining role in labor unionism.

Coal was a declining industry in the United States soon after 1947. It lost market share to other fuels, and production declined from 688 million tons in 1947, to 516 million in 1950, and to 392 million in 1954. The operators attempted to maintain a competitive position by increased mechanization and greater use of less costly strip mining. The number of nonunion mines increased, since that meant a saving in benefit payments even if wages were equal to those in union contracts. Clashes between union and nonunion miners became more frequent.

At times it seemed that Lewis valued power over principle. Lewis took the UMWA out of the AFL in 1947. He played only a minor role in the unification of the AFL and the CIO in the 1950s. Throughout that time, he continued his efforts to guard miners' wages and benefits in a declining industry. The welfare fund continually operated at a deficit. Some UMWA members claimed he got too cozy with mine management. Cooperation with the forces of capitalism and government in the interests of a stable society defined his career in labor. In the waning years of his long tenure, he was more inclined to seek the company of business leaders. More and more, the practices of the UMWA to unionize the mines of Appalachia turned to violence, behind-the-scenes dealing, and attempts to buy coal properties in order to ensure their functioning as union mines.

In the words of historian Robert Zieger:

> With an enfeebled and often sickly John L. Lewis paying less attention to the actual conduct of UMW affairs, the union by the late 1950s had begun to sink into a cesspool of financial speculation, collusive bargaining, and gangsterish violence. Lewis's years of dictatorial rule left the union with an emerging leadership that combined sycophantic adulation of the chief with contempt for working miners, cynical views of collective bargaining, and a penchant for outright thuggery that soon made the once-proud UMW a pariah among unions.[2]

Lewis voluntarily retired as president of the UMWA in 1960. President Lyndon Johnson awarded him the Medal of Freedom, the nation's highest civilian decoration, in 1964. Lewis remarked that it was in honor of those deeds the government had fought him over. He continued to chair the UMWA Welfare and Retirement Fund until his death in 1969.[3]

On the night of December 30, 1969, a challenger for the position of president of the UMWA, Joseph A. "Jock" Yablonski, was shot to death in his home. His wife and daughter died with him. Six years later, the union president, William A. "Tony" Boyle, was convicted of having hired the murderers and was imprisoned. John L. Lewis had been dead for six months when the shootings occurred. Boyle and Lewis were associates in the management of the UMWA long before Lewis retired. These events raised harsh questions about trends in the UMWA. Did the moral climate that Lewis established during forty years as the union head have a causative effect on the conduct in office of "Tony" Boyle? Did the ends Lewis sought justify the means he employed?

Lewis sought power and the exercise of power as ends in themselves. During a life of contradictions, he had many acquaintances and no friends. He "preached class struggle" and "practiced class collaboration" as he sought "peace, productivity, and social harmony." He often posed as a self-made man yet sought tightly knit group solidarity in the UMWA.[4]

According to Zieger, Lewis was "an associate of big-city leftists and immigrants who was himself a small-town conservative who embraced traditional American morals and values. He spoke and fought for millions of ill-paid, boss-ridden toilers, but he lived in luxury and ruled his own union with the proverbial iron hand. No single career better illuminated the achievements and the defects of the trade union movement in the United States during the twentieth century."[5]

Life stories from the years after the disasters at the Centralia and West Frankfort mines offer tantalizing ingredients for a study of human nature and survival. Unfortunately, a scholarly project directed at the two events would be hampered by a shortage of documentation and the diminishing number of people who experienced the aftermath personally. Researchers might ache for more details and documentary evidence, but the fact is that they do not exist. While frailties of memory and lack of written accounts are a plague to social scientists, family chronicles and anecdotes are quite adequate for putting a satisfying "period" on the coal mine stories.

A case in point is Joe Vancil Jr., the last survivor of the Centralia disaster. Vancil remembers events leading up to the explosion with clarity, and he is specific about the years after. But he does not remember a thing about what happened to him underground on March 25, 1947, or for several more months. Vancil's memory is blocked by an explosion that rendered him unconscious. Without eyewitnesses, Vancil has depended on verbal accounts of people who rescued him for some idea of what happened to him. Only a miracle could make Vancil's story more complete.

Picking up his life months after recovery in hospitals and at home, Vancil went back to Centralia No. 5 mine in an attempt to confront his demons.

Sadly, that didn't work. Newly married and needing to find work, Vancil moved to the St. Louis area, where he worked successfully at a number of jobs. Drawn back to his southern Illinois roots in DuQuoin, Vancil and his wife, Jean, opened a machine shop. Through the decades, Vancil has done all he can to cope with the lingering memory gap, the images of his father and uncle, both of whom died in the mine, and the challenges of keeping a life and family on track.

An appreciation of Vancil's life is not diminished by the gap in his memory but rather is enhanced by what is known and what it means. In the greater scheme of events of the last half-century, Joe Vancil's story is remarkable for its simplicity. Anyone who has struggled along life's pathways can relate to the challenges Vancil faced and met successfully. The larger significance for the thousands of people directly affected by West Frankfort and Centralia is that the Vancils are representative of the many who went ahead with their lives. This is not to say there weren't further tragedies or that everyone got back on her or his feet and soldiered on. No one knows the complete toll on survivors and families of the dead. Nevertheless, there are signs that lead us to conclusions.

Many of the young widows left behind married again and started new families. Ella Bradley Sweet of Carbondale is a good example of one who found happiness after starting life over. Other women who were less inclined to start a new family went to school, found jobs, and kept their equilibrium. That may sound easy enough to today's younger generations, but in the 1940s and 1950s, women had more limited educational and work opportunities. These were people whose lives had been consumed by coal mining and for whom breaking clean in another, entirely new direction was easier said than done.

Comfort and encouragement came from families and church affiliations. These relationships stretched back through the decades. When many families came to work in the mines of southern Illinois, they spoke little English, had virtually no education, and were not welcomed by native citizens. In order to live in a hostile environment, immigrants depended on families, friends, and neighbors of similar background, culture, and religion. In 1947 and 1951, during a time of crisis and loss, cultural connections served survivors well.

The literature of coal mining makes the point over and over again that death and injury were considered acceptable risks for miners and their families, and workers took this reality in stride. They knew from history that men would die mining coal. The unanswered questions were where, when, and how many. The random nature of coal mining death may have made it easier to dismiss the dangers. The chances of massive death in a single event seemed nearly impossible by the midpoint of the twentieth century. However, the explosions at Centralia and West Frankfort rattled even the most self-confident mining families. The loss of one life or two, while lamentable, still meant everyone else kept on working. When scores died, the spirit, the continuity of generations, and the way of life were threatened.

Importantly, relatives today remember survivors for their courage, determination, and sacrifice. This legacy comes from observations and assessments reached by admiring descendants rather than firsthand accounts of those directly affected. A half-century ago, people were less inclined to express their feelings openly or share their innermost thoughts. People of that generation did not devote much time to self-analysis of their emotions. They judged each other by their actions.

How can people today relate to those who survived West Frankfort and Centralia in the distant past? One comparison is with the aftermath of September 11, 2001. While on a much larger scale than anything that happened in the mines, the tragedies of New York City, Washington, D.C., and a field in rural Pennsylvania had immediate impact on families, in neighborhoods, and for the future of survivors. The casualties drew people together. Churches and clergy rose to the occasion by opening doors and counseling any who came inside. These were rallying points for survivors in 2001, just as they were in 1947 and 1951.

There also are notable differences in the reaction of mine disaster survivors and those who were touched deeply and personally on 9/11. There are no records of lawsuits seeking redress for survivors or placing blame for the coal mine disasters. Also, by today's standards, the financial aid for coal miners' survivors was meager. The mine workers' union provided payments to help cover funeral costs or immediate survival needs. Local charities came to the rescue for a while. Funds collected by community efforts provided short-term financial aid, mining company operators chipped in a few dollars, and survivors received some workers' compensation money. However, there were no legislated awards and no resources paid for the unfulfilled promise of lost lives.

Under these circumstances, the accomplishments of mine disaster survivors are all the more amazing. The safety nets so often discussed today were within reach but cradled relatives only until they could stand alone. The rest was up to them.

Immediately after a disaster—any disaster—there is a desire, actually a demand, for the final word on blame and responsibility. Toward this end, investigations are held, experts are sought to issue their conclusions, and governmental bodies pronounce the official verdict with conviction. The end? Not a chance. Debates, discussions, and arguments continue for decades, sometimes even longer.

Having said that, what about Centralia No. 5 mine and New Orient No. 2 mine? The questions remain. Do we know what happened deep underground where scores of miners died? Is there some way for families and friends to find closure? The answers, given within weeks of the disaster, in both cases reflect good intentions, guesswork, bias, politics, hard feelings, and the perspective that only time provides.

Only the survivors of those who died can answer the question about closure. It is an intensely personal matter that authors of a book are unable to answer. Time helps healing, but it cannot replace lost lives and tender moments. Occasionally, having more information provides solace. In that case, we hope this book may offer a small measure of assistance.

The preceding pages provide the results of investigations and the words of experts. In regard to Centralia No. 5, most parties agreed on the approximate origin of the explosion, what happened after ignition, and the death toll. Left unanswered are questions about who caused the ignition and what conditions existed underground that can be identified and blamed for providing the elements of disaster. Company officials claimed that careless miners with disregard for their own safety were to blame. Miners pointed the finger at politicians and inattentive company officials. Politicians blamed their political enemies. Federal officials said their hands were tied by lack of authority.

After the explosion in New Orient No. 2 mine in 1951, there was a perfect orgy of effort to avoid blame and responsibility and to point a finger at some other actor in the tragic drama. Governor Stevenson, embarrassed by a disaster so similar to the one he had capitalized on in running for office in 1947 and 1948, was quick to explain all that he had tried to do to prevent the recurrence. Mine management wished to place blame on mine workers. The UMWA and its president, John L. Lewis, sought to fault management. The U.S. Bureau of Mines appeared to be more interested in expanding its authority than in locating the true cause of the explosion. Walter Eadie, director of the Department of Mines and Minerals, came down on the side of the companies. Only Professor Harold Walker seemed to be intent on getting to the root of the matter.

None of this is to suggest that everyone intentionally worked at covering up for negligence and irresponsibility. Abundant evidence exists to conclude that the actions of most parties were predictable, based on how they had reacted before, during, and after countless other mining deaths. In fact, pinpointing the blame is not easy, and no matter how many years pass, opinions will differ. If it were simple, the issues would have been decided long ago and locked up for posterity. Instead of simply shrugging shoulders and allowing the subject to rest entirely on the statements and reputations of people long dead, the tragedy's survivors and families deserve a further attempt to define responsibility.

Was it an electric arc or spark or careless smoking that touched off the New Orient No. 2 explosion? The perspective of fifty years strongly suggests the latter. It is probable that the last action on earth of one of the "two dead timbermen" was to light a cigarette.

There is no figure in the prelude to the West Frankfort disaster comparable to Inspector Driscoll Scanlan and his reports of conditions in the mine at Centralia. Nor was there any document similar to the "please save our lives" letter. It is true that the UMWA warned the Department of Mines and Minerals in July 1951 that No. 2 was "extremely dangerous," but little attention seemed to be paid to that warning. It was known in the days before the explosion that the mine was highly gassy, that methane was being "squeezed" out of the coal at an accelerated rate, and that smoking underground was a prohibited and dangerous practice. Mine management in 1951 did not have, as a defense, the wartime need for coal that sheltered management in 1944 and 1945 from cleaning up a dirty mine. The UMWA local itself, in 1951, seemed to be largely passive in regard to the dangers of everyday work. If there are heroes to be found in the account of the New Orient No. 2 explosion, they are the men, both union members and management, who boldly entered the smoking mine, compelled only by a sense of duty, to attempt to rescue and succor those who were dying in its depths.

As for Centralia No. 5, looking back at what transpired before the explosion and who did what during and after, these conclusions are supported by evidence:

• The Department of Mines and Minerals, and its official leadership, was so completely stoked by politics and preservation of turf that most of its time was spent keeping constituencies happy with inaction rather than finding ways to improve mine safety. This situation resulted from decades of coal politics in Washington, D.C., in Springfield, and in every mine in the state. Officials did everything they could to keep from taking action that might upset mine operators and contributors to election campaigns.

• While the UMWA local union at No. 5 tried repeatedly to bring the attention of officials and mine operators to safety problems in the mine, it received little or no visible support from union officials in Springfield or

Washington. Of course, after the fact, those officials, including the king of coal, John L. Lewis, mounted rhetorical assaults on every party to the matter. At almost every turn, the complaints and charges leveled by local miners were ignored.

• Operators and owners of No. 5 followed the line of least resistance in assuming responsibility for not rock dusting the mine or introducing an efficient sprinkling system. They questioned the dependability of those measures in reducing risk and said they were sorry so many died. Their statements and testimony of sympathy lacked conviction. Company people did everything possible to deflect their negligence.

• The U.S. Bureau of Mines went through the motions but in the end did nothing to prevent the disaster. Its bureaucracy and inspectors became slaves to mine history at No. 5, proclaiming it had been dusty for fifteen years or more, as if that had relevance for current conditions. Federal inspector Perz made detailed inspection reports, but until 1946, the bureau had no legal right to close the mine. When government seizure of the mines gave the bureau the right to close a mine if "imminent danger" was proclaimed, the bureau chose to stick with outdated standards, claiming that dust did not qualify. The bureau finally changed its attitude toward dust as a condition for "imminent danger," but only after the disaster.

At the center of the Centralia story is the figure of state inspector Driscoll O. Scanlan. In the days and weeks after the explosion, the media proclaimed him a hero, the only person who had tried for years before the disaster to get the parties to lessen the dangers and risks to miners. In an attempt to save lives, he battled with bureaucrats and fought the inaction and selfishness of mine operators. With the perspective of a half century, he looks far and away the best of a lamentable assemblage of people and organizations involved. His ethical standards, determination, guts, and devotion to working men and mine safety shine brightly.

However, the center of attention rarely is perfect. And, as might be expected, those who discovered Scanlan's Achilles heel were the parties who sought a scapegoat to avoid responsibility for their own behavior and complicity. They said, almost in unison, that Scanlan should have declared the mine in violation of state safety laws and closed it until the problems were corrected. How easy it was for them to point the finger at the one person without a company, government, or constituency behind him. Scanlan fought back fiercely, with help from a sympathetic media.

Scanlan said that if he had tried to close the mine, his state bosses would have overruled him, fired him on the spot, and replaced him with someone who would not rock the boat. From all previous appearances and actions, that is exactly what would have occurred. His claim that the State Mining Board had the authority to take such action, too, has merit. But, again with hindsight, Scanlan cannot be fully excused by stating the obvious. He was on point as the person with the most information about serious conditions in the mine. Generations forever after will never know what would have happened if Scanlan had said, "Close this mine." That shadow hangs over the one person who valiantly battled for those who died. In Scanlan's further defense, without his willingness to go public, provide documentation for his accusations, and bring public attention to the weaknesses of the system, students of the disaster would have much less basis for deciding who was responsible.

The memory of those who died deserves a declaration of blame for the Centralia tragedy. These are so named:

- William Young and all the officials and supervisors of the Centralia Coal Company, for looking out for their own welfare to the exclusion of all others.
- Regional and national union officials, especially John L. Lewis, who preferred to fight big, visible battles on the federal level rather than direct attention and pressure at the state level, where they could save lives.
- Robert Medill, those for whom he worked (including Governor Dwight Green), and those who worked for him in the Department of Mines and Minerals and on the State Mining Board, for relentlessly striving to preserve the status quo and political harmony at all human costs.

When all is said and done, Driscoll O. Scanlan is the only one who fought the good, and long, and ultimately futile fight to save the miners' lives.

Appendixes
Notes
Glossary
Bibliography
Index

Appendix 1.
Miners Killed in the Centralia Mine Disaster

Joe Altadonna	Sandoval
Rodrigo Alvarez	Beckemeyer
Joe Ballantini	Centralia
Pietro Ballantini	Centralia
Alvin M. Barnes	Centralia
Martin Basola	Sandoval
Nick Basola	Sandoval
Domenick Beneventi	Centralia
Harry A. Berger	Centralia
Celso Biagi	Centralia
Harold Bryant	Sandoval
Joe Bryant	Sandoval
Edward Bude	Centralia
Otto Buehne	Centralia
Raymond Buehne	Centralia
Thomas M. Bush	Centralia
John Busse	Centralia
Charlie Cagle	Centralia
Theo Carriaux	Centralia
Arthur H. Carter	Centralia
Joe Cerutti	Centralia
Dominic Cervi	Sandoval
Anton Chariottino	Sandoval
Paul Comper	Centralia
Clifford Copple	Centralia
Frank Copple	Centralia
Leo R. Dehn	Centralia
Eugene Erwin	Centralia

Source: Table 6, "Welfare of Miners," in U.S. Senate, Special Subcommittee of the Committee on Public Lands, *Investigation of Mine Explosion at Centralia, Illinois*, 80th Cong., 1st sess., 1947 (Washington, D.C.: Government Printing Office, 1947), 165. The addresses used do not differentiate among small towns in the vicinity of Centralia that were not incorporated or did not have a post office in 1947.

George Evans	Sandoval
Frank Famera	Centralia
Andrew Farley	Beckemeyer
Walter H. Fetgatter	Centralia
John Figielek	Centralia
William F. Fortmeyer	Irvington
Ray Fouts	Centralia
Odis Lee Francis	Centralia
Luther Frazier	Beckemeyer
Martin Freeman Jr.	Sandoval
Martin Freeman Sr.	Centralia
Albert Friend	Rickview
Bruno Gaertner	Centralia
Angelo Gallassini	Centralia
Tony Giovannini	Sandoval
John Grotti	Mt. Vernon
Louis Grotti	Centralia
Adolph Gutzler	Centralia
Fred W. Gutzler	Centralia
John H. Gutzler	Centralia
John W. Gutzler	Centralia
Henry Hoeinghaus	Woodlawn
Edward Hofstetter	Centralia
Gustave Hohman	Centralia
Ned Jackson	Odin
Warrie L. Jackson	Centralia
Henry Knicker	Centralia
Philip Knight	Centralia
Joseph Koch Sr.	Beckemeyer
Charles Kraus	Centralia
Fred Laughbunn	Centralia
Dominick Lenzini	Centralia
Pete Lenzini	Centralia
John Mazeka	Beckemeyer
Miles McCollum	Centralia
Charles McGreavey	Centralia
Charles McHenry	Centralia

William Mentler	Centralia
Fred Moore	Centralia
Elmer G. Moss	Sandoval
Henry Niepoetter	Sandoval
Charles Oestreich	Centralia
George Panceroff	Centralia
Frank Paulauskis	Centralia
John Pawlisa	Centralia
Charles Peart	Sandoval
Joseph H. Peiler	Beckemeyer
Walter Pelker	DuBois
Alva Petrea	Centralia
Pete Piasse	Sandoval
Julius Piazzi	Centralia
Louis Piazzi	Centralia
John Pick Sr.	Centralia
John Placek	Beckemeyer
Alfredo Pollacci	Centralia
George Powell	Odin
Richard Privette	DuBois
Glenn Purcell	Centralia
Nick Reggo	Centralia
Jacob Rethard	Centralia
Forrest Rhodes	Sandoval
Carl Rohde	Centralia
Daniel C. Sanders	Irvington
Jacob Schmidt	Centralia
Archie Schofield	Centralia
Lee Gerard Shaw	Centralia
Anton Skrobul	Beckemeyer
Clarence Smith	Centralia
Ray O. Smith	Centralia
Andrew Spinner	Sandoval
Joe Spinner	Centralia
Alfred Stevens	Beckemeyer
H. W. Sundermeyer	Centralia
James Tabor	Centralia

Stanley Teckus	Centralia
Anthony Tickus	Centralia
Anton Tillman	Centralia
Emmett Uhls	Sandoval
Desmond Vancil	Centralia
Joseph Vancil Sr.	Centralia
Mark Watson	Centralia
Joe Zinkus	Centralia
Max Zonarini	Centralia

Appendix 2.
Miners Killed in the West Frankfort Mine Disaster

Arthur Adams	Benton
Bill Akins	Benton
Rivers Ashmore	Carterville
Fay Austin	Benton
Oscar Bartley	Johnston City
Charles Bartoni	West Frankfort
Roy B. Beaty	Benton
Lawrence Bell	Benton
Wilburn Bell	West Frankfort
William W. Bell	Benton
John F. Bennett	Thompsonville
James L. Black	West Frankfort
Charles E. Boyd	Marion
Estel J. Bradley	Logan
Oral Bradley	Logan
Carroll Bridges	Benton
Aston L. Bufford	Benton
Lonnie J. Cairel	Logan
James O. Cantrell	West Frankfort
Thomas Clark	West Frankfort
Paul Coats	Herrin
Jesse Connor	Zeigler
Andrew Cunningham	West Frankfort
John Dobruff	West Frankfort
Paul V. Dollins	Benton
George R. Dunlop	West Frankfort
Clyde Dupree	Pittsburg
Clarence Eubanks	Sesser
Frank Evrard	West Frankfort
James W. Fairbanks	Johnston City
John Farkas	Johnston City

Source: Edwin Hair, *Our Christmas Disaster* (Privately printed, 1952).

Archie Ferbus	Johnston City
Joseph L. Fitzpatrick	Benton
James Fowler	West Frankfort
Harry Gunter	Benton
Henry O. Harper	West Frankfort
Herschel C. Harris	West Frankfort
John E. Haynes	Johnston City
Robert Hines	Benton
Audrey Huffstutler	Benton
Roy Hutchins	Benton
Guy Johnson	Macedonia
Rolla Jones	Sesser
Roscoe Karnes	West Frankfort
Ralph Kent	Marion
John Kucewesky	Benton
Otis Lewis	West Frankfort
Lafet Lipsey	Benton
Mynett Lockhart	West Frankfort
John Matelic	West Frankfort
Bill McDaniel	West Frankfort
Wallace Miller	Benton
Claude Milligan	West Frankfort
Warren Mitchell	Benton
Sam Montgomery	Sesser
Harry Morthland	West Frankfort
Clyde Moses	Marion
Edward Mundy	West Frankfort
Roy L. Neibel	West Frankfort
R. L. Newell	West Frankfort
Max P. Nolen	West Frankfort
George Novak	Benton
Marion Odle	West Frankfort
Earl Overturf	Benton
Shelby Pauley	Benton
Earl Payne	Buckner
Andy Peska	Benton
Pete Petroff	Johnston City

Thomas Pierson	Benton
John Polic	West Frankfort
George Pollock	West Frankfort
Vallie Pritchett	Benton
John Quayle	West Frankfort
Joseph Quayle	West Frankfort
Alexander Ramsey	West Frankfort
Ellis Reach Jr.	West Frankfort
Ellis Reach Sr.	West Frankfort
Earl R. Rees	Elkville
Joe Revak	Benton
Guy Rice	Christopher
Robert Rice	Benton
Tom Roberts	West Frankfort
Claude Roland	Herrin
Charles Rose	Benton
Thomas Runnels	Benton
John Sadoski Jr.	West Frankfort
William D. Sanders	Benton
Stanley Sandusky	West Frankfort
Mike Senkus	West Frankfort
Charles H. Smith	Benton
Charles R. Smith	West Frankfort
Earl H. Smith	West Frankfort
George R. Smith	West Frankfort
William R. Smith	West Frankfort
Charles Southern	Benton
Burton Spencer	Whittington
Wayne Spencer	Whittington
Silas Stewart	Benton
Carrol Stubblefield	Johnston City
Hearstel Summers	Benton
Leon Summers	West Frankfort
Ted Tapley	West Frankfort
Paul Taylor	Benton
John D. Thomas	Benton
Louis A. Trapper	Benton

Alberic Vancouwelaert	Johnston City
Howard Wall	West Frankfort
Max Wawrzyniak	West Frankfort
Roy Westray	Thompsonville
Charles H. Whitlow	Benton
B. R. Williams	West Frankfort
Carl Williams	Benton
James H. Williams	Thompsonville
W. E. Wilson	West Frankfort
Walter L. Woodward	Johnston City
William Z. Yates	West Frankfort
Victor Younkin	West Frankfort
Louis Zanauchi	West Frankfort
Joe Zeboski	West Frankfort

Notes

Introduction

1. Priscilla Long, *Where the Sun Never Shines* (New York: Paragon, 1989), 3–5.

2. *Encarta*, s.v. "Coal," <http://encarta.msn.com/encnet/refpages/RefArticle.aspx? refid=761558734>, 1–3. (All website URLs cited were current as of 2004.)

3. See Robert L. Galloway, *A History of Coal Mining in Great Britain* (London: Macmillan, 1882).

4. "Disasters," <http://www.haig1.freeserve.co.uk/page5.htm(cmhrc 2)>.

5. U.S. Department of Labor, Mine Safety and Health Administration, "History of Anthracite Coal Mining," <http://www.msha.gov/district/dist01/history/history.html>, 1–2.

6. Andrew Roy, *A History of the Coal Miners of the U.S.* (Westport: Greenwood, 1970), 134–37.

7. John McDowell, "The Life of a Coal Miner," *World's Work*, 4 Oct. 1902.

8. William Graebner, *Coal Mining Safety in the Progressive Period* (Lexington: University Press of Kentucky, 1976), 9.

9. Graebner, 3.

10. "Monongah Mining Disaster," Boise State University, <http://www.idbsu.edu/history/ncasner/hy210/mining.htm>, 1–3.

11. Graebner, 2, 163.

12. Illinois Department of Natural Resources, Office of Mines and Minerals, <http://www.dnr.Stateil.us>.

13. Dianne Throgmorton, "Early Mining History—A Miner's Life," in *Concerning Coal*, ed. Magdalen Mayer et al. (Carbondale: Coal Research Center, 1997), 8.

14. Illinois State Historical Society, "Mining and the Cherry Mine Disaster," *Dispatch/News* 7, no. 2 (Fall 1999): 4.

15. Graebner, xi, 4.

16. Graebner, xi, 2, 4.

17. Robert P. Howard, *Illinois: A History of the Prairie State* (Grand Rapids: Eerdmans, 1972), 75, 109–10.

18. Malcolm Brown and John N. Webb, *Seven Stranded Coal Towns* (New York: Da Capo, 1971), 3–4.

19. Brown and Webb, 109.

20. Herman Lantz, *People of Coal Town* (New York: Columbia University Press, 1958), 13, 17, 20, 26, 27, 30, 37, 38, 43, 59, 61, 87.

21. Throgmorton, 10.

22. Paul Angle, *Bloody Williamson: A Chapter in American Lawlessness* (New York: Knopf, 1952), 89–116, quote on 116.

23. Brown and Webb, 4–5.

24. Angle, 119.

25. C. William Horrell, *Southern Illinois Coal: A Portfolio* (Carbondale: Southern Illinois University Press, 1995); Herbert A. Russell, ed., *A Southern Illinois Album: Farm Security Administration Photos, 1936–1943* (Carbondale: Southern Illinois University Press, 1990).

26. Throgmorton, 11.

27. Angle, 117.

28. Angle, 133.

29. Angle, 3-71.

30. George J. Mavigliano, "Paul Cadmus's Painting of the Lester Strip Mine Disaster," in *Concerning Coal*, ed. Magdalen Mayer et al. (Carbondale: Coal Research Center, 1997), 52-53.

31. Brown and Webb, xxiii.

32. Brown and Webb, 7, 111.

33. "Progress 2003," *West Frankfort Daily American* (special issue, 2003), 2.

34. Brown and Webb, 109-10.

35. David Conrad, "Coal Field Recreation," in *Concerning Coal*, ed. Magdalen Mayer et al. (Carbondale: Coal Research Center, 1997), 29.

36. Lantz, 2.

37. Brown and Webb, xxiii.

38. Brown and Webb, v.

39. David J. Maurer, "Unemployment in Illinois During the Great Depression," in *Essays in Illinois History*, ed. Donald F. Tingley (Carbondale: Southern Illinois University Press, 1968), 120-21.

40. Lantz, 187.

41. Brown and Webb, 25-29.

42. Brown and Webb, iv.

43. Brown and Webb, iii.

44. Brown and Webb, xxiv.

45. Brown and Webb, 121.

46. Maurer, 121.

47. Milton Derber, *Labor in Illinois* (Urbana: University of Illinois Press, 1989), 1.

48. Robert H. Zieger, *John L. Lewis: Labor Leader* (Boston: Twayne, 1988), xi-xii.

49. Melvin Dubofsky and Warren Van Tine, *John L. Lewis: A Biography* (New York: Quadrangle/New York Times, 1977), xvi.

50. Elsie Gluck, *John Mitchell: Labor's Bargain with the Gilded Age* (New York: John Day, 1929).

51. The Illinois Labor History Society, *John Mitchell*, <http://www.kentlaw.edu/ilhs/mtchell.htm>, 1-2.

52. Gluck, 257-61.

53. Long, 323-24; Dubofsky and Van Tine, 38; Zieger, xiv.

54. Dan Reitz, "A Brief History of the UMWA," in *Concerning Coal*, ed. Magdalen Mayer et al. (Carbondale: Coal Research Center, 1997), 13; Zieger, xv, 43.

55. Dallas M. Young, "Origin of the Progressive Mine Workers of America," *Journal of the Illinois State Historical Society* (Sept. 1947): 315-17.

56. Dubofsky and Van Tine, 178.

57. Zieger, 64-65.

58. Dubofsky and Van Tine, 220-21; Zieger, 82-83.

59. Dubofsky and Van Tine, 247.

60. Zieger, 83.

61. David McCullough, *Truman* (New York: Simon and Schuster, 1992), 506.

62. Reitz, 13.

63. Frank J. Bietto, "A Study of the Federal Government's Attempts to Promote Safety

in the Bituminous-Coal Mines of the United States" (master's thesis, Southern Illinois University, 1952), 35. The text of parts 2(a) and 2(b) follows:

> 2. *Mine safety program.—(a) Federal mine safety code.*—As soon as practicable and not later than 30 days from the date of the making of the agreement, the Director of the Bureau of Mines after consultation with representatives of the United Mine Workers and such other persons as he deems appropriate, will issue a reasonable code of standards and rules pertaining to safety conditions and practices in the mines. The Coal Mines Administrator will put this code into effect at the mines. Inspectors of the Federal Bureau of Mines shall make periodic investigations of the mines and report to the Coal Mines Administrator any violations of the Federal Safety Code. In cases of violation the Coal Mines Administrator will take appropriate action which may include disciplining or replacing the operating manager so that with all reasonable dispatch said violation will be corrected. From time to time the Director of the Bureau of Mines may, upon request of the Coal Mines Administrator or the United Mine Workers, review and revise the Federal Mine Safety Code.
>
> *(b) Mine safety committee.*—At each mine there shall be a mine safety committee selected by the local union. The mine safety committee may inspect any mine development or equipment used in producing coal for the purpose of ascertaining whether compliance with the Federal Safety Code exists. The committee members while engaged in the performance of their duties shall be paid by the union, but shall be deemed to be acting within the scope of their employment in the mine within the meaning of the workmen's compensation law of the State where such duties are performed.
>
> If the committee believes conditions found endanger the life and bodies of the mine workers, it shall report its findings and recommendations to the management. In those special instances where the committee believes an immediate danger exists and the committee recommends that the management remove all mine workers from the unsafe area, the operating manager or his managerial subordinate is required to follow the recommendation of the committee, unless and until the Coal Mines Administrator, taking into account the inherently hazardous character of coal mining, determines that the authority of the safety committee is being misused and he cancels or modifies that authority.
>
> The safety committee and the operating manager shall maintain such records concerning inspections, findings, recommendations and actions relating to this provision of the agreement as the Coal Mines Administrator may require and shall supply such reports as he may request.

64. McCullough, 528.
65. Zieger, 165–66.

1. More Than a Coal Town

1. James E. Davis, *Frontier Illinois* (Bloomington: Indiana University Press, 1998), 356.

2. Arthur Charles Cole, *The Era of the Civil War, 1848–1870* (Urbana: University of Illinois Press, 1987), 8–9.

3. Catherine Phee, "The Centralia Mine Disaster of 1947 (Ph.D. diss., St. Louis University, 1971), 16. Also based on the text of a speech by Marietta Broughton on the history of Centralia, from *Centralia Sentinel* archives provided to the authors in 2003; and George E. Ross, *Centralia, Illinois: A Pictorial History* (St. Louis: G. Bradley, 1992).

4. John E. Stover, *History of the Illinois Central Railroad* (New York: Macmillan, 1975), 15–16. Stover provides a comprehensive story of the railroad and its place in Illinois history.

5. Broughton speech, 1.

6. Stover, 65.

7. Broughton speech, 2.

8. "State Fair Came to Centralia in 1858," *Sentinel*, 26 Feb. 2003, 9B; Stover, 73.

9. Broughton speech, 3; Phee, 16.

10. Phee, 16–17; Broughton speech, 3.

11. Phee, 17–18, 58.

12. "Wamac Resembled Dodge City of Old West Thirty-Odd Years Ago," *Sentinel*, 9 Apr. 1947, 6. The 2000 U.S. census listed Wamac's population as 1,378.

13. "Lake Centralia Oil Field Sets Record," *Sentinel*, 26 Feb. 2003, 3B; Broughton speech, 4; Robert M. Medill, "World's Richest Deposit of Coal Located in Illinois," in *Illinois Blue Book, 1945–46* (Springfield: State of Illinois, 1947), 510–11.

14. "Cities, Counties Reap Huge Rewards from Oil Industry," *Sentinel*, 26 Feb. 2003, 6B; Broughton speech, 5.

2. "Please Save Our Lives"

1. See "Previous Explosions in This Mine," in U.S. Department of the Interior, Bureau of Mines, *Final Report of Mine Explosion, No. 5 Mine, Centralia Coal Company, Centralia, Marion County, Illinois, March 25, 1947*, reprinted in Phee, appendix 7, 228, in which federal inspectors quote statements from employees about three death events; and Illinois Department of Mines and Minerals, *Report of the Mining Industry of Illinois* (Springfield, 1955), 146, which lists the deaths in 1909 and 1921. Harry Niermann said he recalled a third fatality in 1915, in testimony, 3 Apr. 1947, U.S. Senate, Special Subcommittee of the Committee on Public Lands, *Investigation of Mine Explosion at Centralia, Illinois*, hearings, 80th Cong., 1st sess., 1947 (Washington, D.C.: U.S. Government Printing Office, 1947), 4 (hereafter cited as U.S. Senate hearing).

2. Dust in coal mines has been a problem since the earliest days of mining around the world and continues to be one in the United States today. In the *Handbook for Dust Control in Mining*, by Fred N. Kissell (Pittsburgh: U.S. Department of Health and Human Services, June 2003), 16, the list of dust control methods does not include rock dusting. Those considered most effective by the department are dilution ventilation, displacement ventilation, wetting by sprays, airborne capture by high-pressure sprays, foam, dust collectors, and dust avoidance.

3. Frequently during testimony at public hearings after 25 March 1947, mining operator officials, mine inspectors, longtime workers in the mine, and federal officials acknowledged the mine's history as dusty.

4. William P. Young, testimony, U.S. Senate hearing, 5 Apr. 1947, 287. Young clarified the corporate relationship of Bell and Zoller of Chicago and the Centralia Coal Company. He said Bell and Zoller was an affiliate of Centralia, with responsibility for coal sales.

5. H. B. Humphrey, *Historical Summary of Coal-Mine Explosions in the United States, 1810–1958*, Bulletin 586, rev. ed. (Washington, D.C.: U.S. Government Printing Office, 1976), 227–29; Phee, 49–51, citing *U.S. Statutes at Large* 55: part 1, 177.

6. R. R. Sayers, testimony, U.S. Senate hearing, 17 Apr. 1947, 416. Sayers recounted the full history of mine inspections at Centralia No. 5.

7. Frank Perz, testimony, U.S. Senate hearing, 3 Apr. 1947, 40.

8. Driscoll O. Scanlan, testimony, U.S. Senate hearing, 3 Apr. 1947, 79. Scanlan's father was working at the Mt. Olive and Staunton Coal Company Mine No. 2 in 1947. See also "Scanlan Won't Gamble with Men's Lives Because He Was 'Raised in a Coal Mine,'" *St. Louis Post-Dispatch* (hereafter cited as *SLPD*), 1 Apr. 1947.

9. John Bartlow Martin, "The Blast in Centralia No. 5: A Mine Disaster No One Stopped," *Harper's*, Mar. 1948, 196, 198. Martin's account a year after the disaster praised the work of Scanlan.

10. State of Illinois, "Fact-Finding Committee Appointed by Governor Dwight H. Green to Investigate the Disaster at the Centralia Coal Company Mine No. 5, at Wamac, Illinois, Occurring on March 25, 1947," in *Report to the Governor and People of the State of Illinois* (Springfield, 11 Apr. 1947), 10 (hereafter cited as Fact-Finding Committee). Phee, 27–35, discusses the history of coal mining laws in Illinois.

11. State of Illinois, *Mining Code*, p. 64, sec. 28, subpara. (b), "Penalties," as quoted by Senator Joseph C. O'Mahoney, U.S. Senate hearing, 3 Apr. 1947.

12. Biographical information on Robert M. Medill in *Illinois Blue Book, 1945–46*, 509; "Medill Has Served as Mine Director under 3 Governors," *SLPD*, 2 Apr. 1947, 3; "Medill Owed Job as Mine Bureau Head to Operators," *SLPD*, 9 Apr. 1947, 3.

13. Robert M. Medill, testimony, U.S. Senate hearing, 4 Apr. 1947, 118.

14. "Medill Owed Job," 3.

15. Marjorie Hornbein, "Josephine Roche: Social Worker and Coal Operator," *Colorado Magazine* 53 (Summer, 1976): 243–60.

16. Medill, testimony, 119.

17. Martin, "Blast in Centralia No. 5," 198. Illinois Department of Mines and Minerals files do not contain a copy of the 1942 inspection report.

18. Robert Weir to William H. Brown, Centralia Coal Co., 26 Mar. 1947, Driscoll Scanlan Papers. Scanlan's personal files, retained by his nephew, Gerald Scanlan, include personal documents and correspondence, copies of official correspondence from the Department of Mines and Minerals, handwritten notes, and copies of inspection reports. The authors are grateful to Gerald Scanlan for allowing copies of the papers to be made.

19. This observation by the authors resulted from a personal inventory of the files of the Centralia and West Frankfort Coal Mine Disasters, Illinois Department of Natural Resources, Office of Mines and Minerals, Benton, Illinois, 30 Sept. 2003 (hereafter cited as Department of Mines and Minerals files). Art Rice of the Benton office maintains the only existing official state file of papers regarding the Centralia disaster.

20. William E. Rowekamp to Robert M. Medill, 4 Nov. 1944, Scanlan Papers.

21. Weir to Scanlan, 10 Nov. 1944, and Weir to Rowekamp, 10 Nov. 1944, Scanlan Papers.

22. Scanlan to Weir, 13 Nov. 1944, Scanlan Papers.

23. Scanlan to Rowekamp, 13 Nov. 1944, and Weir to Rowekamp, 28 Nov. 1944, Scanlan Papers.

24. Rowekamp to Scanlan, 2 Dec. 1944, Scanlan Papers.

25. Weir to Brown, 27 Dec. 1944, Scanlan Papers. The letter provides details of observations and recommendations from Scanlan's inspection report, 1–2.

26. Weir to Brown, 27 Dec. 1944, Scanlan Papers.

27. Scanlan, testimony, U.S. Senate hearing, 3 Apr. 1947, 80.

28. Scanlan to Medill, 21 Feb. 1945, Scanlan Papers.

29. William Young to Medill, 28 Feb. 1945, Scanlan Papers.

30. Scanlan to Norman Prudent, 28 Feb. 1945, Scanlan Papers.

31. UMWA Local No. 52 to Weir, 7 Apr. 1945, Scanlan Papers.

32. Medill, testimony, 125.

33. Scanlan, testimony, 83–84.

34. Scanlan, testimony, 85.

35. Weir memo to State Mining Board, 11 May 1945, Scanlan Papers.

36. Frank Perz, "Coal-Mine Reinspection Report No. 4" (July 16–19, 1945), 19, in U.S. Department of the Interior, Bureau of Mines, *Coal Mine Inspection Report, No. 5 Mine, Centralia Coal Company, Centralia, Marion County, Illinois*, by Frank Perz (Vincennes, Indiana), copy, Department of Mines and Minerals files.

37. Perz, "Coal-Mine Reinspection Report," 18.

38. Scanlan to Medill, 8 Dec. 1945, Scanlan Papers.

39. Scanlan, testimony, 86.

40. Driscoll Scanlan, "Mine Inspection Report" (13 and 14 Dec. 1945), 2, in Illinois Department of Mines and Minerals, *Mine Inspection Report: Centralia Coal Company, No. 5 Mine*, by Driscoll O. Scanlan, photostat, Department of Mines and Minerals files.

41. Centralia No. 5 employees to Medill, 26 Dec. 1945, Scanlan Papers.

42. Prudent and Brown to members of commission appointed to investigate charges filed by Local 52 against them, 28 Dec. 1945, Scanlan Papers.

43. Special Investigation Commission Report to State Mining Board, 2 Jan. 1946, Scanlan Papers.

44. Local 52 to Medill, 26 Feb. 1946, Scanlan Papers.

45. Martin, "Blast in Centralia No. 5," 205.

46. Local 52 to Governor Dwight Green, 3 Mar. 1946, Scanlan Papers. The letter was stamped "received Mar 9- 1946" at the governor's office. It was stamped "Mar 13 1946" in the Department of Mines and Minerals file. The *Sentinel* published contents of the letter in "Miners Protested 'State Negligence,'" 27 Mar. 1947, 1.

47. John William Chapman to Medill, 11 Mar. 1946, Scanlan Papers.

48. Medill to Chapman, 13 Mar. 1946, Scanlan Papers.

49. Perz, "Coal-Mine Inspection Report" (5–8 Mar. 1946), 8, copy, Illinois Department of Mines and Minerals files.

50. Scanlan, "Mine Inspection Report" (6–7 Mar. 1946), 2, photostat, Illinois Department of Mines and Minerals files.

51. Scanlan, testimony, 106.

52. Interior Secretary Julius Krug, testimony, U.S. Senate hearing, 10 Apr. 1947. He explained the agreement between the federal government and the UMWA in detail.

53. Scanlan, "Mine Inspection Report" (18–19 June 1946), 2, photostat, Illinois Department of Mines and Minerals files.

54. Scanlan, "Mine Inspection Report" (3–4 September 1946), photostat, Illinois Department of Mines and Minerals files.

55. Perz, "Coal-Mine Inspection Report" (4–6 Nov. 1946), 1, copy, Illinois Department of Mines and Minerals files.

56. Perz, "Coal-Mine Inspection Report" (4–6 Nov. 1946), 5–6.

57. Capt. N. H. Collisson, testimony, U.S. Senate hearing, 10 Apr. 1947, 323–24.

58. Scanlan, "Mine Inspection Report (18–19 Nov. 1946), 7, photostat, Illinois Department of Mines and Minerals files.

59. Joe W. Rafby to Medill, 8 Dec. 1946, Scanlan Papers.

60. James Sneddon to Medill, 17 Dec. 1946, and Weir to William Brown, 19 Dec. 1946, Scanlan Papers.

61. Niermann to Weir, 23 Dec. 1946, Scanlan Papers.

62. The lack of written comment on Niermann's letter must be considered intentional, either to avoid putting anything in writing on the record or to ignore requests for information.

63. Walter J. Johnson, testimony, U.S. Senate hearing, 5 Apr. 1947, 278.

64. Frank Perz, testimony, U.S. Senate hearing, 3 Apr. 1947, 42, 51; Scanlan, testimony, 103–4; Johnson, testimony, 273.

65. Scanlan, testimony, 107.

66. Perz, testimony, 42.

67. Scanlan, testimony, 104.

68. Scanlan, statement, 24 Apr. 1947, Illinois General Assembly, *Report of the Legislative Mine Investigating Committee to the 65th General Assembly* (Springfield: Illinois State Archives, 1947), 5; Perz, "Coal-Mine Inspection Report" (18–19 Mar. 1947), copy, Illinois Department of Mines and Minerals files.

69. Johnson, testimony, 279.

70. Fact-Finding Committee, 11 Apr. 1947, 38.

3. Day of Reckoning

1. "Explosives and Blasting," in U.S. Department of the Interior, Bureau of Mines, *Final Report of Mine Explosion, No. 5 Mine*, reprinted in Phee, appendix 7, 226.

2. Sam Wilkinson, telephone interview with author, 26 Oct. 2003, and subsequent correspondence; Bill Niepoetter (son of Henry), telephone interview with author, 12 Nov. 2003, and subsequent correspondence. (All interviews were conducted by Robert Hartley.) Wilkinson also provided an audiotape of comments by his father, Earl, who survived the disaster. Bill Niepoetter, a longtime Centralia newspaper reporter and radio personality, shared newspaper clippings and reminiscences by survivors. At the peak, Glenridge had about three hundred residents.

3. Martin, "Blast in Centralia No. 5," 215–16; "Dying Miners' Notes Tell of Love and Concern for Their Families," *SLPD*, 31 Mar. 1947; "Dying Miners Wrote Notes to Their Families as Deadly Gas Swept on Them in Illinois Pit," *New York Times*, 31 Mar. 1947 (AP dispatch).

4. "No. 5 Coal Mine Disaster Survivor Tells of Fateful Day 15 Years Ago," *Sentinel*, 25 Mar. 1962.

5. Mrs. Donald (Elvera) Kirkland, interview with author, 1 Oct. 2003; report of No. 5 mine safety committee, quoted during testimony of William Rowekamp, U.S. Senate hearing, 4 Apr. 1947.

6. August Holzhauer, testimony, U.S. Senate hearing, 4 Apr. 1947, 174–75.

7. John Pick Jr. quoted in "'Knocked Cold' by Mine Blast, Says Digger," *SLPD*, 26 Mar. 1947, 1 (UPI story).

8. Henry Goforth, testimony, U.S. Senate hearing, 4 Apr. 1947, 180.

9. "Like Cyclone Hit Mine, Eyewitness Survivor Relates," *Sentinel*, 29 Mar. 1947, 7; "All of 111 Miners Trapped at Centralia Found Dead," *SLPD*, 29 Mar. 1947, 1.

10. Descriptions of the mine are from many sources, including a final report by federal inspectors of the Bureau of Mines and files of the *SLPD*, the *St. Louis Globe-Democrat* (here-

after cited as *SLGD*), and the *Sentinel*. Many who later testified before investigating groups speculated on how miners killed by the blast and its aftereffects might have survived.

11. "12 Miners Leave Notes," *Sentinel*, 31 Mar. 1947, 1; see also articles of the same date in the *SLPD* and *SLGD* and by all the wire services. Officials who released the messages intentionally omitted the names of writers, although some notes did not contain the writers' names. A few writers later were identified in magazine articles. The *SLPD* provided the most extensive reconstruction of what happened while the notes were being written.

12. "12 Miners Leave Notes," 2.

13. Harry Niermann, testimony, U.S. Senate hearing, 3 Apr. 1947, 10–11. Other miners' testimony presented differing versions of times and events during the confusion of the first minutes after the explosion. Several others mention experiences like Niermann's.

14. Scanlan, statement to press, 31 Mar. 1947, quoted in "Accuses Superiors," *Sentinel*, 1 Apr. 1947, 1.

15. Goforth, testimony, 180.

16. "104 Miners Still Trapped in Illinois, 30 Rescued, Repeated Hazard Warnings," *SLPD*, 26 Mar. 1947, 1; "17 Known Dead, 110 Trapped in Explosion at No. 5 Mine," *Sentinel*, 26 Mar. 1947, 1.

17. "104 Miners Still Trapped," 1.

18. "A Statement of the Centralia Mine Disaster by R. R. Sayers, Director, Bureau of Mines," during testimony, U.S. Senate hearing, 16 Apr. 1947, 415–25; *Final Report of Mine Explosion, No. 5 Mine*, presented by M. J. Ankeny, federal mine inspector, at U.S. Senate hearing, 16 Apr. 1947, 317–414.

19. "104 Miners Still Trapped," 1.

20. Goforth, testimony, 181.

21. Most news organizations settled on the figure of 500 persons at the mine, although no official or unofficial sources were cited.

22. Harry Wilensky, "How 111 Men Died in Illinois Pit, Repeated Warnings by Inspector on Hazards," *SLPD*, special section, 30 Apr. 1947, 1. Wilensky's reporting work on the explosion and his leadership of a team of seven reporters were cited when the newspaper was awarded the Pulitzer prize for public service for coverage of the disaster. He retired in 1979 after thirty-seven years at the newspaper and died on 29 November 1996. "Harry Wilensky: Led Team That Won a Pulitzer Prize," *SLPD*, 1 Dec. 1996, 9D.

23. "Miners' Lives Depend on 'If,'" *Sentinel*, 26 Mar. 1947, 2.

24. "Whose Guilt?" (editorial), *SLPD*, 26 Mar. 1947, reprinted in special section, 30 Apr. 1947.

25. "Illinois' Mine Disaster," *SLGD*, 27 Mar. 1947, 9C.

26. "Move in House to Investigate Mine Disaster," *SLPD*, 27 Mar. 1947; "Senate Votes Mine Blast Inquiry as Hope Dims for 104 in Illinois," *New York Times*, 27 Mar. 1947, 1. Congressman Charles Vursell spoke on the floor of the House of Representatives on 26 March. During his remarks, he mentioned meeting with four Centralia No. 5 miners during the previous Christmas holidays about safety problems at the mine. The spokesman for the four was Dominick Lenzini, who died in the disaster. 80th Cong., 1st sess., *Congressional Record* 93, pt. 2:2635–36.

27. "Impeachment Threat to Green in Mine Disaster," *SLPD*, 27 Mar. 1947, 1.

28. Scanlan quoted in "Near End of Grim Search for 111 Trapped in Mine," *Sentinel*, 29 Mar. 1947, 1; "Last of 111 Miners' Bodies Found, Are Being Removed," *SLPD*, 29 Mar. 1947, 1.

29. "Rescuers Rebel at State Bureau Chief's Order to Turn on Power in Gas-Filled Tunnel," *SLPD*, 29 Mar. 1947, 1. In testimony at the Senate hearing on 4 April 1947, Medill commented on Scanlan's activities during the search for bodies. "Inspector Scanlan was interviewing the press nearly every time the shift changed, telling them his story and broadcasting a lot of gossip" (138).

30. Elvera Kirkland, interview.

31. "All of 111 Miners Trapped at Centralia Found Dead," *SLPD*, 30 Mar. 1947.

32. The first mention of survivors and dependents appeared 29 March 1947 in the *SLPD*, reporting information compiled by Hugh White, president of UMWA District 12.

4. Years of Strife

1. R. J. Branson, testimony, U.S. Senate hearing, 4 Apr. 1947, 209.

2. "Scanlan Won't Gamble with Men's Lives Because He Was 'Raised in a Coal Mine,'" *SLPD*, 1 Apr. 1947. Additional information about Scanlan's background from Phee, 59–60, based on her interview with Scanlan; and Martin, "Blast in Centralia No. 5," 197–98.

3. Sam Day to Robert Medill, 19 Apr. 1941, Scanlan Papers.

4. Scanlan, testimony, U.S. Senate hearing, 3 Apr. 1947, 108–9.

5. State of Illinois files regarding Centralia contain mostly copies of inspection reports, a few copies of correspondence, and miscellaneous documents. The most complete copies of state records exist in the Scanlan Papers.

6. Medill to William Young, 27 Feb. 1945, and Young to Medill, 28 Feb. 1945, Scanlan Papers.

7. Medill to Scanlan, 7 Mar. 1945, Scanlan Papers. Regarding the Benton meeting, Scanlan attached a handwritten note to the correspondence saying, "On March 1-2-3, 1945, discussed this with Mr. Medill at Benton."

8. Scanlan, testimony, 82.

9. Scanlan, testimony, 83; "Medill Denies Some of Charges Made by Scanlan," *SLPD*, 31 Mar. 1947, 1.

10. Scanlan, testimony, 86–87.

11. Scanlan, testimony, 89. Scanlan attached a handwritten note to his mine inspection report of 13-14 December 1945, saying, "December 21, 1945, called into Springfield regarding this complaint. Conference with Ben Schull—not called before the mining board."

12. Special Investigation Commission memorandum to the State Mining Board, 2 Jan. 1946, "Conditions at Centralia Coal Company, Mine No. 5, Centralia, Illinois"; Scanlan, testimony, 88.

13. "Inspector Blames Medill, Says He 'Took Chance': Illinois Miners Won't Work till Mines Are Safe," *SLPD*, 31 Mar. 1947, 1; Scanlan, testimony, 97–98. Notes by Scanlan attached to his report of 6-7 March are from the Scanlan Papers.

14. Robert M. Medill, testimony, U.S. Senate hearing, 4 Apr. 1947, 136; "Medill Denies Some of Charges Made by Scanlan," *SLPD*, 31 Mar. 1947, 1.

15. Branson, testimony, 208; Scanlan, testimony, 238.

16. Martin, "Blast in Centralia No. 5," 210–11; Richard Biles, *Richard J. Daley: Politics, Race, and the Governing of Chicago* (DeKalb: Northern Illinois University Press, 1995), 15–17.

17. Medill, testimony, 139.

18. Medill, testimony, 139, 142.

19. "Scanlan Asserts Director Ordered $25,000 Lug on Coal Operators," *SLPD*, 31 Mar. 1947, 1; Scanlan, testimony, 110–15. After March 25, Scanlan repeated his version of

the solicitation of campaign contributions frequently, before all the investigating groups and to reporters.

20. Medill, testimony, 109–10.

21. Harry Wilensky, "Mine Operators 'Shaken Down' by G.O.P. for Funds in Chicago Fight," *SLPD*, 19 Mar. 1947, 1.

22. "Scanlan Asserts Director Ordered $25,000 Lug," 1.

5. A Pox on All Houses

1. "'We're Going to Have an Explosion,' Miner Who Was Killed Told Wife," *SLPD*, 5 Apr. 1947, 3.

2. John L. Lewis, testimony before the U.S. Senate Public Lands subcommittee, 28 Mar. 1947, quoted in "Lewis Blames Krug for Mine Disaster," *New York Times*, 29 Mar. 1947, 8A; "Lewis Charges Negligence by Krug 'Murdered' Miners," *SLPD*, 28 Mar. 1947, 1.

3. "Lewis Orders Mines Closed a Week as Tribute to Dead, 400,000 to Quit April 1 to 6," *New York Times*, 30 Mar. 1947, 1.

4. John L. Lewis, "Testimony of John L. Lewis Before the House of Representatives Subcommittee on Miners' Welfare of the Committee on Education and Labor, April 3, 1947" (Washington, D.C.: Labor's Non-Partisan League, n.d.), 6, 15–16.

5. "U.S. Closes 518 Mines Believed Unsafe," *SLPD*, 3 Apr. 1947, 1 (AP dispatch); "48 Illinois Mines among the 518 Closed by Krug," *SLPD*, 3 Apr. 1947, 1.

6. "Inspector Blames Medill, Says He 'Took Chance,' Illinois Miners Won't Work till Mines Are Safe," *SLPD*, 31 Mar. 1947, 1; "Scanlan Asserts Precautions He Urged Could Have Averted Disaster," *SLPD*, 29 Mar. 1947, 1.

7. "Scanlan Won't Gamble with Men's Lives Because He Was 'Raised in a Coal Mine,'" *SLPD*, 1 Apr. 1947; "Medill Replies to Scanlan's Charges of Mine Negligence," *Sentinel*, 1 Apr. 1947, 1.

8. "Text of Gov. Green's Order for Closing of Coal Mines That Violate Safety Rules," *SLPD*, 1 Apr. 1947, 3; "Illinois to Close All Unsafe Mines," *New York Times*, 31 Mar. 1947, 12.

9. "Medill Resigns, Gov. Green Here," *Sentinel*, 1 Apr. 1947, 1; "Medill Quits under Fire, Gov. Green Orders Inquiry Board to 'Pull No Punches,'" *SLPD*, 1 Apr. 1947, 1; "Medill Quits as Illinois Mines Director," *St. Louis Star-Times*, 1 Apr. 1947, 1.

10. "Medill Denies Some of Charges Made by Scanlan," *SLPD*, 31 Mar. 1947, 1.

11. "Medill Replies to Scanlan's Charges," 1; "Medill Blames Inspector for Mine Disaster," *SLPD*, 1 Apr. 1947, 1.

12. State Mining Board, "Inspection of Mine No. 5, Centralia Coal Company, Centralia, Illinois" (Apr. 3 and 10, 1947), in *Report to Harold L. Walker, Director, Department of Mines and Minerals* (Springfield, 11 Apr. 1947), 4–5.

13. State Mining Board, "Inspection of Mine No. 5," 7.

14. Bureau of Mines report, in Phee, appendix 7, 218–55.

15. "Explosion Laid to Dust and 'Dangerous' Blasting Method in Federal Report," *SLPD*, 16 Apr. 1947, 1.

16. Fact-Finding Committee, 1.

17. "Dust Spread Centralia Disaster, Probers Find," *SLPD*, 3 Apr. 1947, 1.

18. "Dust Spread Centralia Disaster," 1.

19. Fact-Finding Committee, 40–46.

20. Jo Anne McCormick Quatannens, comp., *Senators of the United States: A Historical Bibliography, 1789–1995* (Washington, D.C.: U.S. Government Printing Office, 1995), 68, 89, 215.

21. Harry Niermann, testimony, U.S. Senate hearing, 3 Apr. 1947, 2–31.

22. Frank Perz, testimony, U.S. Senate hearing, 3 Apr. 1947, 47–51.

23. Perz, testimony, 49, 55.

24. Scanlan testified on three different occasions during the Senate hearings. The first was during the afternoon of 3 April, the second that evening, and the third on 4 April, after he had been in the mine with federal inspectors. Most of the third testimony regarded that inspection. Scanlan, testimony, 79–115, 228–38.

25. Obviously, Scanlan had kept copies of his reports, correspondence with various officials, and personal notes and had done research on state laws.

26. Robert M. Medill, testimony, U.S. Senate hearing, 4 Apr. 1947, 117–44. Medill spent most of his time refuting assertions and accusations of Scanlan, offering his version of confrontations, and stating repeatedly that Scanlan should have shut down the mine.

27. R. J. Branson, testimony, U.S. Senate hearing, 4 Apr. 1947, 208–12.

28. Hugh White, testimony, U.S. Senate hearing, 5 Apr. 1947, 212–28.

29. W. H. Brown, testimony, U.S. Senate hearing, 5 Apr. 1947, 268.

30. M. J. Ankeny, testimony, U.S. Senate hearing, 16 Apr. 1947, quoted in "Explosion Laid to Dust and 'Dangerous' Blasting Method in Federal Report," *SLPD*, 16 Apr. 1947, 1.

31. Subcommittee report, 5 June 1947, 80th Cong., 1st sess., *Congressional Record* 93, pt. 5:6428; "Senators Blame Illegal Blast for Centralia Deaths," *SLPD*, 6 June 1947, 1 (AP dispatch).

32. "Illinois Senate Votes to Set Up Mine Inquiry Body," *SLPD*, 2 Apr. 1947, 1.

33. Illinois General Assembly, *Minority Report of the Legislative Mine Investigating Committee to the 65th General Assembly of Illinois*, 27 May 1947 (Springfield: Illinois State Archives, 1947), 24A.

34. Scanlan, statement to Legislative Investigating Committee, 24 Apr. 1947, copy provided to the author by Gerald Scanlan. Gerald Scanlan said copies of the printed version were distributed by his uncle's father at the hearing. See also "Statement of Driscoll Scanlan to the Press," clipping from a Nashville, Illinois, weekly newspaper, 27 Apr. 1947.

35. Illinois General Assembly, *Report of the Legislative Mine Investigating Committee to the 65th General Assembly*, 21 May 1947 (Springfield: Illinois State Archives, 1947), 6–7.

36. "G.O.P. Legislators Are Accused of Trying to 'Shield Wrongful Acts,'" *SLPD*, 25 Apr. 1947, 1; Illinois General Assembly, *Minority Report*, 19–21.

37. Illinois General Assembly, *Report of the Legislative Mine Investigating Committee*, 6–9; see also, "Operators Oppose Proposed Ban of On-Shift Shooting," *Sentinel*, 13 May 1947, 1; and "Probers of Mine Disaster Recommend Law Revision," *Illinois State Journal*, 22 May 1947, 4.

38. "Operators Oppose Proposed Ban."

39. Illinois General Assembly, *Report of the Legislative Mine Investigating Committee*, 10; Illinois General Assembly, *Minority Report*, 15–16.

40. Illinois General Assembly, *Report of the Legislative Mine Investigating Committee*, 10.

41. Phee, 130–31.

42. "Scanlan Resigns as Mine Inspector," *SLGD*, 12 Dec. 1947, 4 (AP dispatch).

6. Miners' Lives

1. Material for the Ballantini brothers' story came from a special section of the *Sentinel*, 23 Mar. 1997, commemorating the fiftieth anniversary of the mine disaster.

2. "List of Men Killed in Mine Explosion," U.S. Senate hearing, 165. The address of each man was published in addition to name, age, and occupation.

3. Mrs. Wilma Gutzler, interview with author, 17 June 2004. She was unsure whether the children's parents had come to Centralia.

4. Saundra Ebbs, interview with author, 16 June 2004.

5. Wilma Gutzler, interview.

6. Dickson Terry, "Life in the Grim Shadow of Death," *SLPD*, 30 Mar. 1947.

7. Bill Knight, interview with author, 26 June 2004.

8. Philip Knight obituary, *Sentinel*, 30 Mar. 1947.

9. Betty Pick, interview with author, 29 Sept. 2003; interview with Dorothy Pick, Jack Jr.'s sister, in the *Sentinel*, 23 Mar. 1997.

10. Ralph Spinner, interview with author, 1 Oct. 2003; obituary, *Sentinel*, 27 Mar. 1947.

11. The primary source of information about Harry Niermann on 25 March 1947 is his testimony, U.S. Senate hearing, 3 Apr. 1947, 2–31; see also interview with Niermann in "Number Five Mine Disaster" (oral history on computer disk, Centralia Public Library, 2002); and interview with Niermann, 29 Sept. 1969, in Phee, 105–6.

12. Humphrey, *Historical Summary of Coal-Mine Explosions*, 213; Harold L. Walker, "Report of Explosion, Centralia Coal Company Mine No. 5, Centralia, Washington County, Illinois," in *66th Coal Report of Illinois* (Springfield: Department of Mines and Minerals, 1947), 233.

13. Niermann, testimony, 16.

14. Mike Jones, "No. 5 Mine Disaster Lives in Memories of Survivors," *Sentinel*, 24 Mar. 1982, 3.

15. In correspondence and e-mail messages in December 2003 and January 2004, Karen Crouse, William Rowekamp's great-niece, provided reminiscences and biographical documents to the author.

16. William Rowekamp, testimony, U.S. Senate hearing, 4 Apr. 1947, 148.

17. The *SLPD*, the first newspaper to publish the "please save our lives letter," did not reveal the source of the correspondence. There is no copy of the letter in the files of the Department of Mines and Minerals. Driscoll Scanlan's personal papers include a copy of the letter and correspondence generated by it. The *Sentinel* said the letter was released to the press by William Rowekamp. "Miners Asked State to Enforce Laws at Shaft, 'Save Our Lives,'" *SLPD*, 27 Mar. 1947; "Miners Protested 'State Negligence,'" *Sentinel*, 27 Mar. 1947.

18. Rowekamp, testimony, 150–51.

19. Rowekamp, testimony, 152.

20. Crouse, reminiscence, 7 Jan. 2004.

21. Joe Vancil Jr., interview with author, 30 Sept. 2003, DuQuoin, Illinois. His wife, Jean, attended.

22. "No. 5 Victims Honored in Service," *Sentinel*, 24 Mar. 1997, 1.

7. The Reality of Coal Politics

1. The *SLPD* used the quote from a 1940 campaign appeal to organized labor by candidate Dwight H. Green in an editorial on 11 April 1947, concluding, "In other words,

the man who wanted to be Governor forgot all about mine safety after he was elected." Gubernatorial candidate Adlai E. Stevenson picked up the item during his 1948 campaign and used it frequently; see Stevenson speech, Centralia, 24 Mar. 1948, in *The Papers of Adlai E. Stevenson*, ed. Walter Johnson and Carol Evans, vol. 2 (Boston: Little, Brown, 1973), 488–89; and Stevenson speech, 27 July 1948, Salem, Illinois, in "Speeches of Adlai E. Stevenson, 1948," 13, Department of Rare Books and Special Collections, Princeton University Library.

2. Robert P. Howard provides background on Green in *Mostly Good and Competent Men: Illinois Governors, 1818–1988*, Illinois Issues, Sangamon State University (Springfield: Illinois State Historical Society, 1988), 267–73. See also Robert P. Howard, *Illinois: A History of the Prairie State* (Grand Rapids: Eerdmans, 1972), 539–45; and Mary Watters, "The Green Machine: McCormick-Brooks Domination," in *Illinois in the Second World War: The Production Front*, vol. 2 (Springfield: State of Illinois, 1952), 480. As the *Chicago Tribune* political reporter in Springfield during the 1948 campaign, Howard knew Green well and was employed by Robert McCormick.

3. Watters, 481–83; Robert P. Howard, "Illinois Statecraft" (oral history, Springfield: Sangamon State University, 1982), 102.

4. Howard, "Illinois Statecraft," 102–3, provides details of Green's personal traits and shortcomings.

5. Watters, 491–97, provides information on the 1944 campaign. See also Howard, "Illinois Statecraft," 109. For official vote results, see *Illinois Elections, 1818–1990: Candidates and County Returns for President, Governor, Senate, and House of Representatives*, ed. Howard W. Allen and Vincent A. Lacy (Carbondale: Southern Illinois University Press, 1992), 61.

6. Watters, 498.

7. Watters, 510–11.

8. "Whose Guilt?" 26 Mar. 1947, *SLPD*, reprinted in special section, 30 Apr. 1947, 12.

9. Illinois General Assembly, *Minority Report*, 30.

10. Walter Eadie, director, Department of Mines and Minerals, to George Postich, 16 Nov. 1951, Department of Mines and Minerals files.

11. Howard, "Illinois Statecraft," 103–4; "Dwight Green Once Denounced Third Term as 'Dictatorship,' Now Seeks One for Himself," *SLPD*, 20 May 1948.

12. "The Unfitness of Gov. Green" (editorial), *SLPD*, 27 May 1948.

13. Richard Norton Smith, in *Thomas E. Dewey and His Times: The First Full Scale Biography of the Maker of the Modern Republican Party* (New York: Simon and Schuster, 1982), says Senator Robert Taft of Ohio was the favorite of Robert McCormick for the presidency, and Green never was seriously considered as a vice presidential candidate for Taft or Dewey. Walter Trohan, in *Political Animals: Thirty-Eight Years of Washington-Watching by the Chicago Tribune's Veteran Observer* (Garden City: Doubleday, 1975), 232, says *Tribune* insiders conspired to team Dewey and Green, and McCormick accused them of treason.

14. John Bartlow Martin, *Adlai Stevenson of Illinois* (New York: Doubleday, 1976), is the essential source on the life and career of the biographical subject. See also Jean H. Baker, *The Stevensons: A Biography of an American Family* (New York: W. W. Norton, 1996).

15. See Martin, "Blast in Centralia No. 5."

16. *Papers of Stevenson*, 2:488.

17. *Papers of Stevenson*, 2:466.

18. Stevenson speech, 10 Apr. 1948, McLeansboro, Illinois, 1–2, in "Speeches of Stevenson, 1948."

19. Robert E. Hartley, *Paul Powell of Illinois: A Lifelong Democrat* (Carbondale: Southern Illinois University Press, 1999), 43–64.

20. Stevenson speech, 27 July 1948, Salem, 15.

21. Martin, *Adlai Stevenson of Illinois*, 336.

22. Stevenson speech, 6 Sept. 1948, Mt. Vernon, Illinois, 6–7, in "Speeches of Stevenson, 1948."

23. Dwight Green speech, 16 Mar. 1948, Rock Island, Illinois, Dwight H. Green Papers, Box 5, Illinois State Historical Library.

24. UMWA Local 52, statement, 7 Aug. 1948, Box 5, Dwight H. Green Papers.

25. Stevenson speech, 15 Sept. 1948, Bloomington, Illinois, in *Papers of Stevenson*, 2:573.

26. Martin, *Adlai Stevenson of Illinois*, 347. See also *Illinois Elections, 1818–1990*, 63.

27. Martin, *Adlai Stevenson of Illinois*, 358.

28. State of Illinois, 65th General Assembly, Senate Bills 634, 635, Illinois State Archives; Phee, 128–29; Eadie to Postich, 16 Nov. 1951.

29. State of Illinois, 66th General Assembly, House Bills 1084, 1086, 1088, 1089, 1092, Illinois State Archives.

30. State of Illinois, 67th General Assembly, House Bills 583, 584, 1168, 116, Illinois State Archives.

31. *Papers of Stevenson*, 3:400.

32. *Papers of Stevenson*, 3:401–2.

8. "It's All Blown to Hell"

1. *History of West Frankfort, Illinois* (West Frankfort: Frankfort Area Historical Society, 1948).

2. "Fear 80 Killed in Orient Mine Disaster," *Benton Evening News*, 22 Dec. 1951, 1.

3. "Hope Dwindles for Men Missing," *SLPD*, 23 Dec. 1951, 1A.

4. "Death Toll Rising in One of State's Worst Explosions," *West Frankfort Daily American*, 23 Dec. 1951, 1.

5. "218 Men at Work in Mine," *SLPD*, 22 Dec. 1951, 3C; Edwin Hair, *Our Christmas Disaster* (privately printed, 1952), 14.

6. "90 Believed Dead in Illinois Mine Blast," *SLPD*, 22 Dec. 1951, 1.

7. "91 Known Dead in Mine, 30 Missing," *SLGD*, 24 Dec. 1951, 1.

8. "Hope Fades for Missing at West Frankfort," *SLGD*, 23 Dec. 1951, 1.

9. Illinois Department of Natural Resources, Office of Mines and Minerals, *Paul McCormick: Mine Rescue Experiences, 1926–1980*, video.

10. "Hope Fades for Missing," 1.

11. "Fear 80 Killed," 1.

12. "Disaster Cuts Holiday Joy in Mine Area," *SLGD*, 23 Dec. 1951, 1.

13. "Disaster Cuts Holiday Joy," 1.

14. Hair, 18–19.

15. Hair, 16–17.

16. Hair, 14–16.

17. "Funeral Wreaths Go Up in Stricken West Frankfort," *SLPD*, 23 Dec. 1951.

18. *SLPD*, 31 Dec. 1951, Pictures, 3.

19. "Fire Fighting Equipment and Gas Masks Used," *SLPD*, 23 Dec. 1951, 2.

20. "Hope Fades for Missing," 1.

21. Hair, 21.

22. Hair, 21.

23. Illinois Department of Natural Resources video.

24. "'Almighty God Took Care of Me'—Sanders," *Benton Evening News*, 26 Dec. 1951, 1.

9. Burying the Dead

1. Howard, *Mostly Good and Competent Men*, 272–73; "Governor at Scene of Mine Tragedy," *West Frankfort Daily American*, 23 Dec. 1951, 6.

2. Martin, *Adlai Stevenson of Illinois*, 308.

3. "Hope Fades for Missing at West Frankfort," *SLGD*, 23 Dec. 1951, 1.

4. "Lewis Blames Mine Management for Blast," *Benton Evening News*, 29 Dec. 1951, 1.

5. "Safety Comes Second," *SLPD*, 27 Dec. 1951, 2; Dubofsky and Van Tine, 470–71.

6. "Hope Fades for Missing," 1.

7. "Joint Inquiry Planned into Illinois Mine Blast," *SLGD*, 26 Dec. 1951, 3; "John L. Lewis Is Shocked by Mine Tragedy," and "Prepare Dead for Burial in Central Gym," *West Frankfort Daily American*, 23 Dec. 1951, 1.

8. "The Women They Left Behind," *SLGD*, 30 Dec. 1951, 4F.

9. For another view of the coal town culture in Franklin County, see Robert Coover, *The Origin of the Brunists* (New York: Putnam, 1966). The fictional Brunist cult developed around a man named Bruno who was a survivor of the New Orient No. 2 disaster. Coover grew up in Herrin and was educated at Southern Illinois University.

10. "Grief in the Wake of Mine Disaster," *SLPD*, 28 Dec. 1951, 3D.

10. Seeking the Cause and Greater Safety

1. "Unsafe Safety in Illinois Mines," *SLPD*, 29 Dec. 1951, 4.

2. "Unsafe Safety," 4.

3. "Stevenson Says Explosion Must Be Used to Learn How to End Peril," *SLPD*, 24 Dec. 1951, 1.

4. Martin, *Adlai Stevenson of Illinois*, 504.

5. "Inspection Team Spends 8 Hours in Orient No. 2," *SLGD*, 27 Dec. 1951, 2; "Methane Gas Blamed for Orient Mine Blast," *SLGD*, 28 Dec. 1951, 3.

6. "Lewis Blames Mine Management for Blast," *SLPD*, 29 Dec. 1951, 1.

7. Hair, 85.

8. Hair, 49.

9. "Pass the Mine Safety Bill," *SLPD*, 31 Dec. 1951, 2B.

10. "Governor May Call Special Session," *SLGD*, 1 Jan. 1952, 3.

11. Walter Eadie, director, Department of Mines and Minerals, "Explosion in Orient No. 2 Mine, Chicago, Wilmington, and Franklin Coal Company, West Frankfort, Illinois" (1952, mimeograph), Department of Mines and Minerals files.

12. Adlai Stevenson to Walter Eadie, 9 Jan. 1952, Department of Mines and Minerals files.

13. Eadie to Stevenson, 11 Jan. 1952, Department of Mines and Minerals files.

14. Martin, *Adlai Stevenson of Illinois*, 503–4.

15. U.S. Department of the Interior, Bureau of Mines, *Final Report on Major Explosion Disaster, Orient No. 2 Mine, Chicago, Wilmington and Franklin Coal Company, West Frankfort, Illinois, 21 December 1951* (Washington, D.C.: Government Printing Office, 1953), 45.

16. Bureau of Mines, *Final Report on Orient No. 2 Mine*, 48.

17. Bureau of Mines, *Final Report on Orient No. 2 Mine*, 47–50.

18. Eadie to Stevenson, 14 Jan. 1952, Department of Mines and Minerals files.

19. Harold L. Walker, "A Summarizing Report to Governor Adlai E. Stevenson on the Chicago, Wilmington and Franklin Orient Mine No. 2 Explosion Which Occurred on December 21, 1951" (1952, mimeograph), 17, Department of Mines and Minerals files.

20. Illinois Mine Investigation Commission, *Hearing*, West Frankfort and Springfield, Feb. 1952, 1087 (hereafter cited as MIC, *Hearing*). The correct name of the commission is as given here. The verbatim record of this hearing incorrectly used the word *Mining* instead of *Mine*. Apparently there exists only one copy of the hearing account in a library setting, in the Illinois State Archives in Springfield. Through the courtesy of the archives, the authors secured a copy. It is their intention to place it in the collection of the Office of Mines and Minerals in Benton, Illinois.

21. MIC, *Hearing*, 1095.

22. Hair, 84; MIC, *Hearing*, 1055–60.

23. Hair, 83–84.

24. MIC, *Hearing*, 96, 348.

25. MIC, *Hearing*, 425–26; *History of West Frankfort*, 130.

26. MIC, *Hearing*, 298.

27. Hair, 35, 87.

28. MIC, *Hearing*, 210, 211.

29. MIC, *Hearing*, 691–93.

30. MIC, *Hearing*, 878–79.

31. MIC, *Hearing*, 789–90.

32. MIC, *Hearing*, 630.

33. MIC, *Hearing*, 637.

34. MIC, *Hearing*, 645.

35. MIC, *Hearing*, 674.

36. MIC, *Hearing*, 633.

37. MIC, *Hearing*, 155, 181, 182, 226.

38. MIC, *Hearing*, 660.

39. MIC, *Hearing*, 840–41, 858.

40. MIC, *Hearing*, 836.

41. MIC, *Hearing*, 999, 1001.

42. MIC, *Hearing*, 836.

43. MIC, *Hearing*, 528, 449.

44. MIC, *Hearing*, 724–25.

45. MIC, *Hearing*, 56–59, 72–74.

46. MIC, *Hearing*, 84–85.

47. "Senator Martin Criticized for Fighting Mine Safety," *SLGD*, 1 Jan. 1952, 2.

48. Written statement of Governor Adlai E. Stevenson to the Subcommittee on Mine Safety of the Senate Committee on Labor and Public Welfare, in Division of Department Reports, *Illinois State News*, 28 Jan. 1952, 4, 5.

49. Martin, *Adlai Stevenson of Illinois*, 504.

50. Testimony of John L. Lewis, 29 Jan. 1952, U.S. Senate, Committee on Labor and Public Welfare, *Welfare of Coal Miners*, 82nd Cong., 2nd sess., 1952, S. Rep. 1223, 7.

51. Senate Committee, *Welfare of Coal Miners*, 7.

52. "Senator Martin Criticized," 3.

53. "No Money to Enforce Mine Bill, Interior Department Declares," *SLPD*, 17 July 1952, 1.

54. *Illinois Blue Book, 1953–1954* (Springfield: State of Illinois, 1955), 562–64.

11. Affected Lives

1. "In Memoriam," *Benton Evening News*, 20 Dec. 1952, 7.

2. "Memorial Services for New Orient Mine Disaster Victim in West Frankfort," *Benton Evening News*, 20 Dec. 1952, 1.

3. "Tenth Anniversary of Orient Two Mine Disaster," *Benton Evening News*, 21 Dec. 1961, 1.

4. "Odds and Ends," *Benton Evening News*, 21 Dec. 1976, 2.

5. Ella Sweet, interview with author, 13 July 2004.

6. "Progress 2003," *West Frankfort Daily American* (special issue, 2003), 5, 7.

7. Sharon Raymond and Georgia Colp, interviews with author, 21–22 July 2004.

8. Charles McDaniel, interview with author, 23 July 2004.

9. Jack Westray, interview with author, 7 Aug. 2004.

Conclusion

1. Phil Gonet, president of the Illinois Coal Association, in "Will Coal Be King Again?" *Southern Illinoisan*, 12 Aug. 2004, 1, 2.

2. Zieger, 170.

3. Dubofsky and Van Tine, 491–517.

4. Dubofsky and Van Tine, xi.

5. Zieger, x.

Glossary of Coal Mining Terms

Afterdamp: The mixture of nonflammable gases left after a firedamp explosion that is low in oxygen and may contain carbon monoxide.

Air course: Underground ventilating passage.

Airdox: An appliance for breaking coal by the release of high-pressure air at the back of a shot hole.

Airshaft: An opening into the mine, primarily for completion of the ventilating system, which might have a stairway built into it for escape and other purposes.

Blackdamp: Carbon monoxide, often the product of rapid combustion, as in an explosion of methane gas or coal dust; a suffocating gas.

Brattice: Canvas material impregnated with a tarlike preservative, used for construction partitions, ordinarily to direct air flow and ventilation; also a wooden framework, covered with canvas, erected in a passageway, usually for the same purposes.

Buddy: A partner in underground work.

Buggy: A vehicle for carrying coal away from the working face, where there are no rail lines.

Cage: A structure used in a mine shaft for conveyance of men and materials.

Carbon monoxide (white damp): A tasteless and almost odorless gas, a product of incomplete combustion; mere traces of it are dangerous to life.

Caving: Collapse of the roof in worked-out areas.

Coal-dust explosion: Explosion caused by the ignition of coal dust, most commonly caused by a firedamp explosion.

Crosscut: A cut made across the working face of a room every 60 or 70 feet for ventilation that connects with other entries; also, a tunnel driven at an angle into the strata, seeking another vein of coal.

Cutting machine: Machine for undercutting the working face of a room, work that in the past was done by hand.

Damp: Dangerous gases underground, as in *afterdamp, blackdamp, chokedamp,* and *firedamp.*

Driller: The worker who drills holes in the working face of a room for the insertion of an explosive charge, or a compressed air valve, for the purpose of bringing a quantity of coal down on the floor.

Dummy: A package of explosive material, such as dynamite, that is stuffed in a hole at the mine face and contains a fuse.

Engine room: The covered space near the mine shaft that houses the equipment used in moving workers in and out of the mine and hoisting coal to the surface.

Entry: A passageway between the surface and the working face of a mine.

Face: The point or points at which coal is being knocked down for loading and removal to the hoisting shaft; thus, the working face.

Fan: The large fan, usually driven by electricity, that forces air into, or draws air out of, the mine for ventilation.

Firedamp: Explosive gas, usually methane.

Gopher hole: A small mine, often in a horizontal entry.

Sources: A. Nelson, *Dictionary of Mining* (New York: Philosophical Library, 1965); E. J. Prior, *Dictionary of Mining Technology* (London: Mining Publications, 1962).

Haulage road: The passageway along which coal is taken toward the hoisting shaft, usually in vehicles that run on rails.

Hoist: Drum on which the hosting rope is wound in the engine room.

Hoisting shaft: The shaft in which personnel are lowered to the bottom and taken out and coal is raised to the surface.

Ignition point: The flash point of combustible gases. The place at which an explosion was ignited.

Inbye: Path toward the working face from the shaft.

Incombustible material: Material such as limestone particles and clay that will not explode; when the mixture of materials on the floor of the mine at a given point is 65 percent or more incombustible, it is considered unlikely to explode.

Lignite: Intermediate form between peat and bituminous coal.

Loading machine: A machine that loads the coal that has been knocked down on the floor of a room into a vehicle for removal toward the haulage road.

Main airway: Principal airway connecting with the shaft.

Mainline: A principal passageway of the mine from which entries are opened that is used for haulage and ventilation.

Motor: A machine used to haul coal cars.

Outby: A path from the working face to the shaft.

Permitted explosive (permissible explosive): An approved explosive charge for dropping the coal on the floor of the mine.

Pit: Mine or mine shaft.

Pit head: Landing stage at the top of a shaft.

Portal: Entrance to the mine shaft.

Return aircourse: The path of contaminated air to the surface.

Rock dust: Pulverized stone, often limestone, with which the mine is dusted to render the mixture with coal dust at least 65 percent incombustible.

Room: A space in the mine, off an entry, where the work of extracting the coal from the working face is carried out.

Room-and-pillar: The method of taking coal and leaving roof supports of pillars of coal.

Safety lamp: Miner's lamp with a shielded flame so that it does not ignite methane gas.

Shaft: Opening, usually rectangular, to underground coal. It has a variety of uses including moving coal, and hoisting.

Shooting: Use of explosives in breaking coal.

Shot: The charge of powder or compressed air used to drop coal onto the floor of the room.

Tamping: Filling the hole containing an explosive charge around a fuse, so that the force will be contained in order to bring coal down onto the floor of a room.

Timbers (timbering): Wooden props used to support the roof of a passageway.

Tipple: The structure above ground where loaded coal cars are "tipped" to be emptied.

Tracklayer: A worker with the assignment of laying rails for the coal cars.

Trackman: A worker involved with the making of railways within the mine.

Trip: Vehicle used to carry personnel within the mine.

Triprider: The person being transported in a trip.

Undercut: The cut made into the face of the coal at the floor of a room for the purpose of having coal brought down by an explosive charge or compressed air.

Ventilation split (air split): A division of the intake current of air in order to direct a portion of it in a desired area.

Wash house: The building above ground near the shaft where miners' street clothes are kept while they are at work; bathing facilities often are included.

Bibliography

Manuscript Sources

Files of the Centralia and West Frankfort Coal Mine Disasters. Illinois Department of Natural Resources. Office of Mines and Minerals, Benton, Illinois.

Dwight Green Papers. Speeches 1940–49. Abraham Lincoln Presidential Library, Springfield, Illinois.

Personal Papers of Driscoll O. Scanlan. Collection of Gerald Scanlan, Venedy, Illinois.

"Speeches of Adlai E. Stevenson, 1948." Department of Rare Books and Special Collections. Princeton University Library.

Newspapers, Wire Services

Associated Press
Benton (Ill.) Evening News
Centralia (Ill.) Sentinel
Chicago Tribune
New York Times
St. Louis Globe-Democrat
St. Louis Post-Dispatch
St. Louis Star-Times
United Press International
West Frankfort (Ill.) Daily American

Books

Allen, John W. *Legends and Lore of Southern Illinois.* Carbondale: Southern Illinois University Press, 1963.

Angle, Paul M. *Bloody Williamson: A Chapter in American Lawlessness.* New York: Knopf, 1952.

Baker, Jean H. *The Stevensons: A Biography of an American Family.* New York: W. W. Norton, 1996.

Baratz, Morton S. *The Union and the Coal Industry.* New Haven: Yale University Press, 1955.

Bietto, Frank J. "A Study of the Federal Government's Attempts to Promote Safety in the Bituminous-Coal Mines of the United States." Master's thesis, Southern Illinois University, 1952.

Biles, Roger. *Richard J. Daley: Politics, Race, and the Governing of Chicago.* DeKalb: Northern Illinois University Press, 1995.

Brown, Malcolm, and John N. Webb. *Seven Stranded Coal Towns.* New York: Da Capo, 1971.

Casey, Robert J., and W. A. S. Douglas. *The Midwesterner: The Story of Dwight H. Green.* Chicago: Wilcox and Follett, 1948.

Clayton, John. *The Illinois Fact Book and Historical Almanac, 1673–1968.* Carbondale: Southern Illinois University Press, 1970.

Cole, Arthur Charles. *The Era of the Civil War, 1848–1870.* Urbana: University of Illinois Press, 1987.

Conrad, David. "Coal Field Recreation." In *Concerning Coal*, edited by Magdalen Mayer et al. Carbondale: Coal Research Center, 1997.

Coover, Robert. *The Origin of the Brunists*. New York: Putnam, 1966.

Curran, Daniel. *Dead Laws for Dead Men: The Politics of Federal Coal Mine Health and Safety Legislation*. Pittsburgh: University of Pittsburgh Press, 1993.

Davis, James E. *Frontier Illinois*. Bloomington: Indiana University Press, 1998.

Derber, Milton. *Labor in Illinois*. Urbana: University of Illinois Press, 1989.

Dubofsky, Melvin, and Warren Van Tine. *John L. Lewis: A Biography*. New York: Quadrangle/New York Times, 1977.

Duckham, Helen, and Baron. *Great Pit Disasters*. Newton Abbot: David and Charles, 1973.

Freese, Barbara. *Coal: A Human History*. Cambridge: Perseus, 2003.

Galloway, Robert L. *A History of Coal Mining in Great Britain*. London: Macmillan, 1882.

Gluck, Elsie. *John Mitchell: Labor's Bargain with the Gilded Age*. New York: John Day, 1929.

Graebner, William. *Coal Mining Safety in the Progressive Period*. Lexington: University Press of Kentucky, 1976.

Gregory, Clark E. *A Concise History of Mining*. New York: Permagon, 1980.

Hair, Edwin. *Our Christmas Disaster*. Benton: Privately printed, 1952.

Hartley, Robert E. *Paul Powell of Illinois: A Lifelong Democrat*. Carbondale: Southern Illinois University Press, 1999.

History of West Frankfort, Illinois. West Frankfort: Frankfort Area Historical Society, 1948.

Horrell, C. William. *Southern Illinois Coal: A Portfolio*. Carbondale: Southern Illinois University Press, 1995.

Howard, Robert P. *Illinois: A History of the Prairie State*. Grand Rapids: Eerdmans, 1972.

———. *Mostly Good and Competent Men: Illinois Governors, 1818–1988*. Illinois Issues, Sangamon State University. Springfield: Illinois State Historical Society, 1988.

Kaiser, John H. *Building for the Centuries: Illinois, 1865–1898*. Urbana: University of Illinois Press, 1977.

Kenney, David, and Robert E. Hartley. *An Uncertain Tradition: U.S. Senators from Illinois, 1818–2003*. Carbondale: Southern Illinois University Press, 2003.

Lantz, Herman R. *People of Coal Town*. New York: Columbia University Press, 1958.

Laslett, John H. M. *The United Mine Workers of America: A Model of Industrial Solidarity?* University Park: Pennsylvania State University Press, 1996.

Long, Priscilla. *Where the Sun Never Shines*. New York: Paragon, 1989.

Martin, John Bartlow. *Adlai Stevenson of Illinois*. New York: Doubleday, 1976.

———. *It Seems Like Only Yesterday*. New York: William Morrow, 1986.

Maurer, David J. "Unemployment in Illinois During the Great Depression." In *Essays in Illinois History*, edited by Donald F. Tingley. Carbondale: Southern Illinois University Press, 1968.

Mavigliano, George T. "Paul Cadmus's Painting of the Lester Strip Mine Disaster." In *Concerning Coal*, edited by Magdalen Mayer et al. Carbondale: Coal Research Center, 1997.

McCullough, David. *Truman*. New York: Simon and Schuster, 1992.

Morris, Edmund. *Theodore Rex.* New York: Random House, 2001.

Munn, Robert F. *The Coal Industry in America: A Bibliography and Guide to Studies.* Morgantown: West Virginia University Library, 1965.

The Papers of Adlai E. Stevenson. Edited by Walter Johnson and Carol Evans. Vol. 2, *Washington to Springfield, 1941–1948.* Boston: Little, Brown, 1973.

The Papers of Adlai E. Stevenson. Edited by Walter Johnson and Carol Evans. Vol. 3, *Washington to Springfield, 1949–1953.* Boston: Little, Brown, 1974.

Quatannens, Jo Anne McCormick, comp. *Senators of the United States: A Historical Bibliography, 1789–1995.* Washington, D.C.: U.S. Government Printing Office, 1995.

Reitz, Dan. "A Brief History of the UMWA." In *Concerning Coal,* edited by Magdalen Mayer et al. Carbondale: Coal Research Center, 1997.

Ross, George E. *Centralia, Illinois: A Pictorial History.* St. Louis: G. Bradley, 1992.

Roy, Andrew. *A History of the Coal Miners of the U.S.* Westport: Greenwood, 1970.

Russell, Herbert A., ed. *A Southern Illinois Album: Farm Security Administration Photos, 1936–1943.* Carbondale: Southern Illinois University Press, 1990.

Selvin, David F. *The Thundering Voice of John L. Lewis.* New York: Lathrop, Lee and Shepard, 1969.

Shapiro, Bruce. *Shaking the Foundations: 200 Years of Investigative Journalism in America.* New York: Thunder's Mouth, 2003.

Smith, Richard Norton. *The Colonel: The Life and Legend of Robert R. McCormick, Indomitable Editor of the Chicago Tribune.* New York: Houghton Mifflin, 1997.

———. *Thomas E. Dewey and His Times: The First Full Scale Biography of the Maker of the Modern Republican Party.* New York: Simon and Schuster, 1982.

Stover, John E. *History of the Illinois Central Railroad.* New York: Macmillan, 1975.

Tingley, Donald F. *The Structuring of a State: The History of Illinois, 1899 to 1928.* Urbana: University of Illinois Press, 1980.

Tintori, Karen. *Trapped: The 1909 Cherry Mine Disaster.* New York: Atria Books, 2002.

Trohan, Walter. *Political Animals: Thirty-Eight Years of Washington-Watching by the Chicago Tribune's Veteran Observer.* Garden City: Doubleday, 1975.

U.S. Department of Interior. Coal Mines Administrator. *A Medical Survey of the Bituminous-Coal Industry.* Washington, D.C.: U.S. Government Printing Office, 1947.

Watters, Mary. *Illinois in the Second World War: The Production Front.* Vol. 2. Springfield: Illinois State Historical Library, 1952.

Zieger, Robert H. *John L. Lewis: Labor Leader.* Boston: Twayne, 1988.

Selected Sources

"Agreement Between the Secretary of the Interior and the United Mine Workers of America, Covering Government Possession, Subject to Executive Order No. 9728, 21 May 1946." Washington National Records Center, Record Group No. 70: 22000-436.

Bruchman, Cynthia. "Two Coal Towns in 1900 Bureau County: Seatonville and Ladd." *Journal of the Illinois State Historical Society* 97, no. 3 (Autumn 2004): 226–37.

Changnon, Stanley A. "The Rise and Fall of Illinois Coal." *Historic Illinois,* June 2004, 6–8.

"Coal." *Encarta.* <http://encarta.msn.com/encnet/refpages/RefArticle.aspx?refid=761558734>.

Franklin, Ben A. "The Scandal of Death and Injury in the Mines." *New York Times Magazine,* 30 Mar. 1969.

Harris, Roy J., Jr. "An Era of Crusaders." *Quill Magazine*, May 2003, 13.

Hornbein, Marjorie. "Josephine Roche: Social Worker and Coal Operator." *Colorado Magazine* 53 (Summer, 1976): 243–60.

Howard, Robert P. "Illinois Statecraft" (oral history). Springfield: Sangamon State University, 1982.

Humphrey, H. B. *Historical Summary of Coal-Mine Explosions in the United States, 1810–1958*. Bulletin 586. Rev. ed. Washington, D.C.: U.S. Bureau of Mines, 1976. First published 1959.

Illinois Department of Mines and Minerals. *Mine Inspection Report: Centralia Coal Company, No. 5 Mine*, by Driscoll O. Scanlan. Springfield. (Reports for 13–14 Dec. 1945; 6–7 Mar., 18–19 June, 3–4 Sept., 18–19 Nov. 1946; 21–22 Jan., 18–19 Mar. 1947.)

————. *Report of the Mining Industry of Illinois*. Springfield, 1955.

Illinois Department of Natural Resources. Office of Mines and Minerals. *Paul McCormick: Mine Rescue Experiences, 1926–1980*. Videocassette.

Illinois State Historical Society. "Mining and the Cherry Mine Disaster." *Dispatch/News* 7, no. 2 (Fall 1999).

Indiana Division of Reclamation. "Formation of Coal." <http://www.state.in.us/dur/reclamation/coalhistory.htm>.

Kissell, Fred N. *Handbook for Dust Control in Mining*. Pittsburgh: U.S. Department of Health and Human Services, June 2003.

Lewis, John L. "Testimony of John L. Lewis Before the House of Representatives Subcommittee on Miners' Welfare of the Committee on Education and Labor, April 3, 1947, and Subcommittee of the Senate Committee on Public Lands to Investigate the Centralia Mine Explosion, April 17, 1947." Washington, D.C.: Labor's Non-Partisan League, n.d.

Martin, John Bartlow. "The Blast in Centralia No. 5: A Mine Disaster No One Stopped." *Harper's*, Mar. 1948, 193–220.

McDarrell, John. "The Life of a Coal Miner." *World's Work* no. 4 (Oct. 1902).

Medill, Robert M. "World's Richest Deposit of Coal Located in Illinois." *Illinois Blue Book, 1945–46*. Springfield: State of Illinois, 1947.

"Milestones in the History of Coal Energy." <http://www.eia.doe.gov/kids/milestones/coal/htm>.

"Monongah Mining Disaster." Boise State University. <http://www.idbsu.edu/history/ncasner/hy210/mining.htm>.

Phee, Catherine. "The Centralia Mine Disaster of 1947." Ph.D. diss., St. Louis University, 1971.

The President, 1943–1948 Compilation. Containing the Full Text of Presidential Documents Published in the *Federal Register* During the Period 2 June 1943 to 31 December 1948. In *Code of Federal Regulations*, Title 3. Washington, D.C.: U.S. Government Printing Office, 1957.

Throgmorton, Dianne. "Early Mining History—A Miner's Life." In *Concerning Coal*, edited by Magdalen Mayer et al. Carbondale: Coal Research Center, 1997.

U.S. Department of Labor. Mine Safety and Health Administration. "History of Anthracite Coal Mining." <http://www.msha.gov/district/disto1/history/history.html>.

U.S. Department of the Interior. Bureau of Mines. *Coal Mine Inspection Report, No. 5 Mine, Centralia Coal Company, Centralia, Marion County, Illinois*, by Frank Perz. Vincennes, Indiana. (Reports for 16–19 July 1945; 5–8 Mar., 4–6 Nov. 1946.)

Young, Dallas M. "Origin of the Progressive Mine Workers of America." *Journal of the Illinois State Historical Society* 40, no. 3 (Sept. 1947).

Investigations and Hearings

Illinois General Assembly. *Minority Report of the Legislative Mine Investigating Committee to the 65th General Assembly of Illinois*, 27 May 1947. Springfield: Illinois State Archives, 1947.

———. *Report of the Legislative Mine Investigating Committee to the 65th General Assembly*, 21 May 1947. Springfield: Illinois State Archives, 1947.

State of Illinois. "Fact-Finding Committee Appointed by Governor Dwight H. Green to Investigate the Disaster at the Centralia Coal Company Mine No. 5, at Wamac, Illinois, Occurring on March 25, 1947." In *Report to the Governor and People of the State of Illinois*. Springfield, 11 Apr. 1947.

———. Illinois Mine Investigation Commission. *Hearing*. West Frankfort and Springfield, 1952.

———. State Mining Board. "Inspection of Mine No. 5, Centralia Coal Company, Centralia, Illinois" (3, 10 Apr. 1947). In *Report to Harold L. Walker, Director, Department of Mines and Minerals*. Springfield, 11 Apr. 1947.

U.S. Department of the Interior. Bureau of Mines. *Final Report of Mine Explosion, No. 5 Mine, Centralia Coal Company, Centralia, Marion County, Illinois, March 25, 1947*. Reprinted in Phee, "Centralia Mine Disaster," appendix 7.

———. *Final Report on Major Explosion Disaster, Orient No. 2 Mine, Chicago, Wilmington and Franklin Coal Company, West Frankfort, Illinois, 21 December 1951*. Washington, D.C.: U.S. Government Printing Office, 1953.

U.S. Senate. Committee on Labor and Public Welfare. *Welfare of Coal Miners*. 82nd Cong., 2nd sess., 1952, S. Rep. 1223.

———. Special Subcommittee of the Committee on Public Lands. *Investigation of Mine Explosion at Centralia, Illinois*. 80th Cong., 1st sess., 1947. Washington, D.C.: U.S. Government Printing Office, 1947. (Hearings held on 3, 4, 5 Apr. 1947 in Centralia, Illinois, and 10, 16, 17 Apr. in Washington, D.C.)

Walker, Harold L., director. "Report of Explosion, Centralia Coal Company Mine No. 5, Centralia, Washington County, Illinois." *66th Coal Report of Illinois*. Springfield: Department of Mines and Minerals, 1947.

———. "A Summarizing Report to Governor Adlai E. Stevenson on the Chicago, Wilmington and Franklin Orient Mine No. 2 Explosion Which Occurred on December 21, 1951." Springfield, 1952.

Index

Altadonna, Joe, 64
Ankeny, M. J. (U.S. Bureau of Mines), 90, 98, 150, 165–68
Avery, Noah, 153
Avondale (Pa.) mine disaster, 3

Bailey, Fred, 168
Balabos, Alex, 139–40
Ballantini, Joe, 64, 105, 106
Ballantini family, 105–6
Barkley, Sen. Alben, 6
Barnett, Dr. Andy, 138
Barnfield, Elzie, 144
Bell and Zoller Coal Company, 26, 50, 66
Beaty, Rev. E. B., 71
Benton Evening News, 176
Berger, Harry, 64, 71
Biaga, Celso, 71
Bishop, C. W. "Runt," 173
Bishop, Oliver, 90
Blakeney, Charles, 44
Block, J. L., 141
Boles, Era, 67
Bonacorsi, Leo, 143, 144, 145
Boyd, James, 83
Boyle, William A. "Tony," 183
Brashear, Lee, 151
Bradley, Ella, 176
Bradley, Oral, Jr., 145, 176
Branson, Rep. R. J., 133; support of Scanlan by, 74, 78; testimony before Senate committee by, 98
Bridges, Sen. Styles, 69
Brooks, Sen. C. Wayland, 69
Brush, Samuel (St. Louis and Big Muddy mine), 9
Brown, William H. (No. 2 mine manager), 38, 40, 43–44, 45, 51, 53, 65, 88, 97–98
Bryant, Harold "Jack," 59
Bryant, Joe, 59, 60, 64, 105
Bude, Edward, 108
Buehne, Raymond, 64
Bush, Thomas, 40, 47

Cadmus, Paul, 12
Cantrell, James, 150
Cardox Corporation, 169
Carter, Arthur, 82
Carter, Edith, 82
cause of No. 2 explosion, 172, 176
Centralia, 23–29
Centralia No. 5 mine, 26, 30, 57. *See also* Mine No. 5
Cerutti, Joseph, 64
Centralia Coal Company, 104
Centralia Sentinel, 67
Chapman, John, 47–48
Chapman, Oscar (Interior Secretary), 149, 157)
Cherry (Ill.), 4
Chicago, Burlington, and Quincy Railroad, 9, 25
Chicago, Wilmington, and Franklin Coal Company, 138, 157–58
Choate, Clyde, 133
Clayton, David, 165
coal camps, 5
coal dust explosions, 30–31
coal economy in southern Illinois, 13–15
coal industry, 1, 82, 181–82
Coal Mines Administration, 52, 50
coal mining: disasters in, 1, 5; in early twentieth century, 12; in England, 1; growth of, 3–4; in Illinois, 4; and immigration, 4; in nineteenth century, 3, 5; traditional method of, 2
Coal Mining Act, 1953 changes in, 173–74
coal production and World War II, 31
coal town culture, 13
Collisson, Capt. N. H., 52
Colp family (Georgia, Deon, David, and Michelle), 178–79
company houses, 10
company towns, 5
contract between Krug and Lewis, (1946), 19
Cook, Arlie, 140, 164–65

Copple brothers (Clifford and Frank), 62, 70
Crouse, Karen, 117, 118

Dahn, Leo R., 64
"Dark as a Dungeon," 3
Deason, Paul, 143, 144
Deneen, Gov. Charles S., 6
Devonald, David H., 90
Donohue, Paul, 140, 141
Douglas, Sen. Paul, 173
Dunlop family (George, Lucille, Sharon, and Georgia), 178–79
Dupree family (Clyde and Lloyd), 141
Dworshak, Sen. Henry C., 93, 97–98

Eadie, Walter, 145–46, 150, 157, 186; and Department of Mines and Minerals, 131; and No. 2 mine, 149; and Stevenson, 160, 161–62
Ebbs, Saundra, 109
election of 1948, 132–33
Evans, George, 59
explosions. See coal dust explosions; Mine No. 2; Mine No. 5

fact-finding committee, 90–93
farewell notes, 64
federal inspectors, 89–90
Fetgatter, Walter H., 64
Forbes, John (U.S. Bureau of Mines), 149, 157
Ford, Charles, 57, 88
Ford, Tennessee Ernie, 3
Foster, John R., 150, 169
Frankfort Heights, 137
Franklin, Williamson, and Saline counties coal field, 12–13, 14
Frazer, Luther, 64
Freeman, Martin, Jr., 64
Frisco Lines, 10

Gaertner, Bruno, 64
Gallagher, W. A., 90
Garwood, Thomas, 165, 167–68
Gates, John W. "Bet-a-Million," 7
German, Luther, 175
Giovannini, Tony, 64

Glenridge Seven, 59–60
Glodich, Mrs. Sam, 153
Goforth, Henry, 62, 67, 91
Golden, John, 44
Gospelaires, the, 175
Green, Gov. Dwight W., 66, 68, 69, 121–23; appoints DMM personnel, 74; names fact finding committee, 90; is defeated by Stevenson, 125–30; elections of, 173; fires Medill, 89; on mine safety, 121; and "please save our lives" letter, 45–47; on Root for Chicago mayor, 79–80
Gunter, Mrs. Harry, 155
Guthrie, Woody, 105
Gutzler family, 64, 105, 107–8

Haley, Tom, 144
Hall, Floyd, 141–43
Haskell, Marie Joan, 151
Hepburn Act, 7
Herrin Massacre, 12
Hohman, Gus, 60
Horrell, Bill, 10
Howe, Robert E. (UMWA lobbyist), 159
Humphrey, Sen. Hubert, 169

Illinois Central Railroad, 7, 24–25
Illinois Department of Mines and Minerals, 33, 148
Illinois Mining Act, 34
Illinois Steel Company, 7
immigration, 2

Jackson, Ned, 63, 64
"John Henry," 3
Johnson, Walter, 51, 54, 55, 56, 98
Johnston City, 7, 12

Kaskaskia Community College, 29
Kelly, Mayor Edward J., 78
Kent, Ralph, 140, 150
King, Rev. T. H., 175
Kirkland, Elvera, 60
Knight, Bill, 109–10
Krug, Julius A. (Interior Secretary), 69, 83, 85

Lake Centralia–Salem oil field, 28
Lappin, Les, 140
Legislative Investigating Committee,
    (1947), 99–103, 186
Leiter, Joseph (Zeigler Coal Company), 9
Lenzini, Adolf, 67–68
Lenzini, Domenico, 71
Lewis, John L., 151, 157; and CIO, 18;
    early life and career of, 15–16, 17; and
    FDR, 19; and Krug, 19; on No. 2 di-
    saster, 149, 158, 186; on No. 5 disaster,
    83–85; statement to Senate subcom-
    mittee by, 171; and Truman, 19; waning
    power of, 181–83
Lichtenfeld, Fred, 57
Lingo, Omar, 139
Link, Ted, 128
Local 52, UMWA, 36, 45
Lorenzini, John, 61–62, 64, 91, 117
Louden, Gov. Frank O., 34
Lucas, Sen. Scott, 69

Madison Coal Company, 9
Marion County Coal Company, 26
Martin, Sen. Edward, 173
Martin, John Bartlow, 126, 170–71
Mazeka, John, 64
McCormick, Paul, 140, 147
McDaniels, Wilfrid, 140, 164
McDonald, N. F. (Bell and Zoller Coal
    Co.), 52
Medill, Robert M., 37, 39, 48, 49, 53, 66,
    70, 79, 88–89; appointed to IDMM,
    34–35; background of, 34; firing of,
    104; miners' letter to, 44; and Scanlan,
    73–81, 87; at Senate committee hear-
    ing, 96–99; and UMWA, 49–50
mine examination procedure, 57
Mine Investigation Commission, 134, 148,
    156–57, 168
Mine No. 2: anniversary of, 175; beginning
    of, 157; burying the dead of, 150–55;
    condition of, 139; crowd gathers at,
    138; explosion in, 139; and federal
    inspectors, 157; number of employees
    in, 138; production in, 137; recovery
    of dead from, 145; relief fund for, 159;
    rescue efforts at, 195–97

Mine No. 5, 63; blame for explosion in,
    187–88; closing of, 176; condition of,
    38; death toll in, 59; distribution of
    workers in, 58; explosion in, 59, 62;
    family vigils at, 67; funerals of dead
    from, 71; identification of dead from,
    70; newspaper on, 68; Red Cross
    at, 67; rescue crews in, 65, 66, 67,
    70; Salvation Army at, 67; search for
    survivors in, 69; shot firing in, 58;
    ventilation of, 58
miners: ethnic character of, in U.S., 8;
    wages for, 9, 14
mine safety bill S.1310, 173
mining law changes: in 1947, 131–32; in
    1949, 133; in 1951, 133–34
Missouri Pacific Railroad, 7
Mitchell, John, 16–17
Monongah, West Virginia, 4
Moss, Elmer, 40, 45, 47

Nash, Patrick, 78
Neely, Sen. Matthew M., 169
New Orient No. 2 coal mine. See Mine
    No. 2
New York Central Railroad, 10
Nicholson, Charlene, 141
Niepoetter, Henry, 59
Niermann, Harry "Cotton," 51, 53, 55,
    64–66, 98; on No. 5 mine, 52, 112–15;
    as No. 5 superintendent, 51; before
    Senate committee, 93–94
"Nine Pound Hammer," 3

Oestreich, Charles, 107–8
Oestreich, Clara, 107
O'Mahoney, Sen. Joseph, 93, 94–95
O'Neal, T. H., 32

Patton, L. Goebel, 175
Paulaskis, Frank, 71
Pauley, Mrs. Shelby, 154
Peiler, Joseph, 64
Perz, Inspector Frank (U.S. Bureau of
    Mines), 49, 50, 51, 55, 78; additional
    power of, 50; background of, 32–33; on
    No. 5 mine, 41, 42, 51, 52, 54–55, 56;
    and Senate committee, 45, 94–95

Petroff, John, 140
Piasse, Pete, 59
Piazzi, Louis, 64
Pick, Betty, 110–11
Pick, Jack Jr., 62, 110–11, 117
Pick, Jack Sr., 62, 91, 101
Placek, John, 64
"please save our lives" letter, 45–47, 116–17
Powell, Paul, 66, 99, 102, 127, 133
Preihs, Carl, 69, 102, 133
Price, Rep. Melvin, 173
Progressive Mine Workers, 34
Prudent, Norman, 40, 43, 44, 45, 51;
    charges against, 43–44; response to
    miners' complaints by, 44; as superin-
    tendent of No. 5, 37
Pullum, Charles, 140

Quayle brothers (John and Joseph), 151, 155

Rafly, Joe W., 53
Ramsey, Alexander, 155
Ramsey, Betty, 152
Raymond family (James, Sharon, Sabrina,
    and Lisa), 179
Reach, Mrs. Ellis, Jr., 153
Reach, Ellis, Sr., 155
Reach, Ellis, Jr., 145, 155
Reak, Murrell, 44
Revak, Joe, 147
Rhodes, Forrest, 59
Rice brothers (Guy and Robert), 155
Roberts, "Cowboy," 144
Rohde, Carl, 64
Roland, Claude, 147
Root, Russell W., 79, 123
Rowekamp, William E., 37, 40, 44, 88, 89;
    and "please save our lives" letter, 45,
    115–18; as secretary of UMWA Local
    52, 36–37

Sanders, Cecil, 141, 146–47, 175, 176
Sandusky, Stanley, 152–53
Sandusky family, 152–53
Saunders, Mark, 80
Scanlan, Driscoll O., 38, 39, 44, 45, 54,
    55, 56, 64, 65, 66, 69–70, 88, 89, 103,

188; background of, 33; and cleanup
    of No. 5 mine, 40–41; evaluation of,
    188–89; as inspector, 33, 36, 104; later
    life of, 104; before legislative commit-
    tee, 100; and Medill, 39, 46, 50, 73–81,
    86–88; on No. 5 mine, 37, 38, 42, 43;
    reports by, 49, 50, 51, 53, 54–55, 56,
    75–78; resignation of, 104; before Sen-
    ate committee, 95–96; on State Mining
    Board, 48
Schmidt, Jake, 40, 47
Schofield, Utah, 4
Schreiber, Georges, 105
Schull, B. H., 44, 76–77
seizure of coal mines by federal author-
    ity, 19
Senate Report 1223, 171–73
Senate Special Subcommittee on Mine
    Safety, 170–71
"seven stranded coal towns," 12
Sever, Frank, 93
Short, Clarence, 140
"Sixteen Tons" (Travis), 3
Smith, Frank, 142
Sneddon, James, 53–54, 90
Soper, Don, 63
Southern, Charles, 154
Southern, Charles, Mrs., 215
southern Illinois, 6–7, 8s, 9
Spinner brothers (Joseph and Andrew),
    111–12
Spinner, Ralph, 112
State Mining Board, 33–34, 44, 48, 88–89
Stevenson, Adlai E., 157, 160, 161; and
    governorship, 130; and IDMM, 156; on
    mining laws, 134; on No. 2 explosion,
    186; at No. 2 mine, 148; before Senate
    Subcommittee on Mine Safety, 170;
    and presidency, 173
St. Louis and Big Muddy mine, 9
St. Louis Globe Democrat, 68, 151, 173
St. Louis Post-Dispatch, 67, 128; on Green,
    124; on Lewis, 159; on No. 2 explosion,
    149–50; Pulitzer Prize for, 125; on sup-
    port for Root by Medill, 123
St. Paul Coal Company, 5–6
Summers, Hearstel, 141

Summers, Roy, 140
Sweet, Dick, 177–78
Sweet, Ella Bradley, 176–78, 184
Swofford, "Red," 144

Taft-Hartley Act, 20
Taylor, Paul, 141–42
Thomas, Marie, 145, 146
Thomas, Ted, 144–45
Tickus, Stanley, 71
Tillman, Anton, 64
Tomlinson, W. H., 164
Travis, Merle, 3
Terry, Dickson, 154
Treadwell, H. H., 157
Truman, Harry, 173

United Mine Workers of America
    (UMWA), 6, 9, 34; current status of,
    250; and funds for survivors of No. 2
    disaster, 159; and operation of seized
    mines, 19; opposition of, to Green in
    1948, 129
University of Illinois, Department of Min-
    ing and Metallurgical Engineering, 148
U.S. Bureau of Mines, 186; creation of,
    6; and Federal Mine Safety Code, 19;
    report of No. 2 disaster by, 161–62
U.S. Farm Security Administration, 10, 14
U.S. Senate: on No. 5 disaster, 93–99
U.S. Steel, 10

Vancil, Joe, Jr., 40, 118–20, 183–84
Vaughn, Clayton, 138
Vursell, Rep. Charles W., 69

Walker, C. M. "Chalk," 140, 150, 164

Walker, Harold L., 157, 186; and DMM,
    87; on No. 2 explosion, 163–64; and
    recodification of mining laws, 134
Wall, Howard, 141
Wamac, Illinois, 27
Warner, A. M., 25
Watson, Mark, 65
Weaver, Leo, 143, 144
Weir, Robert (DMM), 35–36, 38, 41, 44,
    51, 54, 57, 99
Westfield, James, 166–68, 150
West Frankfort, 12, 137, 153
Westray family, 151–52
Westray, Jack, 180
White, Hugh, 86, 97, 164
Whitlow, Sherman (UMWA Local
    No.1265), 168
Wieb, Edward, 156–57
Wilensky, Harry, 67, 80, 125
Williams, Earl "Blink," 59
Williams, William, 65, 146
Williams family (Carl and James), 151
Williamson-Franklin-Saline counties coal
    field, 7
Wilson, James, 161
Wilson, Tom, 143–45
Wright, O. W. (Centralia mayor), 72

Yablonski, Joseph A. "Jock," 182–83
Yates, Zell, 155
Young, William P. (Centralia Coal Co.),
    31–32, 39, 44, 52, 55, 70, 75, 91, 98

Zeigler, Illinois, 10
Zeigler Coal Company, 9, 10
Zeigler No.1 mine, 10–12
Ziegler, Elaine, 106–7

Robert E. Hartley is the author of *Charles H. Percy: A Political Perspective*, *Big Jim Thompson of Illinois*, *Paul Powell of Illinois: A Lifelong Democrat*, and *Lewis and Clark in the Illinois Country: The Little-Told Story* and co-author of *An Uncertain Tradition: U.S. Senators from Illinois, 1818–2003*. He was a journalist for Lindsay-Schaub Newspapers in Illinois from 1962 to 1979 and also served as executive editor of the *Toledo (Ohio) Blade* and as publisher of the *Bellevue (Wash.) Journal-American*.

David Kenney served in the cabinet of Illinois governor James Thompson and is a professor emeritus of political science at Southern Illinois University Carbondale. His books include *Making a Modern Constitution*, *Basic Illinois Government: A Systematic Explanation*, and *A Political Passage: The Career of Stratton of Illinois*, and he is the coauthor of *An Uncertain Tradition: U.S. Senators from Illinois, 1818–2003*. He has also served as an elected member of the Sixth Illinois Constitutional Convention and as the founding director of the Illinois Historic Preservation Agency.